Praise for *The Financial Times Guide to Business Ethics*

"In a world with contested trust, it has never been more important for business leaders to do the right thing. Pablo has written an excellent pragmatic guide and we are all better for it."

Charles Conn, Chair, Patagonia

"A must-read for today's leaders. This book will give you real insight into your organisation's ethics and provide a practical tool kit to help put your conscience to work."

Dame Sally Dicketts, Chair, Brook

"Business ethics is about brand integrity. Pablo has created a unique and practical tool kit that allows committed leaders to turn ethics into sustainable differentiation."

Ronan Dunne, Former CEO, Verizon Wireless and O2

"This is an impressively clear and well-written guide to business ethics in the 21st century. Pablo offers sharp, jargon-free insights, evidence, and a wealth of tools and case studies to back up his robust, practical advice."

Professor Alison Taylor, Clinical Professor, NYU Stern School of Business

"Essential reading for those who view business ethics as critical to both moral responsibility and commercial success. It provides actionable advice and real-world examples to address everyday business challenges."

Sean Williams, CEO, AutogenAI

"Pablo has produced a book that we desperately need in a complex world. Exceptionally clear and readable, with superb use of examples and case studies. It is essential reading for anyone who aspires to make their contribution to society more meaningful."

Mark Malcomson CBE, CEO, City Lit

"This is an essential book for leaders who want to make principled decisions that drive long-term value. The practical insights, case studies and toolkits are clear and useful guides for navigating complex ethical challenges and ultimately shaping a better world."

Sarah Gillard, CEO, A Blueprint for Better Business

"This book works across the realities of public and private sector leadership, offering practical tools for navigating ethical challenges. Its ethical compass provides a clear and actionable framework to make values-driven decisions. Well worth the read."

Michael Davis, CEO, National Centre for Social Research

"An easy-to-read guide to business ethics that includes its origins, the role of culture, ESG and voluntary standards. The insight and practical examples will be valuable for any business leader."

Katherine Marshall, Director of Ethics and Financial Crime, SSE plc.

"Powerful, actionable insights on how to lead with authenticity and compassion. It shows you how to put culture, ethics and people at the heart of your business".

Hayden Taylor, CEO, Unloc

"A guide for the perplexed business person who just needs a reliable steer on the ethical thing to do."

Professor Laura Spence, Professor of Business Ethics & Sustainability, King's Business School

"Ethics is not something you either 'have or you don't', it's a skill you must develop. This book offers a clear, practical toolkit to help managers develop that skill and make better decisions."

Professor Guido Palazzo, Professor of Business Ethics, University of Lausanne

"I cannot think of a more important topic at this time, offering actionable insights to leaders who want to step up and play their part in the field of responsible business, helping re-establish trust in institutions and leadership"

Sarah Walker-Smith, Group CEO Ampa LLP

THE FINANCIAL TIMES GUIDE TO BUSINESS ETHICS

)»Pearson

At Pearson, we believe in learning – all kinds of learning for all kinds of people. Whether it's at home, in the classroom or in the workplace, learning is the key to improving our life chances.

That's why we're working with leading authors to bring you the latest thinking and best practices, so you can get better at the things that are important to you. You can learn on the page or on the move, and with content that's always crafted to help you understand quickly and apply what you've learned.

If you want to upgrade your personal skills or accelerate your career, become a more effective leader or more powerful communicator, discover new opportunities or simply find more inspiration, we can help you make progress in your work and life.

Every day our work helps learning flourish, and wherever learning flourishes, so do people.

To learn more, please visit us at **www.pearson.com**

The Financial Times

With a worldwide network of highly respected journalists, *The Financial Times* provides global business news, insightful opinion and expert analysis of business, finance and politics. With over 500 journalists reporting from 50 countries worldwide, our in-depth coverage of international news is objectively reported and analysed from an independent, global perspective.

To find out more, visit **www.ft.com**

THE FINANCIAL TIMES GUIDE TO BUSINESS ETHICS

THE COMPREHENSIVE GUIDE FOR MAKING A POSITIVE IMPACT

PABLO HEPWORTH LLOYD

Harlow, England • London • New York • Boston • San Francisco • Toronto • Sydney
Dubai • Singapore • Hong Kong • Tokyo • Seoul • Taipei • New Delhi
Cape Town • São Paulo • Mexico City • Madrid • Amsterdam • Munich • Paris • Milan

PEARSON EDUCATION LIMITED
KAO Two
KAO Park
Harlow CM17 9NA
United Kingdom
Tel: +44 (0)1279 623623
Web: www.pearson.com

First edition published 2026 (print and electronic)
© Pearson Education Limited 2026 (print and electronic)

The right of Pablo Hepworth Lloyd to be identified as author of this work has been asserted by him in accordance with the Copyright, Designs and Patents Act 1988.

The print publication is protected by copyright. Prior to any prohibited reproduction, storage in a retrieval system, distribution or transmission in any form or by any means, electronic, mechanical, recording or otherwise, permission should be obtained from the publisher or, where applicable, a licence permitting restricted copying in the United Kingdom should be obtained from the Copyright Licensing Agency Ltd, Barnard's Inn, 86 Fetter Lane, London EC4A1EN.

The ePublication is protected by copyright and must not be copied, reproduced, transferred, distributed, leased, licensed or publicly performed or used in any way except as specifically permitted in writing by the publishers, as allowed under the terms and conditions under which it was purchased, or as strictly permitted by applicable copyright law. Any unauthorised distribution or use of this text may be a direct infringement of the authors' and the publisher's rights and those responsible may be liable in law accordingly.

All trademarks used herein are the property of their respective owners. The use of any trademark in this text does not vest in the author or publisher any trademark ownership rights in such trademarks, nor does the use of such trademarks imply any affiliation with or endorsement of this book by such owners.

Pearson Education is not responsible for the content of third-party internet sites.

ISBN: 978-1-292-75251-8 (print)
    978-1-292-75250-1 (ePub)

British Library Cataloguing-in-Publication Data
A catalogue record for the print edition is available from the British Library

Library of Congress Cataloging-in-Publication Data
A catalog record for the print edition is available from the Library of Congress

10 9 8 7 6 5 4 3 2 1
30 29 28 27 26

Cover design by Michelle Morgan
Cover credit: Cagkan Sayin/Alamy Stock Photo

Print edition typeset in 9.5/14pt Stone Serif ITC Pro by Straive

NOTE THAT ANY PAGE CROSS REFERENCES REFER TO THE PRINT EDITION

Contents

About the author ix
Foreword x
Author's note xii
Acknowledgements xiii
Introduction xv

Part 1 Ethics in action 1

1. The four key ethical principles 3
   Toolkit A: Ethical decision making 13
2. The purpose of business 17
3. Putting ethics into practice 25
   Toolkit B: Ethical health 39
4. Corporate responsibility for the natural environment 43
   Toolkit C: The natural environment 48
5. Corporate responsibility for social equity 53
   Toolkit D: Social equity 62
6. Corporate responsibility for emerging technology 67
   Toolkit E: Emerging technology 73
Ethics in action: **Quick read summary** 77

Part 2 Ethical leadership	**79**
7. The ethical compass	81
8. Empathy	87
9. Traction	95
10. Higher purpose	101
11. Ingenuity	109
12. Courage	115
Toolkit F: The Ethical Compass (ETHIC)	121
Ethical leadership: **Quick read summary**	126
Part 3 Organisational culture	**127**
13. Moral psychology	129
14. Learning from responsible cultures	141
15. Learning from ethical failures	157
Toolkit G: Ethical culture (employer viewpoint)	168
16. Speaking up (employee viewpoint)	173
Toolkit H: Improving ethical practice (ILEAP – employee viewpoint)	183
Organisational culture: **Quick read summary**	185
Part 4 Regulations, standards and impact	**187**
17. Directors' duties and anti-corruption laws	189
18. The UN global compact, ESG and SDGs	201
19. Non-government standards	215
20. Making a positive impact	231
Regulations, standards and impact: **Quick read summary**	266
Index	269

About the author

Pablo Hepworth Lloyd advises boards and leaders on performance, culture and ethics.

After graduating from the University of Cambridge, he qualified as a chartered accountant and served as a CFO in the banking and music sectors in his early career. As a social entrepreneur for 25 years, he co-founded and led educational businesses that have helped four million people achieve leadership, business and technical qualifications. He also works with charities to enrich mainstream education and was recognised with an OBE in 2019.

Elsie Kibue-Ngare, EK13 Photography

Foreword

If you are here, congratulations! You're already demonstrating what we need more of in today's business landscape: curiosity, reflection and the willingness to engage with challenge and innovation.

The word *ethics* can sometimes feel off-putting – too abstract, too academic, perhaps even a little uncomfortable. But, in practice, ethics is about how we make decisions when the stakes are high, the answers aren't obvious, and the pressure is on. It's about values in action. And in a volatile world, it's a critical differentiator between leadership that endures and leadership that unravels.

Pablo has spent the last two years listening carefully to leaders around the world – people navigating real decisions in real time. Using his extensive expertise as a business leader, mentor and educator, this is not just a guidebook; it's a strategic resource. The stories he shares and the insights and frameworks he distils offer a powerful reminder: ethical leadership isn't an add-on. It's the foundation of long-term business success.

In 1992, I stood in a phone box, calling my father. I was studying Ecology at UCL and had just come out of a lecture on climate change. I didn't have the words for it then, but I now know what I felt: anxiety, uncertainty and urgency. Today, that sense of urgency is no longer a student's private concern. It is a boardroom priority, a global conversation, and a test of how seriously we take our responsibility to future generations.

The challenges we face – social, technological, environmental and economic – are not theoretical. They are present, material and accelerating. In this context, ethics is not a constraint on performance. It is a compass for navigating ambiguity, building trust and creating sustainable value for all stakeholders.

This guide offers both inspiration and practical insight.

First, I hope you use it not just to think differently, but to behave differently – to shape decisions and cultures that are as principled as they are pragmatic.

And then, I hope you also realise that business is not invincible in the face of these challenges – individual businesses cannot do this alone. This is a collaborative sport. We need the systems we have relied on for a long time, including regulations and laws, to change as well. Everyone has a responsibility to speak up and ask for the help they need to lead ethically, in collaboration with others.

Because business is not defined by profit, it is defined by purpose, integrity and the courage to do what's right, in all our interests.

Lauren Branston, CEO, Institute of Business Ethics

Author's note

When I was a child our parents, Maria and Trevor, took us on summer holidays to see my mother's brother, Uncle Nori, in Madrid. He was a philosopher and engineer at the Spanish research institute Consejo Superior de Investigaciones Científicas where he wrote the first and only book on preology. He dreamt of hosting a global philosophical symposium in a new conference centre that he started to build in the Gredos mountains outside the city.

He loved to provoke a lively discussion and had a strong sense of right and wrong. My sisters, Rosario and Elena, would listen and argue and, as the youngest of the three, I would mostly listen. When a homeless person came to the door of the institute asking for food, it was Uncle Nori who fed them, then told everyone else off for being slow to help. When young men were fighting in the street, it was Uncle Nori who broke them up, shouting and waving his walking stick.

He was not a practical person. He never finished the conference centre. His work on preology is obscure. However, he loved ideas and debate and taught us about wonder, curiosity and fairness.

He died many years ago and my dear sister Elena died more recently. The original idea for this book came to me soon afterwards while thinking of them both and owes much to those childhood summers.

Acknowledgements

My greatest thanks are to my partner in life and work, Cathy Hepworth Lloyd, for her patience, research and sharp-eyed comments on countless drafts.

For two years, Veronica Heaven, founder of the Heaven Company and ESG-sustainability specialist, and I have collaborated as writing buddies, egging each other on through the ups and downs of authorship on related subjects. I have also found common cause with Lauren Branston, CEO of the Institute of Business Ethics, who contributed the foreword and many other insights. I am deeply grateful for Veronica's and Lauren's generous expertise and encouragement.

Key insights were curated from interviews with 50 leaders. Any flaws are mine, but I hope to have done justice to the wisdom and expertise of these exceptional interviewees: Alastair Da Costa CBE, Amanda Dickens, Andy Brown, Ann Swain, Ben Rowland, Brian Harpur, Caroline Fox, Charles Conn, David Grayson CBE, David Schofield, Gunther Jancke, Hayden Taylor, James Barbour, Josh Peasley, Judy Hadden, Julian Richer, Justin Rix, Justin Skinner, Katherine Chapman, Katherine Marshall, Katie Hill, Kevin McKee, Lauren Branston, Malcolm Bachhus, Mark Huxley, Mark Malcomson CBE, Matt Trott, Michael Davis, Mike Bullock, Peter Beeby, Peter Marks, Pierre Chauvineau, Robert Newry, Ronan Dunne, Sarah Gillard, Sarah Walker-Smith, Sateesh Pillai, Sean Vernell, Sean Williams, Sharon Saxton, Simon Rogerson, Veronica Heaven and several others who asked to remain anonymous.

I am also grateful for the inspiration in conversation and in action from: Alice Hepworth, Andrew Pullman, Angela Joyce, Annie Warburton, Ben Blackledge, Ben Glazier, Casita Sumner, Cathy Hepworth Lloyd, Charlie Martin,

Chris Blackwell, Chris O'Reilly, Chris Simmance, David Dangana, Fiona Stilwell, Freya Hepworth Lloyd, Ian Hopkins, Ian MacGregor, Ian McNeill, Inger Breitenstein, Isis Lloyd, Jasbir Sondhi, Jason Holt CBE, Jenny Garrett OBE, Jenny Herrera, Jill Goddard, John Hutchinson, Laura Edralin, Liam Black, Loree Gourley, Mark Adams, Mark Smith, Matt Cruice, Michael Ingemann, Mike Jennings, Natalie Hunt, Pete Ashby, Rick Lowe, Roger Steare, Roger Wilson, Roy O'Shaughnessy, Dame Sally Dicketts, Sarah Rozenthuler, Sarah Samuel, Sheila Lumsden OBE, Simon Biltcliffe, Tabby Bunyan, Trovene Hartley, Valerie Hopkins and Xavier White.

Thanks also to Matthew Stevenson and his colleagues at the independent bookshop *Everybody Reads* for procuring most of the reference books.

Finally, a huge thank you to the Pearson/FT team, particularly editor Eloise Cook for her trust and professional guidance.

Introduction

If you are striving to be ethical and want to lead or influence better business practice, read on to find out how to make a positive impact. What follows is for anyone in large, small, public, private and third sector organisations,[a] drawn from the practical experience of a broad range of leaders and decision makers.

At the start of my career, I was asked in a job interview whether an oil company should give bribes to win contracts. My answer was, 'If that's the common practice, then yes.' It removed any doubt about my lack of suitability. The interviewer explained that my answer was wrong because of the reputational impact. It turned out to be a lesson that has stayed with me ever since. Many years later, leading a business in the education sector, I faced a decision with a clear trade-off between short-term profits and ethics.[1] I thought back to the interview and how my conscience had changed over the years. This time, the ethical imperative was clear.

Experiences like this took me on a quest to find the real point of business and to translate ethics into practical insights and tools.

Key insights came from interviews with 50 leaders[b] who provided case studies on their experience of business ethics.

---

a   I typically use the terms 'business' and 'organisation' interchangeably. If different forms of organisation need different treatments, I spell that out.
b   I interviewed 50 leaders and decision makers about business ethics in 2023, 2024 and 2025. They represent large, small, public, private and third sector organisations. About a third work in founder-led businesses, a third in charities and social enterprises and a third in large and listed businesses. These and other case studies illustrate key points throughout the book.

They allowed me behind the scenes into their private discussions and thoughts about ethical dilemmas. Some of the details were too confidential to share but, in all cases, I have permission to provide enough information for you to learn from their experience, with toolkits to help you apply their practical wisdom.

The result is aspirational, practical and jargon-free, so you can:

- achieve competitive advantage
- reduce ethical risk and raise standards
- learn from real-world case studies
- understand mandatory and voluntary regulations
- influence an organisation positively from any level within it.

Why should a business be ethical?

The first reason is because it is right. Global temperatures, social inequality and civil unrest are increasing while trust in institutions is falling. In a global market where 30% of the largest economies are companies, not countries, businesses have the economic power and responsibility to make a positive impact in three key areas: the natural environment, social equity and emerging technology.

The second reason is competitive advantage. Successive studies[2] have shown the correlation between ethics, trust and profits. As Yvon Chouinard, founder of Patagonia, said, 'Every time I do the right thing, it is good for business.'

Who sets the ethical bar?

Since the 1990s, there have been more regulations and a growing market in voluntary standards. However, we still have no common measures of business ethics: unlike financial health, measured by profits, assets and share price, the ethical health of a business is hard to measure and easy to over-estimate.

Transparency is growing. Whether you are a listed company rated by investors or a small business rated on social media, you will be judged increasingly by other people's standards.

More than ever, businesses are competing by being clear what they stand for, setting and meeting their own standards.

What can businesses do?

My conversations with leaders highlighted three broad categories of ethical behaviour, with some businesses demonstrating all three, depending on the context:

- **Consistency** – complying with commitments and regulations.
- **Conscience** – going beyond obligations to do what is right.
- **Cause** – pursuing system change for a cause beyond the organisation.

The main influences on ethical performance are leadership and culture, supported by rules and guidelines. As Simon Rogerson, founder and CEO of Octopus Group, said to me, *'People remember stories not spreadsheets.'*

Ethical culture needs as much focus and attention as any other key business process. It is a muscle that needs regular exercise to overcome *'cultural numbness'* as described by psychologist Merete Wedell-Wedellsborg.[3] Throughout the book, you will see examples of businesses creating an 'organisational conscience' by giving employees both guidelines and autonomy to decide what is right.

What can leaders do?

Five key challenges of ethical leadership arose as a clear pattern in my interviews. Together, they form an ethical compass, not a map defining right and wrong, but a guide to help you clarify ethical questions. It is one of the toolkits to help you put your conscience to work. The five challenges are:

1 **Empathy** – how do you build trustful relationships with stakeholders?
2 **Traction** – how do you take an organisation with you?
3 **Higher purpose** – how do you create an ethical direction?
4 **Ingenuity** – how do you find ethical answers to business questions?
5 **Courage** – how do you find the courage to follow your conscience?

Interviewees also discussed the temptation to do the wrong thing by lying, bribery or looking the other way. The chapters on culture explain why there are real risks and opportunities and how to deal with them.

How can you use this book[c]?

Above all, this is a practical guide inviting you to ask questions, find answers and apply them to make an impact. There are four parts:

- **Part 1 Ethics in action** describes ethical principles, the purpose of business and corporate responsibility.
- **Part 2 Ethical leadership** sets out an *ethical compass* for leaders based on case studies.
- **Part 3 Organisational culture** explains moral psychology and lessons from responsible cultures and ethical failures.
- **Part 4 Regulations, standards and impact** explains regulations, ESG frameworks, voluntary standards and how to make an impact.

There are eight toolkits throughout to help you apply the insights and each part ends with a 'quick read' summary.

The final chapter – 'Making a positive impact' – shows you how to continue developing ethical practice beyond the book. It presents all the toolkits in one place with further reading and key organisations that support collaboration on ethical business practice.

---

c Nothing in this book is intended, or should be taken, to constitute any form of professional advice. Particularly with regard to legal matters, you should obtain advice from appropriately qualified professionals.

Notes

1. See: https://www.theguardian.com/media/2007/oct/01/advertising.television?CMP=Share_iOSApp_Other.
2. Edmans, A. (2020) *Grow The Pie: How Great Companies Deliver Both Purse and Profit*; Sisodia, R., Wolfe, D. and Sheth, J. (2007) Firms of Endearment: How World-class Companies Profit from Passion and Purpose; EY report, available at: https://www.ey.com/content/dam/ey-unified-site/ey-com/en-uk/insights/workforce/documents/ey-how-to-attain-purpose-led-transformation.pdf.
3. See: https://hbr.org/2019/04/the-psychology-behind-unethical-behavior.

part 1

Ethics in action

chapter 1

The four key ethical principles

'Ethics is about how we make decisions when the stakes are high.'

Lauren Branston

In this chapter you will learn:

- The language of ethics and key definitions
- The four key ethical principles
- The basis of the principles in moral philosophy
- How to apply them to decision making (Toolkit A)

Introduction

The first chapter defines ethics in plain language. Centuries of moral philosophy are boiled down to four key principles so you can apply them to decision making. The roots of the principles are explained if you want to explore moral philosophy in more depth.

How do we talk about ethics?

In 1997, following a General Election victory in the UK, the Foreign Secretary of the new government, Robin Cook, set out his vision[1] including the words: 'Our foreign policy must have an ethical dimension.' In theory, it made sense. In practice, the word 'ethical' became a political problem because it appeared to set an impossible task. His successor, Jack Straw, later admitted that he 'swerved' questions about his predecessor's statement.[2]

My interviews highlighted a similar challenge. Leaders will discuss ethics eloquently but, in their businesses, they are more likely to talk about 'values', 'responsible business' or 'doing the right thing'. The word 'ethics' is normally reserved for specific questions of professional or legal compliance and is otherwise loaded with very high expectations.

Most businesses publish some form of purpose and values, they can also appear as a vision, mission, aims, ethos, standards and myriad similar terms.

For the sake of clarity in the book, I will use the following definitions:

- **Morals** are personal standards to do what is right.
- **Ethics** is a set of organisational principles that guide decisions and behaviour to do what is right.
- **Values** or **principles** are the specific ethics that a business stands for; 'ethics', 'values' and 'principles' are used interchangeably in this book.
- **Ethical business** and **responsible business** are, in practice, interchangeable. I normally use 'ethical business' because, for most people, it sets a higher bar.
- **Corporate responsibility** is the long-term responsibility of an organisation to stakeholders in the broadest sense including the natural environment. Note that 'corporate social responsibility' (CSR) is a similar term, but I will use corporate responsibility to keep the language straightforward.
- **Purpose** is the reason why the organisation exists, beyond profit, to serve the common good.

Please note these are not universal definitions. You may need to adopt or adapt them for your business context.

What are the four key ethical principles?

Moral philosophy has created a web of ideas distinguishing right from wrong. They have been shaped by religious, academic, cultural and political influences and are often contentious. As the philosopher David Hume wrote in the eighteenth century: 'The rules of morality ... are not conclusions of our reason'.[3] A common feature is a bias away from self-interest and towards the common good, but there are no absolutes that command universal commitment.

I have boiled down moral philosophy to four key principles for the practical needs of business. Their basis is explained later in this chapter.

Overall, they are designed to test ethics in decision making and have contributed to the toolkits in this book. The four key ethical principles are:

1 **Integrity** – honesty, self-control and accountability.
2 **Duty** – commitment to the common good.
3 **Fairness** – compassion, care and justice.
4 **Freedom** – autonomy, enlightened self-interest and imagination.

They are defined with room for interpretation, so that you can adapt them to your personal principles and beliefs and the values of your organisation.

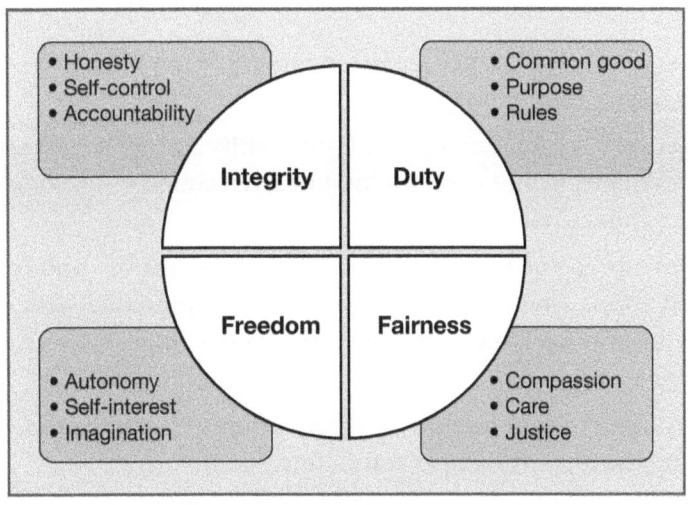

1 Integrity

'In evaluating people, you look for three qualities: integrity, intelligence, and energy. And if you don't have the first, the other two will kill you.'

Warren Buffett

Integrity focuses on truth. It comprises honesty, self-control and accountability.

Honesty includes pursuit of factual truth, disclosure of relevant facts and feelings regardless of self-interest and acceptance of doubt when factual truth is unclear.

Self-control includes moderation, resisting temptation and exercising self-denial in pursuit of ethical goals.

Accountability includes lack of hypocrisy, showing the same behaviour in public and in private. It includes facing up to consequences of unethical behaviour and, as a leader, accepting responsibility for the actions of an organisation, not just personal behaviour.

For some people, integrity goes as far as generosity and altruism, i.e. sacrificing personal benefit in favour of others without anything in return.

In a business context, it is the cornerstone of most definitions of business and professional ethics.

2 Duty

'Ask not what your country can do for you, ask what you can do for your country.'

John F. Kennedy

Duty focuses on the common good. It requires a sense of purpose beyond self-interest with appropriate respect for rules.

At a practical level, it means duty to a community and operates at several levels, for example: family, community, employer, country, society as a whole and the natural environment.

It is normally codified through rules, i.e. laws, regulations and commonly accepted norms. However, ethical principles go beyond rules – the common good is the priority. Ethical dilemmas are often a conflict between rules and conscience.

In a business context, it helps an organisation define its purpose beyond profit and the supporting rules and culture.

3 Fairness

'The trouble with human beings is not really that they love themselves too much ... the trouble is simply that they don't love others enough.'

Mary Midgeley[4]

Fairness focuses on balancing needs. It comprises compassion, care and justice while setting aside self-interest.

Compassion and care include a genuine appreciation of other people's needs (compassion) and the commitment to take action for their benefit (care).

Justice includes the principle of 'universality', i.e. the same rules apply to everyone. It includes the need to balance conflicting interests, for example ensuring ethical dilemmas are weighed up objectively. It provides for an assessment of trade-offs when compromise is unavoidable.

For some people, it goes further than just applying the same set of rights and responsibilities to everyone by allowing for bias in favour of those with disadvantage.

In a business context, this principle encourages collaboration and productive compromise.

4 Freedom

'It is not from the benevolence of the butcher, the brewer or the baker that we expect our dinner, but from their regard to their own interest'.

Adam Smith[5]

Freedom focuses on enlightened self-interest. It comprises autonomy, self-interest and imagination.

It encompasses freedom to compete, innovate, think independently, speak up and take a fair share of resulting benefits. This principle is often overlooked in ethical frameworks but, because business is a competitive and team-based activity, it is important to acknowledge the 'friction' of freedom.

In a business context, freedom enables businesses to seek competitive advantage and encourages individuals to use their imagination and speak up and challenge when appropriate. It helps an organisation maintain perspective, guarding against a conformist culture that prevents innovation or enables unethical behaviour.

What happens when principles are in conflict?

Rushworth Kidder and others at the Institute of Global Ethics define four types of *'right-right'* dilemmas,[6] i.e. where ethical principles are in conflict with each other:

1 **Truth versus loyalty (or integrity versus duty).**
   Challenging loyalty to a person or community when they behave unethically. For example, this is the dilemma for a whistleblower. Do you overrule loyalty to your organisation by calling out unethical or illegal practice?

2 **Individual versus community (or freedom versus duty).**
   Weighing the interests of one person or organisation against a wider community. For example, this is the dilemma for an organisation facing a cyberattack and a demand for ransom to avoid further catastrophic effects. Do you pay the ransom to protect your organisation or take the risk of not paying in order to discourage future attacks on other organisations?

3 **Short-term versus long-term (a consideration for all principles).**
   Judging the long-term benefits of a short-term cost or sacrifice. This is the dilemma for organisations that put ethics above profit in the expectation of earning long-term trust with customers, suppliers and employees. For example, do you pay a premium to source renewable raw materials in the expectation that this creates long-term competitive advantage?

4 **Justice versus mercy (or duty versus fairness)**
   Knowing when to apply rules strictly or make compassionate exceptions. For example, do you give an employee extended compassionate leave or sick pay beyond your obligations when they suffer a personal crisis?

In a business context, right-right dilemmas are likely to demand more time, imagination and consultation.

What is the basis of the four key ethical principles?

I have drawn out the key principles from centuries of moral philosophy in a way that makes sense for business decisions. The following summarises the main sources so that you can understand the root of the principles and, if you want to know more, follow them up beyond this book.

Integrity – virtue and the Golden Rule

The principle of integrity is based on the idea of individual 'virtue' promoted and developed by Aristotle and other philosophers.

Aristotle codified 'virtue' in practical terms, i.e. doing good and achieving a particular purpose, not just knowing what good is. He also emphasised the development of virtue through learning and guidance from others. He saw it as a fundamental character trait including moderation, patience and generosity.

This aspect of moral philosophy is rooted in the *'Golden Rule'* of reciprocity, i.e. treat others as you would want them to treat you. It is a feature of many moral philosophical traditions across the ancient world including the philosophy attributed to Confucius. It tests the morality of an action by looking at the reverse of its effect: 'It would be unacceptable for someone to steal from me, so I should not steal from them.'

Subsequent philosophers, including Adam Smith, added to the definition of virtues, or character traits, to include altruism, restraint, courage and prudence. While he is best known for laying the founding principles of free markets in *The Wealth of Nations*, Adam Smith's other major work was *The Theory of Moral Sentiments*, published in 1759. He prioritised 'the study of wisdom and the practice of virtue' and warned against lack of moderation 'his own passions are apt to mislead him ... to violate all the rules which he himself ... approves of' and 'It is not the soft power of humanity ... that is ... capable of counteracting the strongest impulses of self-love ... it is reason, principle, conscience.'

Virtue and the Golden Rule come close to being a moral absolute, as argued by Elizabeth Anscombe. She rejected the need to consider consequences in the way that some philosophers use utilitarian arguments to judge actions by their consequences.

Duty – deontology, the Categorical Imperative and purpose

The principle of duty is based on the ethics of deontology, which distinguishes right and wrong based on duties and rules that serve the common good.

Immanuel Kant was the leading proponent of deontology in the eighteenth century, proposing the idea of the 'Categorical Imperative' as a test of moral motivation: 'Act only according to that maxim whereby you can at the same time will that it should become a universal law.'[7] It expands the Golden Rule by setting a universal test of reciprocity and reinforces duty to the wider community.

Both virtue and duty rely on a sense of purpose. Aristotle defined ethics in relation to the *'telos'* or purpose of being human which, for him, included achievement of happiness, well-being and practical wisdom (or *'phronesis'*). Aristotle defined practical wisdom as a way of turning moral judgement into action and saw this ability as a critical part of human development.

Fairness – care, the Veil of Ignorance and utilitarianism

The principle of fairness is based on the ethics of distributive justice, care and aspects of utilitarianism that seek to create the greatest good for the greatest number of people.

The principles of the Golden Rule and Categorical Imperative were developed further by John Rawls. He argued in *The Theory of Justice* (1971) for *'distributive justice'* based on the idea of the *'Veil of Ignorance'* as a test of the morality of laws and social norms. The test invites us to set aside our identity, culture, religion, wealth and privilege in deciding whether an action is moral or not. This creates a bias towards actions that are not always the same for everyone but work in favour of people in greater need.

The ethics of care, developed by Carol Gilligan and others in the 1980s, focuses on relationships and the effect of actions on others, with due care for their vulnerability: 'Care is a relational ethic, grounded in a premise of interdependence. But it is not selfless.'[8]

In contrast with the ethics of virtue and duty, utilitarianism evaluates the ethics of an action according to its outcome or consequence, i.e. assessment of ethical cost versus benefit. Jeremy Bentham was the key proponent of utilitarianism in the eighteenth century. He wrote: 'it is the greatest happiness of the greatest number that is the measure of right and wrong.'[9]

Freedom – enlightened self-interest

The principle of freedom is also based on utilitarianism and the aspects of self-interest that serve the common good.

John Stuart Mill was a utilitarian in the nineteenth century, proposing that individuals should have the freedom to act as they please as long as no harm comes to others. He promoted broadening social rights as a result.[10]

Writing at a similar time, Georg Hegel was more focused on the development of freedom and reason to enable both individuals and their communities to develop and thrive. He saw the consequences of actions as a part of the actions themselves, agreeing with Aristotle who said centuries earlier: 'The final cause of anything becomes identical with the good of that thing, so that the end and the good become synonymous terms.'[11] Aristotle believed that, while humans are motivated by self-interest, moral virtues are essential to happiness and fulfilment so there is, ultimately, no conflict between self-interest and the common good.

The term *'enlightened self-interest'* captures the positive interpretation of Aristotle, leaving aside the aspects of self-interest which do not serve the common good.

Please note that the four key ethical principles are not the only way of applying moral philosophy to business ethics. Other examples include:

- The Markkula Center for Applied Ethics: A framework for ethical decision making.[12]
- Roger Steare's *Ethicability*.[13]

Conclusion

The four ethical principles are a practical way of applying ethics in business decisions and in examining your own conscience.

The toolkit that follows shows you how to apply them in decision making.

Notes

1. See: https://www.theguardian.com/world/1997/may/12/indonesia.ethicalforeignpolicy.
2. See: https://www.bbc.co.uk/mediacentre/proginfo/2024/34/the-reunion.
3. The Treatise of Human Nature by David Hume (1740).
4. Midgley, M. (2000) *Utopias, Dolphins and Computers: Problems of Philosophical Plumbing*. Psychology Press, p.78.
5. *Wealth of Nations* (1776) bk. 1, ch. 2.

6 See: https://www.ethicalfitness.org; https://ssbea.mercer.edu/blanke/Kidder.pdf.
7 Kant, I. (1785) *Groundwork of the Metaphysics of Morals*.
8 Gilligan, C. (2011) *Joining The Resistance*.
9 Bentham, J. (1776) *A Fragment on Government*.
10 Ref Mill, J.S. (1861) *Utilitarianism*.
11 Grant, A. (1885) *The Ethics of Aristotle, Illustrated with Essays and Notes*. 4th edn, p. 221. Longmans, Green & Co.
12 See: https://www.scu.edu/ethics/ethics-resources/a-framework-for-ethical-decision-making/.
13 See: https://thecorporatephilosopher.org/.

Toolkit A: Ethical decision making

How do you apply the key ethical principles to decisions?

Every leader and organisation faces ethical dilemmas in their decisions and builds a reputation on their response.

This toolkit is in two sections – process and principles. It supports and challenges decision makers, helping meet their responsibility to make well-balanced decisions ethically and commercially. You should adapt it to complement your organisation's policies and processes.

How to use the toolkit

Section 1 is for the person leading the decision-making process to ensure it is effective.

Score it individually or as a small group and ensure you have evidence for each score.

A total score of 60 or more provides a high level of confidence.

A score of 40–60 shows that there are significant areas that need improving.

A score below 40 indicates that a systemic change may be needed to get to a reliable decision.

In any case, the scores against each individual question will highlight individual areas to improve.

Section 2 is for individuals involved in the decision to complete to ensure ethical rigour.

Dilemmas will rarely score a maximum of 12 marked 'yes'; a score of 9 or more is sound.

The discussion about areas of disagreement or improvement are more important than the score.

Section 1 Process

Heading	Key process questions Ratings: 4 very high, 3 high, 2 medium, 1 low	Level of confidence Rate 1–4
Diagnose the problem	**1** How well defined is the problem and its measure of success? **2** How will it contribute to our long-term purpose? **3** Which stakeholders are affected? **4** What are the commercial and ethical dilemmas? **5** What is needed to reach a balanced decision?	
Apply due process	**6** Who is accountable for the decision? **7** Who should be involved to reduce bias? **8** Which process and regulations should be applied? **9** What are the inputs and assessments of risk? **10** Which organisational values apply?	
Evaluate benefits, costs and options	**11** How well have ethical principles been applied? (Section 2.) **12** How can risks be reduced or eliminated? **13** Which options maximise long-term impact? **14** How effectively have options been weighed up? **15** What is the right decision?	
Follow-through, explain and learn	**16** Who is affected and needs to know the decision? **17** How do we explain how and why we made the decision? **18** How do we ensure we deliver the intended impact? **19** What adjustments should we make during implementation? **20** What can we learn for future decisions?	
Total score		**Max 80**

Section 2 Principles

Everyone involved in the decision can test their conscience as follows in order to decide whether ethical principles have been applied effectively, i.e. to answer question 11 above. This can also be used as a standalone toolkit for personal dilemmas.

Key questions of principle See Chapter 1 for definitions of the four key principles	Yes/No
Integrity – honesty, self-control, accountability	
1 Would you want someone else to copy your decision?	
2 Would you make the same decision if it was openly published?	
3 Have you followed due process including consultation and taking advice?	
Duty – commitment to the common good	
4 If everyone did the same as you, would it serve the common good?	
5 Are you observing recognised laws, regulations and norms?	
6 Are you focused on the common good despite organisational/personal loyalties?	
Fairness – compassion, care, justice	
7 Have you thought through the benefits and costs with validated information?	
8 Will you achieve the greatest benefit for the greatest number of people?	
9 Have you adjusted to compensate for others' disadvantage or vulnerability?	
Freedom – autonomy, enlightened self-interest, imagination	
10 Have you been courageous enough?	
11 Have you taken account of risks to you and those close to you?	
12 Have you applied imagination to maximise benefit and avoid compromise?	
Total 'Yes'	**Max 12**

A dilemma is, by definition, likely to have some questions answered with 'no'.

Consider changing your decision in response to any 'no' answers, particularly if your score is below 10.

Note: the effectiveness of the toolkit depends on how rigorously you apply it and follow through.

chapter 2

The purpose of business

'A great responsibility is the inseparable result of a great power.'

French Revolution Committee of Public Safety (1793)

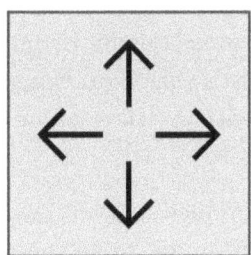

In this chapter you will learn:

- How business and markets have evolved
- The difference between *'shareholder primacy'* and *'stakeholder value'*
- How the wider responsibility of business is changing

Introduction

To understand the purpose of business, I will examine its roots from early co-operation and trade, through its exponential growth in the last two centuries to more recent debate about its wider responsibility.

What are the roots of trade?

About 40,000 years ago, modern humans started settling into communities with evidence of art and specialised tools. At about that time, the physically stronger Neanderthals died out. The ability to cooperate appears to have been our competitive advantage.

About 4,000 years ago, having formed more complex agricultural communities, we started to specialise as bakers, farmers and makers and invented a way to trade specialist expertise. This is when we invented money so that specialist bakers, blacksmiths and farmers did not have to rely on barter to find their customers.

About 400 years ago, the 'joint stock company' or 'company limited by shares' evolved from trade guilds and other late medieval organisations. The root of 'company' was in two words – 'cum pan' meaning 'with bread' – the age-old idea of breaking bread together and cooperating for the common good.[1]

The joint stock company separated the role of financial investors from employees. Money was no longer just a way to exchange goods and services, it was a way of fuelling innovation, with investors taking calculated risks in the expectation of financial returns.

The East India Company, founded in 1600, was the pioneer of this model, separating the roles of investor and worker. A privately funded arm of the British Empire, initially it held a monopoly over the emerging trade routes between South Asia and the rest of the world. Investors in the company could limit risk of losses to the amount they invested, with the opportunity to benefit from future profits with no upper limit. At this very early stage of the company, profit was the only aim of the East India Company, using its wealth and political influence to trade in slavery before and after the practice was made illegal in English law and employing a private army to enforce taxes and low labour costs.

There were other institutional models focused on the common good. For example, The Bank of England Charter of 1694 was 'to promote the good of the people of the UK'.[2] London's Livery companies started in the twelfth century, to provide assurance for the quality and reputation of goods produced by their members.

What are the roots of today's markets?

Adam Smith was a moral philosopher and economist who laid foundations for the free market in the eighteenth century when he published *The Wealth of Nations* in 1776. He was also the author of the *Theory of Moral Sentiments*, published in 1759, promoting the importance of virtue at a time when economics was a branch of philosophy. He argued for greater specialisation and removal of market constraints and tariffs to create greater economic and social value. Adam Smith saw a free market and specialisation as the ways of creating greater prosperity for both investors and society at large.

His writing was, in part, a reaction to the excesses of The East India Company and was rooted in a sense of virtue and serving the public good.

Together with the first industrial revolution, this economic model went on to deliver unprecedented growth in Western economies and the overall trend of growth continued for over two centuries.

As companies became common, intellectual property laws emerged in the eighteenth century. This encouraged investment in new ideas and new ventures, fuelling the first industrial revolution alongside the free-market principles promoted by Adam Smith. New laws gave investors reduced risks in return for their investment in scientific and technical breakthroughs. The breakthroughs were developed, scaled up and sold to other companies and consumers while increasing quality and efficiency through investment, innovation and competition.

Dramatic improvements in quality and reduction in cost were now applied to energy, food, clothing and other essentials. Non-essential and luxury goods and services also flourished.

Six decades after Adam Smith, Karl Marx and Friedrich Engels wrote *The Communist Manifesto* with a different vision. They advocated abolishing the system of class and property ownership and proposed instead central economic planning. Of the two major economies to adopt this model, the USSR disintegrated in 1991 and China has evolved into a 'socialist market economy'. Western capitalism has also evolved, adopting principles of progressive taxation, abolition of child labour and provision of universal free education, which were features of *The Communist Manifesto*.

Governments took the opportunity to tax profits, invest in public services and modify market freedoms, including employee rights, environmental obligations, reporting obligations and restraints on monopolies.

What were early examples of ethical business?

Some private companies rooted in ethical principles emerged in the eighteenth and nineteenth centuries. 'Quaker capitalism' in the UK and USA was an example, serving communities beyond the obligations of the business, based on Quaker values. Food businesses Cadbury, Huntley & Palmers, Clarks footwear, Furness Withy transport and Friends Provident insurance and Lloyds and Barclays banks were all founded by Quakers.

Cadbury paid particular attention to the welfare of its employees. The business built the Bourneville Estate in Birmingham, England, in the late nineteenth century, providing employees and their families with housing, gardens and parkland close to the Cadbury factory. It followed Quaker values, including prohibition of sale of alcohol. The site was given independence from the business through The Bourneville Village Trust, which has since developed further benefits for the residents including education and healthcare and still prohibits the sale of alcohol. It has acted as a blueprint for many other housing developments seeking to create communities based on ethical principles.

What has business achieved?

This cooperation and competition on a grand scale fuelled advances in health, education and welfare. The social constructs of money, companies, markets and intellectual property have unlocked phenomenal innovation and prosperity. Increasingly global and technology enabled, each generation builds on the previous generation's advances.

Four hundred years and three industrial revolutions later, limited liability companies are directly responsible for over 60% of employment in the UK and USA. By limiting the liability of investors and protecting their intellectual property, we encouraged speculation and innovation. For all its flaws, business has harnessed advances in science, health and education, doubled life expectancy and enabled human population to grow more than tenfold.

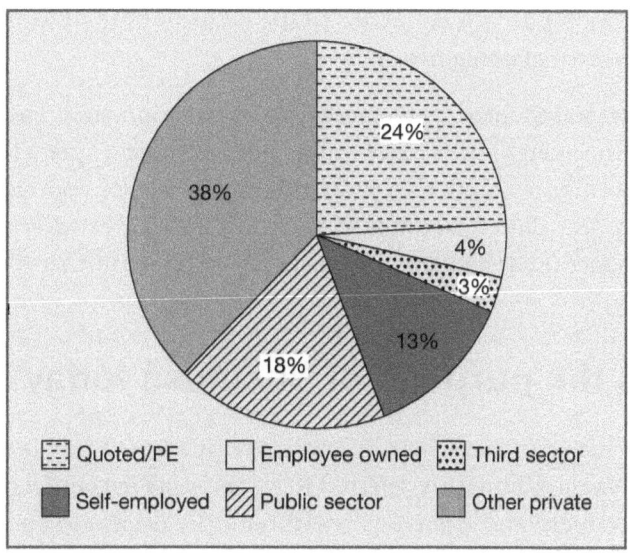

Where do employees work?

Notes: 'Public sector' means government and government-related bodies. 'PE' is Private equity. This is UK data from 2024; US data shows about 5% more in the private sector and 5% less in the public sector.[3]

What is the difference between 'shareholder primacy' and 'stakeholder value'?

Business has the power to create positive social change. However, since the 1970s, two broad schools of thought have competed to define the social responsibility of business.

In the 1970s, the economist Milton Friedman at the Chicago School of Economics promoted shareholder primacy, captured in the phrase: 'The only social responsibility of business is to increase its profits.'[4]

This was challenged in the 1980s by The Stanford Research Institute and Edward Freeman[5] who advocated a broader responsibility based on *'stakeholder value'*. They argued that business should take a wider view of stakeholders, not just shareholders, in their strategy and decision making: balancing the needs of employees, communities and the environment as priorities alongside shareholders. According to Edward Freeman, 'The interest of shareholders is dependent on how well you deal with customers and suppliers and employees and communities.'[6]

These short quotes do not do justice to the nuances of their work,[7] but they draw out an essential difference of view.

By the 1990s, stakeholder value encompassed environmental questions, captured by John Elkington's 'triple bottom line' of 'people, planet and profit', which he recently replaced with 'responsibility, resilience and regeneration'.[8] Initiatives by the United Nations (UN) in the 2000s created environmental social governance (ESG) standards for businesses, explored further in Chapter 18.

What is the purpose of business today?

The world's major markets have increasingly prioritised this broad view of stakeholder value, commonly referred to as *'corporate responsibility'*. From investors', consumers' and regulators' viewpoint, the licence to operate, legally and competitively, requires business to understand its full range of corporate responsibilities.

Markets have also globalised and, comparing market capitalisation with GDP, 30% of the 40 largest economies are companies not countries.[9] The old 'swim lanes', where governments set the rules and businesses maximise profit within the rules, are breaking down.

Larry Fink, chairman and CEO of BlackRock, charted the changing attitudes to ESG in his annual letter to investors. In 2018, he said: 'Society is demanding that companies, both public and private, serve a social purpose. To prosper over time, every company must not only deliver financial performance, but also show how it makes a positive contribution to society.'[10]

In 2019, the Business Roundtable, the association of more than 200 CEOs of the USA's leading companies, published a revised definition of the purpose of a corporation, encompassing a broad range of stakeholders including but not limited to shareholders.[11]

Also in 2019, the British Academy, the UK's national academy for the humanities and social sciences, published 'Principles for Purposeful Business'[12] for business leaders and policymakers covering law, regulations, shareholders, governance, measurement, performance, financing and partnerships.

More recent concerns with over-regulation in the USA have started moving the regulatory pendulum the other way on climate change[13] and diversity, equity and inclusion.[14] Larry Fink has also stopped using the term ESG since it has become politicised. It remains to be seen if this is just a change in labels and language or something more fundamental. For pension funds with long-term objectives, there are signs that corporate responsibility remains a strong priority.[15]

Conclusion

Every market and business within it requires the trust of a social licence to operate effectively. Gillian Tett[16] refers back to Adam Smith when she says '... remember the two sides of Smith. Unfettered competition can certainly drive growth – even crony capitalism can produce a sugar high. But "moral sentiments" – trust and the rule of law – are essential for long-term prosperity.'

Business has the power and responsibility to improve the world around it. The ways that an individual business translates that into action are explored in the chapters that follow.

Questions

- Do you think business has a corporate responsibility beyond profit?
- Has your business defined its corporate responsibilities?

Notes

1 See: https://www.etymonline.com/search?q=company.
2 See: https://www.bankofengland.co.uk/about/history
3 UK ONS, available at: https://www.ons.gov.uk/businessindustryandtrade; similar in the USA, see: https://s-corp.org/wp-content/uploads/2021/09/S-Corp-Association-Slide-deck-Public-Employment-Analysis_.pdf.
4 See: https://www.mckinsey.com/featured-insights/corporate-purpose/from-there-to-here-50-years-of-thinking-on-the-social-responsibility-of-business.
5 See: https://archive.org/details/strategicmanagem00free.
6 See: https://www.hbs.edu/bigs/ed-freeman.
7 See: https://www.ie.edu/insights/articles/the-misquoted-and-misunderstood-milton-friedman/
8 See: https://www.imd.org/ibyimd/audio-articles/regenerative-business-three-rs-are-new-triple-bottom-line/

9 See: https://docs.google.com/spreadsheets/d/1R86JWf6k0lCfcmWcm9mpLrt0KwW II2I7y5Yn_gh-m1o/htmlview#gid=0.
10 L. Fink, letter, 2018.
11 See: https://www.businessroundtable.org/business-roundtable-redefines-the-purpose-of-a-corporation-to-promote-an-economy-that-serves-all-americans.
12 See: https://www.thebritishacademy.ac.uk/publications/future-of-the-corporation-principles-for-purposeful-business/.
13 See: https://www.ft.com/content/8087b0bc-1cd1-4581-9fe6-fa4f8ecf3b38.
14 See: https://www.ft.com/content/f4615bfd-b3dd-4d12-9e5c-55bbd8bc6bd9.
15 See: https://www.ft.com/content/27160b76-b9a8-4eb4-9ea9-582d15637dad.
16 See: https://www.ft.com/content/25974008-ac91-4dde-bd8c-165b8a08fa4a.

chapter 3

Putting ethics into practice

'Great leaders know that money is
the fuel not the destination.'

Simon Sinek

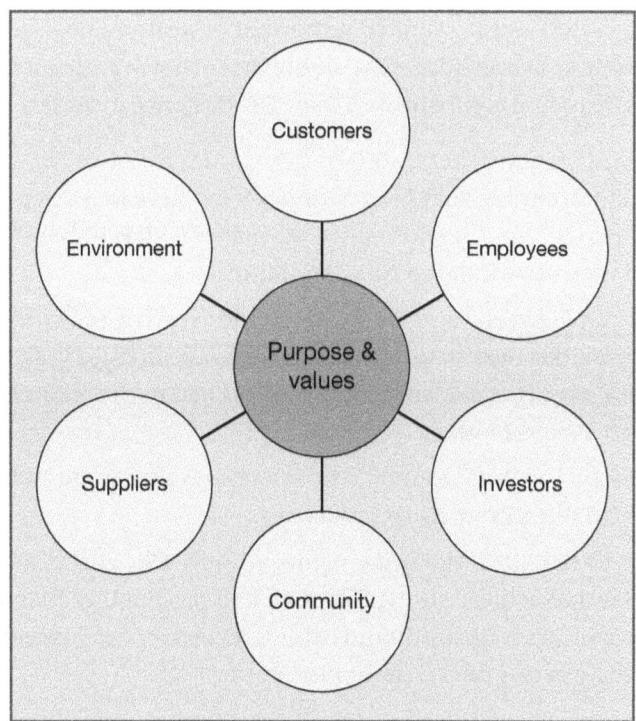

In this chapter you will learn:

- How ethical organisations perform, illustrated by case studies
- How ownership affects priorities
- How to balance stakeholder needs
- The three ways that organisations demonstrate ethical behaviour
- The three key challenges of corporate responsibility

Introduction

As explained in Chapter 1, I define 'ethics' as a set of organisational principles that guide decisions and behaviour to do what is right. 'Values' or 'principles' are the specific ethics that a business stands for; in practice, 'ethics', 'values' and 'principles' are interchangeable in many of the toolkits. These are not universal definitions; feel free to adopt or adapt them to your business context.

How do ethical organisations perform?

There is no consistent definition of 'ethical business', and many other factors are involved, so it is not possible to prove that ethical business causes higher long-term profit. However, successive studies have shown clear correlations between ethics, trust and competitive advantage. Evidence includes:

- Alex Edmans[1] found 'The "100 Best Companies to Work For in America" delivered stock returns that beat their peers by 2.3% to 3.8% per year over a 28 year period.' And 'Performance on material stakeholder issues are ... correlated with superior long-run stock returns.'
- Raj Sisodia, David Wolfe and Jag Sheth[2] found 'firms of endearment outperformed the market over all time frames, ranging from three years to 15 years. They have also outperformed the companies cited in the book *Good to Great* over the last 10 and 15 years.'
- The EY Beacon Institute[3] found '... transformations that put humans at the centre are 2.6 times more likely to succeed'.
- According to the 2023 McKinsey report on how ESG affects performance, 'Companies that achieve stronger growth and profitability than their peers while improving sustainability and ESG scores deliver two percentage points greater annual excess total shareholder return.'[4]

3 PUTTING ETHICS INTO PRACTICE

Here are two case studies of businesses that have delivered successful competitive advantage with an ethical purpose.

The features of both organisations are:

- **Consistency:** long-term commitment to values.
- **Relevance:** ethical behaviour which is relevant to customers.
- **Long-term focus:** prioritise the long term over the short term.
- **Accountability:** being transparent about adherence to stated values.

They also prioritise actions over words, comfortable to change the way purpose and values are publicly expressed.

Case study – Nationwide Building Society[5]

In 1996, the CEO of Nationwide Building Society, Dr Brian Davis, called together his 50 senior managers for a discussion about the organisation's future. Nationwide is and was a UK building society, owned by its savers for over 100 years. At the time of the meeting, most of its competitors were preparing to convert their status to banks, quoted on the London Stock Exchange. That meant more freedom to carry out wider banking activities and investments, regulation by the Bank of England and a windfall for the savers who would receive a windfall in return for giving up their ownership.

It seemed like everybody would win. I was one of those senior managers and, together with my colleagues, fully expected the CEO to set the wheels in motion for conversion. Instead, he talked about the purpose of the building society, about our members and owners, the savers, and the peace of mind they would need from us in the long term.

Soon afterwards, the board initiated the process to get support from members to remain as a building society and remain in their ownership. A group of savers, who stood to gain short-term windfalls and were entitled to call for a vote, challenged the decision in 1997 and lost by a narrow margin.

Other building societies that converted fared less well. Northern Rock collapsed during the financial crisis of 2008. Another, Halifax, was taken over by Bank of Scotland and later needed rescuing by Lloyds Banking Group in 2009. Nationwide, on the other hand, steadily increased its market share and later acquired three building societies and Virgin Money.

Case study – Patagonia[6]

Patagonia's changed its mission in 2018 to: 'We're in business to save our home planet.'[7]

Its original mission was 'To make the best gear, do the least harm and use the business to make change.' It has always been focused on constantly innovating to help people do human-powered outdoor activity.

The founder Yvon Chouinard comes from a modest background in Maine whose family later moved to California. As an unconventional outsider, inventor, rock climber and fanatic for improvement in outdoor equipment, Yvon started his business in the 1960s making climbing equipment. He realised the pitons they were making were being hammered permanently into, and harming, rocks. He designed a new removable device, a 'chock', performing the same role as pitons with no damage to rocks. The organisation is now a global business focused on clothing. Yvon gave the part of the business focused on climbing gear, Black Diamond, to its employees. He also influenced North Face and Esprit, both started by his friend Doug Tompkins.

Patagonia is uncompromising in its pursuit of quality and high environmental standards over and above economic gain. For example, during the COVID restrictions it sacrificed $100 million in sales by shutting off wholesale accounts with distributors that failed to encourage customers to reduce their carbon footprint. It is now examining the effects of microfibres released by the fleece used in its clothing. It is committed to discontinuing it if the environmental impact cannot be solved in the next few years.

Is this commitment to values or just enlightened self-interest? The uncompromising nature of decisions they have made, with clear immediate costs and uncertain long-term benefits, points to the former. This is underlined by the founder's lack of interest in personal wealth – he has lived in the same house for nearly 50 years and has chosen to forgo several $ billion by transferring the business to a charitable foundation fighting climate change and species loss.

Patagonia was one of the first US businesses to become a certified B Corporation, committing to high standards of social and environmental performance, transparency and accountability.

How does ownership affect priorities?

Neither of these businesses is publicly quoted. Only 25–30% of employees in the UK and USA work for publicly listed companies, the rest work for private companies, government bodies and the third sector (non-profits).

Patagonia is a privately owned company, originally owned by its founder Yvon Chouinard, who has transferred the shares to a trust to preserve its purpose beyond his lifetime. Nationwide Building Society decided not to convert to a publicly quoted company and remains owned by its saver customers. They are therefore not subject to the scrutiny of external shareholders who focus on real-time share price movements and are free to sell or buy.

Several leaders of privately held businesses told me that, by not being publicly listed, they felt more confident of prioritising ethical health over short-term profits.

The third sector organisations (including charities and social enterprises) are obliged to prioritise their social purpose and treat profits as a means to an end. Although they are a small part of the economy (3% in the UK), there are lessons to be learned from their experience.

One example is measuring and reporting non-financial value through 'impact statements'. Typically, they include quantitative data on the number of beneficiaries of their service and assessment of the benefits they have received, as well as qualitative case studies to bring the impact to life.

This has already been influential in ESG reporting for large and listed business, explored further in Chapter 18.

Another example is the development of 'purpose and values', which are fundamental to third sector organisations and are now common in commercial organisations.

The following case study draws out a practical ethical dilemma where the purpose delivered the answer.

Case study – Unloc[8]

Hayden Taylor is managing director of Unloc, a successful social enterprise delivering programmes for young and disadvantaged people to build their skills and confidence. He is a self-made social entrepreneur who started Unloc with his co-founder Ben Dowling when he was 16. Eleven years later, it has grown into a vibrant team of 26 people, whose commitment to social impact and ethical practice is prominent in everything they do.

He has grown the organisation by being both highly principled and commercially astute. He is therefore very aware of ethical dilemmas in his work and, in our conversation, was able to refer to several instances of tensions between commercial opportunity and risk to the values and principles of Unloc.

Dilemma

An example was the problem of buying a car for the business. Having decided they needed one, the question was whether to buy a more expensive electric vehicle with a lower carbon footprint or a cheaper hybrid with a higher carbon footprint. The difference in price (£10,000) meant that buying the electric car would mean they could not deliver as many programmes. Should they protect the planet or help more young people with their skills and confidence?

As MD, Hayden had the authority to make this decision. Many MDs would do just that. However, he does not lead in this way and the process to arrive at the decision involving his entire senior team of six people was as revealing about his leadership principles as the decision itself.

Options

The two options had a clear trade-off. A lower carbon-impact car meant fewer programmes for young people, a higher carbon-impact car was within budget and protected the funding earmarked for programmes.

A third option was discussed, which was to seek funding from a sponsor to avoid the dilemma altogether. Hayden was clear this was unrealistic, saying, 'You need green credentials to raise funding but, in practice, the credentials are more about your long-term commitment to improve; nobody in my market will pay you extra to reduce your carbon footprint in the short term.' There are government schemes to help businesses reduce their carbon emissions, but Hayden's social enterprise did not have access to this kind of subsidy for this particular investment, relying instead on corporate sponsors and educational clients who choose their suppliers like Unloc as much on cost as on quality. The dilemma was unavoidable.

Decision

Everyone in the team of six argued from a principled position. At one end was the purpose of the social enterprise: to help as many young people as possible. At the other end was the obligation to reduce carbon emissions by any means. The two were in direct conflict. They weighed up the two by discussion until they reached a decision they could all live with. In the end, it was their organisation's mission (to help young people) that held sway. They went with b – higher carbon emissions and more programmes.

Reflection

Hayden as MD was heavily influential in this outcome: 'I have a strong commitment to sustainability, but I also have a business to run.' As a leader he has to take people with him: 'As a social impact organisation, we have set our ethical bar very high; every difficult decision we make has to be carefully explained to our colleagues and funders; we also have to think about recruitment; most candidates will only join if they know we are serious about our principles.'

He added: 'As a kid, I lobbied uncompromisingly for organisations to behave sustainably. Now, as an adult and social entrepreneur, I realise the world is more complex. I'm accountable for the consequences of my decisions which sometimes leads to compromise, but I'm still driven by my original ideals.'

Unloc sets a high ethical bar because it holds strong beliefs as a team. It also makes commercial sense: funders and sponsors work with them because of their values. However, this example shows that, when values come into conflict, the commitment to discuss and understand different views is as important as the views themselves.

How do you balance stakeholder needs?

Markets and regulators have broadly moved to a stakeholder value view of business but with a wide range of interpretations. It leaves boards and CEOs to juggle their priorities to meet the interests of all stakeholders, including customers, employees, investors, communities, suppliers and the natural environment.

In my conversations with business leaders, the ethical dilemmas they faced were about 'doing the right thing' when their conscience and the interests of stakeholders, such as investors, customers, suppliers or colleagues, were not aligned. It is an age-old challenge.

Resolving the dilemma came down to having clarity of purpose and values to set expectations and shape priorities. When it works, as one leader put it, it achieves a 'dynamic equilibrium' with stakeholder needs held in balance.

There are as many ways of defining purpose and values as there are organisations. There are several examples in cases studies throughout this book with a consistent insight that actions are more influential than words.

Are there generational differences?

The pressure on business to focus on ethical purpose looks set to continue if we look at the emerging generation of consumers and employees.

The so-called Generation Z (or Gen Z) are people born between 1996 and 2012, now in their teens and twenties. I do not know anyone in this category who appreciates being labelled in this way. However, while the research does not do justice to the range and individuality of preferences, this age group marks a shift in ethical expectations.

They were the first generation to grow up with access to an online world at a time of growing concern about climate change and two global economic shocks: the 2008 financial crisis and the 2020 pandemic. They are now 25% of the world population and set to be the highest spending cohort in the next decade.

Research suggests that this generation has a greater commitment than older generations to more ethical business practice:[9]

'They want to buy from and work for companies that share their inclusive values and engage on social issues.

'They encourage people to be themselves and want to make others feel welcomed and respected. And they are far more likely than older generations to believe climate change is an existential threat.

'Generation Z are less loyal to brands and seek those which celebrate their differences and support their fight against rigid gender norms, beauty discrimination, and climate change. They are more reliant on social media for information and seek out unfiltered marketing which shows the imperfections of life and authentic commitment to social causes.'

Another study among Gen Z consumers in Brazil focused on brands that take an ethical stand.[10]

'Generation Z consumers increasingly expect brands to "take a stand." The point is not to have a politically correct position on a broad range of topics. It is to choose the specific topics (or causes) that make sense for a brand and its consumers and to have something clear to say about those particular issues. In a transparent world, younger consumers don't distinguish between the ethics of a brand, the company that owns it, and its network of partners and suppliers.

'The good news is that consumers – in particular Gen Zers – are tolerant of brands when they make mistakes, if the mistakes are corrected. That path is more challenging for large corporations, since a majority of our respondents believe that major brands are less ethical than small ones'"

This also translates into hiring and motivating Gen Z employees:[11]

'Gen Z's support for social and political causes is already boosting activism within workplaces, putting pressure on management teams to be vocal on issues that they may have previously stayed silent on. Maxime Lakat, the 25-year-old co-head of Canadian non-profit Re-generation, which aims to mobilise young people to create a greener economy, says Gen Z's views about work and life have been shaped by the failures of people in power – from the fallout of the global financial crisis and effects of climate change to chaos in politics and minute-by-minute updates to their devices about tragic global wars. They are keen to work somewhere they can make an impact.'

What are the three ways for a business to be ethical?

There is a growing awareness of 'externalities', i.e. the consequence of business activity that has an impact into and out from the business without affecting the balance sheet. Businesses can behave responsibly either by bringing externalities into their decision making, for example reducing their carbon footprint, or going further to pursue a cause or system change by influencing their sector, regulator or government to raise standards.

My conversations with leaders highlighted that businesses demonstrate ethical behaviour in three broad categories. Some businesses demonstrate all three, depending on the context.

1 **Consistency – complying with commitments and regulations.**

   The organisation meets its obligations to legal and good practice, for example protecting the safety and rights of employees and meeting its quality and service commitments to customers and other stakeholders. If it falls short of its commitments, it accepts responsibility and takes compensating action.

   It builds a reputation for doing what it says it is going to do.

   This is sound business practice but is also a source of competitive advantage. An example is the commitment to customers by the UK retailer John Lewis 'never knowingly undersold' introduced in 1925 and, after a short pause, re-introduced in 2023.[12]

2 **Conscience – going beyond obligations to do what is right.**

   The organisation goes beyond legal and contractual obligations by observing principles that define an 'organisational conscience'. It treats stakeholders with care and compassion even if that incurs additional short-term costs or uncomfortable truths. For example, it may provide assistance to employees or suppliers experiencing hardship.

   It builds long-term relationships, guided more by shared purpose than contractual terms.

   An example is the group of 16,000 Living Wage employers in the UK that choose to pay more than the minimum legal wage to their lowest paid employees.

3 Cause – pursuing system change for a cause beyond the organisation.

The organisation applies pressure externally for an ethical cause while living by its principles inside the business. It may include activism to raise awareness, lobbying for more rigorous regulation and collaborating on voluntary standards.

It builds a reputation for moral courage.

An example is the collaboration between Ben & Jerry's and Tony's Chocolonely to end modern slavery and child labour in the chocolate industry.[13]

What are the key challenges of corporate responsibility?

In balancing stakeholder needs and seeking purpose beyond profit, the leaders I spoke to gave a wide range of answers to the question 'What is your wider corporate responsibility?'

One leader said, 'I don't think about ethics, I just take good care of my team because I care about them and it's good for business.' Most were focused on stakeholders close to the business: shareholders, staff and customers.

Others focused on a broader definition of stakeholders including the environment as a whole. For them, the ethical principle of reciprocity 'treat others as you would want to be treated by them' is not enough. They extend the principle in the way philosopher John Rawls' *Veil of Ignorance* invites us to set aside our narrow view of the world – my organisation, my community – and take a universal view that includes remote stakeholders.

In the landmark legal case *Donoghue v Stevenson* (1932), the manufacturer of a bottle of ginger beer contaminated by the remains of a snail was found to have a legal duty of care to the consumer, even though there was no direct contract between them. It extended the responsibility of a business in Scotland and England to a consumer if the business could reasonably foresee they would be harmed by it.

It highlights a 'moral hierarchy': as a business we may care more about some stakeholders than others, our duties may be higher for stakeholders that are close and lower for those that are remote. However, the law, regulations and ethical continue to grapple with the question 'To which communities do I owe a duty of care?'

When environmental changes are affecting a community we don't know, perhaps through droughts and wildfires, does a business have a duty to change its practice and reduce risk for that remote community? This is contentious when there are trade-offs, diverting resources or reducing short-term profits for the benefit of 'remote stakeholders'.

As a leader, you have greater obligations to your team, customers and shareholders than to the communities they live in or wider society. With limited resources, your business pays a salary to its employees, it might provide insurance to help protect their families and it might have a social programme to support projects in the local community but not support charities focused on causes in other communities.

However, boundaries are becoming less clear. The global community is more connected, the workforce is more mobile, there are more multinational businesses, supply chains are more international, pandemic and climate change risks are global.

In short, remote stakeholders are becoming less remote. The question for businesses and leaders is, are you doing your fair share, consistent with your business purpose and personal conscience?

Katie Hill is co-chair of B-Lab Global, the organisation behind B Corp certification. Its aim is to drive change in the global economy to benefit everyone and is described in more detail in Chapter 19. Katie sees particular challenges for business leaders in addressing climate change and social inequality.

My discussions with other leaders added a third challenge – emerging technology. Like previous industrial revolutions, businesses can choose how to apply new technology and how it serves narrower and wider interests. We amplified physical power on a grand scale when we harnessed the new technologies of steam, gas and electricity in the nineteenth century. We now have global connectivity, artificial intelligence and bioengineering to amplify both our mental and physical power with benefits and risks on an equally grand scale.

In the chapters that follow, the three key challenges of corporate responsibility are spelled out under the headings:

- The natural environment
- Social equity
- Emerging technology.

Conclusion

Balancing stakeholder needs has always been a key challenge for any business, but the range of stakeholders and complexity of challenges are both rising.

Choosing the priorities that are most relevant to your business is critical. Well-defined purpose and values that are lived out in practice are the key to meeting these challenges.

Questions

- Does your business have a purpose and values that work in practice?
- Do you have a clear sense of your organisation's ethical health?
  (See Toolkit B that follows.)
- What are your ethical priorities?
  (See Chapters 4, 5 and 6 and accompanying toolkits.)

Notes

1. Edmans, A. (2020) *Grow The Pie*, p. 96.
2. Sisodia, R., Wolfe, D. and Sheth, J. (2014) Firms of Endearment, p. 20.
3. See: https://www.ey.com/content/dam/ey-unified-site/ey-com/en-uk/insights/workforce/documents/ey-how-to-attain-purpose-led-transformation.pdf.
4. See: https://www.mckinsey.com/capabilities/growth-marketing-and-sales/our-insights/next-in-growth/how-do-esg-goals-impact-a-companys-growth-performance.
5. See: https://www.nationwide.co.uk/about-us/our-history/.
6. Author's interview with Charles Conn, Chair, Patagonia.
7. See: https://eu.patagonia.com/gb/en/ownership/.
8. Author's interview with Hayden Taylor, MD, Unloc.
9. The findings from two years of research on Gen Z conducted by the Oliver Wyman Forum and The News Movement, launched at the World Economic Forum in Davos, 2023. See: https://www.oliverwymanforum.com/content/dam/oliver-wyman/ow-forum/template-scripts/a-gen-z/pdf/A-Gen-Z-Report.pdf
10. See: https://www.mckinsey.com/industries/consumer-packaged-goods/our-insights/true-gen-generation-z-and-its-implications-for-companies.

11 *Financial Times*, 17 June 2024, available at: https://www.ft.com/content/ee6fb86c-d2c6-4bc3-ac5c-e7bd7a1db1d4?accessToken=zwAAAZIvTefNk88DntN6-yFDZdO-hosL9HloS3NPub7hs0sZLw9OsXOe9eh2x1NP1bWobnWRDgNOshKRMsb67DwE.MEQCIDckierSH8G9kcx_TUPARaNc3tGC5hfjn8GCAGtkdN7SAiAHw_3_AGatYsFNUjQ12Jvh3i77Wvs1fAXM_E8h_TlN3g&segmentId=85462057-4e57-56c2-164f-e4ce1f09e15f.
12 See: https://www.johnlewis.com/content/a-history-of-john-lewis.
13 See: https://www.fairtrade.org.uk/media-centre/news/ben-jerrys-joins-forces-with-tonys-chocolonely-to-make-chocolate-100-slave-free/.

Toolkit B: Ethical health

What is the ethical health of your organisation?

Background

This toolkit will help you assess ethical health at a high level. You should adapt it to complement your organisation's policies and processes.

Organisations demonstrate ethical behaviour in three broad categories. Some businesses demonstrate all three depending on the context.

1. **Consistency – complying with commitments and regulations.**

    The organisation meets its obligations to legal and good practice, for example protecting the safety and rights of employees and meeting its quality and service commitments to customers and other stakeholders. If it falls short of its commitments, it accepts responsibility and takes compensating action. It builds a reputation for doing what it says it is going to do.

2. **Conscience – going beyond obligations to do what is right.**

    The organisation goes beyond legal and contractual obligations by observing principles that define an 'organisational conscience'. It treats stakeholders with care and compassion even if that incurs additional short-term costs or uncomfortable truths. For example, it may provide assistance to employees or suppliers experiencing hardship. It builds long-term relationships, guided more by shared purpose than contractual terms.

3. **Cause – pursuing system change for a cause beyond the organisation.**

    The organisation applies pressure externally for an ethical cause, while living by its principles inside the business. It may include activism to raise awareness, lobbying for more rigorous regulation and collaborating on voluntary standards. It builds a reputation for moral courage.

How to use the toolkit

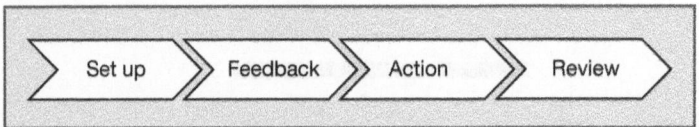

- **Set up with colleagues:**
    - Discuss the toolkit with a cross-section of colleagues; ideally, at a time when you are planning next year's priorities or the long-term strategy.
    - Work out how this toolkit can benefit the business, for example reinforcement of values, stakeholder trust and risk reduction.
- **Gather feedback:**
    - Ask a group of colleagues to complete the toolkit, including examples to back up their answers. If you think colleagues will answer more honestly by completing it anonymously then set up an online poll to collect anonymous answers.
- **Take action:**
    - Review the feedback as a group and identify strengths and areas to improve.
    - Identify actions to make improvements; use the other toolkits in this book, if necessary.
    - Assign responsibilities and follow through.
- **Review the impact:**
    - Revisit this toolkit when you have planned or made changes to test the effect on your scores.
    - Take action to improve further.

Note: the effectiveness of the toolkit depends on how rigorously you apply it and follow through.

Ethical health questions Ratings: 4 consistently/always, 3 often, 2 sometimes, 1 rarely/never	Rate 1–4	Evidence
Consistency		
1 Does the organisation deliver on its commitments?		
2 Does this create competitive advantage?		
Conscience		
3 Are the values (or principles or ethics) clearly understood?		
4 Do values take priority over rules when necessary?		
5 Are customers more loyal because of the values?		
6 Are employees attracted and retained by the values?		
7 Are suppliers more loyal because of the values?		
8 Do the values create competitive advantage overall?		
Cause		
9 Does the organisation stand for an ethical cause or causes?		
10 Is the organisation respected for moral courage?		
Total score	Max 40	
Notes: • Answer these from the viewpoint of either the whole organisation or a division or team. • This refers to 'values'; it works equally well referring to 'principles' or 'ethics'.		

Answer the questions individually, validate the evidence as a group, discuss and agree a score for each of the 10 questions, then add them up (maximum 40).

Total score	How to improve ethical health
30–40	The organisation has sound ethical health. Consider whether there are any areas to improve, in particular if the competitive advantage is not consistently high.
20–30	The organisation can improve its ethical health. Use the other toolkits in this book or other methods to identify specific areas to work on further.
Below 20	The organisation is carrying ethical risks or missing out on ethical potential or both. Use the other toolkits in this book or other methods to identify areas where work can start to develop ethical health.

chapter 4

Corporate responsibility for the natural environment

'If your operations can run on renewable energy, less water, generate less waste and pollution ... it is likely your business will become more attractive to investors and customers.'

Sarah Gillard

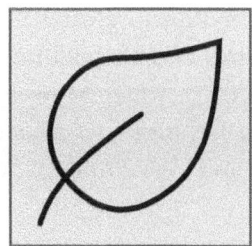

In this chapter you will learn:

- The key challenges in the natural environment
- The role that business can play, including two case studies
- How to use a toolkit to weigh up natural environment priorities in your business

Why should we be concerned about the natural environment?

The context is taken from The Royal Society's 'The Basics of Climate Change' and papers for the World Economic Forum's (WEF) and United Nations.[1]

Carbon dioxide (CO_2), methane and nitrous oxide are the greenhouse gases that, according to Royal Society, WEF and others, have increased significantly since pre-industrial times. CO_2 plays the largest role. Its concentration in the atmosphere has increased by 40% with most of this increase occurring since 1970. According to ice core analysis, greenhouse gas concentration had previously been stable for 800 years. Most of the increase is attributable to humans burning fossil fuels.

The effect is that global average surface air temperature has risen by 1.6°C (2.9°F) in 2024 compared to pre-industrial levels in 1850–1900, with each of the last four decades warmer than any other decade since 1850.

Higher air temperature increases sea temperature, melting ice, expanding sea volume and, therefore, increasing sea levels. The sea level has risen by about 21 cm (8 inches) since 1880. Some of the excess CO_2 in the atmosphere is also being taken up by the ocean, increasing acidity and water vapour, another greenhouse gas.

Our understanding of complex climate systems is that increasing greenhouse gases tend to have a multiplier effect on air temperature. Further increases in greenhouse gases at the same rate will therefore accelerate air temperature at a faster rate.

A warmer earth is already leading to greater incidence of floods, cyclones, hurricanes, typhoons, wildfires and air pollution. Expanding deserts reduce farming land and reduce access to water. More acidic oceans reduce diversity and quantity of sea life. The UN estimates that 13 million people a year die from environmental factors and over 2 million people a year are displaced by weather-related events.

Changes in the climate led to the United Nations setting up an Intergovernmental Panel on Climate Change (IPCC) in 1988 leading to the 'Conference of the Parties' (COP) which first met in 1995 and now has 195 member countries involved. The Climate Change Conference of 2015 (COP21)[2] created the Paris Agreement, which identified anything above a 1.5°C increase as a risk to 'unleashing ... more frequent and severe droughts, heatwaves and rainfall'.

There are some sceptics who see climate change as something that we do not or cannot influence. On the other hand, rising temperatures and other factors are affecting investor behaviour. Norway's vast $1.8 trillion sovereign fund suggests that the long-term impact of climate change would wipe out 19% of the value of its US equity holdings.[3] Regulators, customers and markets are all creating pressure on businesses to take individual and collective action.

It is a challenge to our commitment to the common good.

What can businesses do?

Many practical actions make short-term commercial sense, for example reducing print and packaging costs, improving building insulation to reduce energy costs, reducing pollution to meet regulatory obligations.

Strategic and longer-term commitments should refer to the values of the business to decide what is a priority. A business cannot do everything.

In these three case studies of design-driven businesses, they all have placed environmental concerns at their heart. See Chapters 18 and 19 for examples of larger businesses.

Vitsœ, the UK-based furniture business, is an example of an organisation that cherishes the longevity and sustainability of its product, as this extract from Vitsœ's ethos explains.

Case study – Vitsœ[4]

'For more than 65 years we have stood by our common sense approach of living better, with less, that lasts longer ...

'Every new customer for Vitsœ is another customer who will consume and dispose of less during their lifetime. Some observers are perplexed by Vitsœ's desire to sell less of its self-effacing furniture to more customers and to encourage them to live with it for longer ...

'We charge all our customers a single, fair, honest price and we do not have seasonal sales because our stock does not become obsolete.'

CAUKIN Studio is a small design and architectural practice that has found its niche by going beyond regulatory obligations. It is focused on locally sourced materials and training local communities to maintain the structures they build.

> ### Case study – CAUKIN Studio[5]
>
> Josh Peasley is an architectural designer who co-founded the award-winning design and build business CAUKIN Studio in 2015. The business started as a student project with his co-founders at Cardiff University. In their first project, they designed and built a playground in Cambodia, which they funded via Kickstarter, the funding platform for creative projects. After completing their Master's Degrees in Architecture, three of the founders decided to commit to the business, which is aiming to 'change the face of the built environment'.
>
> They have now completed over 60 projects in 13 countries based on key sustainability principles. They include at least 90% of raw materials sourced within 50 km of the project and a commitment to train local people in maintenance skills.
>
> Josh describes ethical leadership as 'leading by example with solid morals and the integrity to admit to mistakes'. Their business has an ethical heart defined by three public statements:
>
> *'We believe every human being should have the opportunity and tools to shape the spaces they inhabit.'*
>
> *'We should all benefit from the quality of life that is achieved through informed design.'*
>
> *'Construction has to reduce its environmental impact on our planet.'*

RE_CONSIDERED is a small business in the textiles market. Initially, it focused on upcycling, then went on to develop a recycling material in a market where only 13% of discarded textiles are recycled.

> ## Case study – RE_CONSIDERED[6]
>
> According to the founder Tabby Bunyan:
>
> 'One of the first things I wanted to do with RE_CONSIDERED, and what upcycling allows you to do, is produce items that have stories behind them. The difference between 'recycling' and 'upcycling' is that you can still recognise the original item in the upcycled piece, whereas a recycled object is completely different. Stories are inherent to the craft of upcycling and the pieces I create.
>
> 'Fabreco®, on the other hand, is an innovative recycled and multipurpose material made from waste textiles and bio-resin. It can be used to make furniture, jewellery, homeware products and much more.'

Conclusion

See Toolkit C to put these insights into practice.

Notes

1. See: https://royalsociety.org/news-resources/projects/climate-change-evidence-causes/basics-of-climate-change/; https://www.weforum.org/stories/2024/09/rising-sea-levels-global-threat/; and https://www.un.org/en/climatechange/science/causes-effects-climate-change.
2. See: https://unfccc.int/process-and-meetings/the-paris-agreement.
3. See: https://www.nbim.no/contentassets/6fdfd333e6bf460f8e538b9b55a95bb7/gpfg-climate-and-nature-disclosures-2024.pdf; and https://www.ft.com/moral-money?emailId=2370a82f-2c93-467c-9bf1-1cbd91af4ee1&segmentId=a8cbd258-1d42-1845-7b82-00376a04c08f.
4. See: https://www.vitsoe.com/gb/about/ethos.
5. Author's interview with Josh Peasley, co-founder of CAUKIN Studio.
6. See: https://reconsidered.co.uk/blogs/news/items-with-stories-to-tell.

Toolkit C: The natural environment

What is your organisation's responsibility for the natural environment?

This toolkit enables you to create or test your organisation's plans. You should adapt it to complement your organisation's policies and processes.

How to use the toolkit

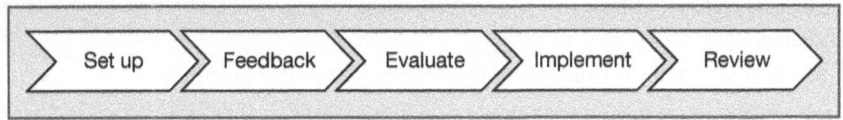

Set up ▶ Feedback ▶ Evaluate ▶ Implement ▶ Review

- **Set up with colleagues:**
  - Discuss the toolkit with a cross-section of colleagues, ideally at a time when you are planning next year's priorities or the long-term strategy.
  - Work out how this toolkit can benefit the business, for example reinforcement of values, stakeholder trust and risk reduction.
- **Gather feedback:**
  - Ask a group of colleagues to complete the toolkit including examples and evidence to back up their answers. If you think colleagues will answer more honestly by completing it anonymously, then set up an online poll to collect anonymous answers.

- If the feedback identifies key risks 'that are hard to discuss', consider creating an independent review. It may need to report to a governance director or senior independent non-executive director to ensure objectivity.
- **Evaluate actions:**
  - Review the feedback as a group and identify strengths and areas to improve, looking at case studies in this book for inspiration, if necessary.
  - Identify actions to make improvements.
  - Evaluate each action against potential benefits, costs and risks, then rank the actions in order of net benefit. Decide which actions to take forward and which to drop or defer.

  Note: use your organisation's normal project evaluation process; if you do not have one, use the *Benefits Scoring Matrix* below.
- **Implement:**
  - Identify risks and enablers and who needs to be consulted and directly involved to achieve the benefits, reduce risks and unlock the resources to deliver the changes.
  - Secure commitment to make changes based on the actions that achieve the greatest benefit.
  - If costs and investment are required, secure the budget required.
  - Assign responsibilities and follow through.
- **Review the impact:**
  - Revisit the impact of your actions.
  - Take action to improve further.

Benefits Scoring Matrix (if needed)

Heading	Ethical	Financial	Total
Benefits (e.g. Low = 1)	1–4	1–4	2–8
Costs and risks (e.g. Low = 4)	1–4	1–4	2–8
Total	2–8	2–8	4–16

- Use judgement to decide criteria for 'very high', 'high', 'medium' and 'low'.
- Use your stated purpose (or mission), values and behaviours as criteria for the ethical column. If you do not have these, use 'stakeholder trust' as a proxy.

- Score 'Benefits' as very high 4, high 3, medium 2, low 1.
- Score 'Costs and risks' as low 4, medium 3, high 2, very high 1.
- Add up total scores in the right-hand column, out of a maximum of 16.
- Rank the highest scoring action at the top and the lowest scoring at the bottom.

Note: the effectiveness of the toolkit depends on how rigorously you apply it and follow through.

The natural environment Ratings: 4 very high, 3 high, 2 medium, 1 low	Priority Rate 1–4	Current Effectiveness Rate 1–4	Action to Improve Effectiveness
Process			
Strategy and planning • Set environmental strategy and principles. • Evaluate benefits, ethics, costs, risks and impact. • Prioritise against overall purpose and values. • Set targets including emissions. • Join external collaborative networks. • Regularly review against best practice.			
Governance and compliance[Note 1] • Agree governance and oversight process. • Understand and comply with regulations. • Determine external review or audit process. • Report against benefits, costs, risks and impact.			
Management and reporting • Assign responsibilities, targets and resources. • Set operational processes and controls. • Manage performance and risks. • Track and report benefits, costs, risks and impact. • Learn and improve against best practice.			

4 CORPORATE RESPONSIBILITY FOR THE NATURAL ENVIRONMENT

The natural environment Ratings: 4 very high, 3 high, 2 medium, 1 low	Priority Rate 1–4	Current Effectiveness Rate 1–4	Action to Improve Effectiveness
Engagement and training • Consult and communicate with stakeholders. • Inform and train employees and suppliers. • Set performance incentives and sanctions. • Publish and promote plans and performance.			
Actions			
Energy and resources • Reduce emissions overall. • Improve efficiency and insulation of property. • Increase renewable energy sources. • Increase use of biofuels. • Reduce travel. • Increase locally sourced suppliers.			
Waste, pollution and circular economy • Reduce waste and pollution overall. • Apply 9R[Note 2] principles. • Reduce production waste. • Reduce packaging. • Reduce use of non-recycled material. • Reduce use of consumables, e.g. paper, ink. • Increase water conservation. • Segregate and recycle waste.			
Biodiversity • Source animal and plant supplies sustainably. • Increase sustainability of business-owned land, plants and animals.			

The natural environment Ratings: 4 very high, 3 high, 2 medium, 1 low	Priority Rate 1–4	Current Effectiveness Rate 1–4	Action to Improve Effectiveness
Supply chain and distribution channels<ul><li>Set standards for suppliers and partners.</li><li>Adapt procurement and partnering criteria.</li><li>Set performance incentives and sanctions.</li><li>Manage performance and risks.</li></ul>			
Note 1: See Chapters 18 and 19 for information on ESG-related regulations and voluntary standards. *Note 2:* The 9Rs of the circular economy comprise 10 strategies numbered 0–9. They are: refuse, rethink, reduce, reuse, repair, refurbish, remanufacture, repurpose, recycle and recover.[1]			

Note

1 See: https://www.weforum.org/stories/2022/05/the-circular-economy-how-it-can-be-a-path-to-real-change/.

chapter 5

Corporate responsibility for social equity

'We cannot afford growth at any cost; any business growth must actively tackle climate change and social inequality.'

Katie Hill

In this chapter you will learn:

- How social equality is correlated with economic growth
- The implications of human rights
- The role of diversity, equity and inclusion
- The difference between equity and equality
- The role that business can play, illustrated by three case studies
- How to use a toolkit to weigh up social equity priorities in your business

What is the relationship between social equality and economic growth?

In an increasingly global economy, the shocks of the financial crash of 2008 and the pandemic of 2020 have led to falling trust in governments and businesses.[1]

At the same time, key measures of income and wealth have shown a marked increase in inequality in developed economies over the last four decades. For example, a key measure of inequality, the Gini Index of income, has increased by between 4% and 15% in the USA, United Kingdom and Germany since 1980. It has also increased by 20% in China. Although income has increased in real terms over that period, the share taken by the highest 1% has approximately doubled.[2]

A study by the IMF showed that greater equality of income increased the duration of countries' economic growth more than other factors such as free trade, low government corruption and foreign investment.[3] As Mark Carney says, 'Greater inequality is correlated with lower growth.'[4]

Social inequality is also a risk. Civil unrest has been rising for several years.[5] Enabling a stable and competent workforce is one way that businesses can contribute positively.

Aside from enlightened self-interest, businesses must also meet a rising bar of obligations to human rights.

What do human rights mean for businesses?

The rising bar is marked by The UN's Declaration of Human Rights of 1948, the International Bill of Rights of 1966,[6] the UN Global Compact of 2000[7] and the Guiding Principles on Business and Human Rights of 2011.[8]

Among the International Bill of Rights are:

- freedom from slavery
- equality and non-discrimination
- privacy
- freedom of speech
- right to strike
- right to an adequate standard of living.

Member governments and civil regulations, such as the UK Equality Act and Fairtrade movement, have followed up with broader and deeper regulations and standards, explored further in Chapters 18 and 19. However, enforceable regulations are still emerging, as Alison Taylor says in *Higher Ground*, 'Much like the early days of anti-corruption efforts, legal efforts have emerged as a patchwork, on a country-by-country basis.'[9]

The effect, according to the World Benchmarking Alliance, is that businesses still have a long way to go to meet the basic rights envisaged by the UN with large variations region by region.[10]

Is diversity good for business?

Principles of diversity, equity and inclusion (DEI) are rooted in the ethical principle of fairness. There are also successive studies that indicate they are good for business.

For example, McKinsey has reported on gender and ethnic diversity in executive teams since 2015. Its 2023 report showed that the likelihood of diverse teams outperforming others has steadily increased year-on-year.[11]

The Wall Street Journal's corporate ranking that examined diversity and inclusion among S&P 500 companies in 2019 concluded 'Diverse and inclusive cultures are providing companies with a competitive edge over their peers.'[12]

In 2023, research by Accenture reported that 'companies that lead in disability inclusion drive more revenue, net income and profit'.[13]

Is the pendulum swinging away from DEI?

Positive business support in the USA for DEI in all its forms gained momentum from the Civil Rights Act of 1964. It continued for 60 years when the pendulum started swinging back.

In March 2025,[14] the *Financial Times* reported:

> 'Over 200 hundred US companies ... removed references to "diversity, equity and inclusion" from their annual reports.
>
> 'In addition, many companies no longer include statistics breaking down their workforce by race or have dropped references to awards for DEI initiatives or internal affinity groups, such as networks for Black professionals.

> 'The number of firms that have opted not to refer to DEI, or its individual components such as diversity, in their latest annual reports far outstrips those that have publicly announced changes to their workplace policies or values. Mastercard, Salesforce, S&P Global, Palantir and American Express are among the companies that changed the language they used about diversity between annual filings published in 2024 and 2025. Many companies have instead stressed "inclusion" or "belonging", saying they want a culture where "all employees" thrive.
>
> 'This was a response to the incoming President signing executive orders prohibiting DEI "discrimination" in federal agencies and requiring federal government contractors to certify that they do not operate inclusion programmes that violate federal anti-discrimination laws. The orders did not clearly define which types of policies the administration views as illegal, leaving companies to assess how to comply.'

It is clear that, under legal pressure from the new administration, businesses have quickly changed their public statements on DEI and are reassessing related programmes.

There are signs that some businesses are retaining their commitments under different labels. Forbes[15] reported that 'most businesses are quietly doing DEI work with less publicity' and the positive business case is still recognised.[16]

Even when DEI initiatives are under pressure, Peter Cheese, CEO of the Chartered Institute of Personnel and Development (CIPD) in the UK says: 'Through the CIPD's own recent research we can see many businesses reconsidering how they are positioning DEI programmes and interventions. But we also see that inclusion and diversity remain an important business focus.'[17]

What is the difference between equity and equality?

Equity and equality sound similar but they are not.

Equality focuses on providing everyone with the same resources and opportunities, regardless of their starting point or vulnerability. It is biased towards the status quo and under-develops potential in a team.

Equity recognises that each person starts with a different set of resources, privileges and vulnerabilities. It seeks to level the playing field by bringing everyone to the same starting point so they can compete fairly for the same opportunities. It realises greater potential from a team and demands more emotional intelligence from the leader.

What can businesses do?

The following case studies illustrate three ways of taking action. In each case, thinking differently and generously about a particular community creates both social and economic value.

The first is an entrepreneur who learned from her own experience of discrimination that there is a better way to do business.

Case study – Judy Hadden[18]

Judy Hadden is an insurance entrepreneur, business founder and Past Master of the Worshipful Company of Entrepreneurs, a City Livery Company.

After leaving school at 17 with 5 poor O-Levels and no family connections, a fortuitous meeting, plus the work experience she'd gained from temporary work while at school, led to her first job as an office junior at a major insurance company. On arrival, she immediately saw the longer-term opportunity and, believing in herself, was determined to seize it by a combination of hard work and gaining professional qualifications which she achieved through evening classes.

Following a blocked promotion opportunity and a poorly phrased reason, not having the 'man qualities' for the position, she moved to a smaller, more forward-thinking insurance company in the City of London.

Aged 27, Judy co-founded her first insurance broking business and, 3 years later, bought out the business with her business partner. They successfully scaled this business and, some 18 years later, sold and exited. Together, they founded and exited two other insurance businesses, one of which, an 'Insurtech' forerunner, they founded at the same time as Judy was on a short period of maternity leave.

In view of her experiences, she realised that, by offering flexible working hours and conditions, they could attract and retain very loyal and productive people who were working parents, particularly mothers with young children.

Judy says '… give the right training, good pay, always treat colleagues with respect and ultimately bring key people into the business as shareholders'.

In this next example, a well-designed series of events between a large business, its clients and groups of young people add value to all the participants.

> # Case study – Solving a recruitment problem[19]
>
> A marketing professional in a large business has developed a way of taking societal issues and creating a compelling business case for a corporate to contribute, with clear benefits both for the corporate and for society. He therefore overcomes the risk of ethical dilemmas by developing solutions that build both social and economic value.
>
> ## Finding talent
>
> He has identified that his business clients had a key challenge in recruiting diverse, talented new employees to certain roles. The solution is to create partnerships that enable businesses and diverse groups of young people to find out more about each other. Working with a social enterprise, who find the young people, events are put on where business managers and young people mentor each other in 'micro-mentoring' sessions. Awareness is raised on both sides, the businesses become more informed recruiters of diverse talent and the young people learn more about opportunities in a sector they may not otherwise consider.
>
> The host organisation enhances its reputation, as some of the businesses involved are his clients.
>
> ## Tracking impact
>
> Every client engaged in these events is tracked, in a similar way to tagging social media engagement. Year by year, enough evidence has built up to put a monetary value on the effect of the events, demonstrating the link between engagement and sales volume, deal value and speed to close. Qualitative feedback is also collected from clients, explaining what they have learnt.
>
> The host organisation builds reputation, relationships and revenue and amplifies PR and marketing resources through partnership. It also contributes to the UN's Strategic Development Goal 17 'Partnerships for the Goals'.

Diversity, innovation and profit

The organisation sees diversity as the key to innovation and profit, supporting research into the causal link from diversity to innovation and from innovation to profit.

Emotion in business relationships

Business-to-business sales and marketing is often more interpersonal than consumer sales, particularly if the buyer and seller only interact online. The emotional connection with clients can act as a key differentiator: 'we feel good by doing good'. There is an intrinsic emotional benefit to a partnership built on shared effort which creates social good.

The marketing professional explains that it meets the 'Instagram story' or 'dinner table conversation' test, i.e. an audience will take more notice if you explain how you have helped young, diverse talent, rather than if you talk about your latest product release.

In the following example, a business helps unemployed people in its community through resolute leadership.

Case study – Fred Keller[20]

Fred Keller, the founder of Cascade Engineering, wanted to show that a for-profit business could also help address society's social ills. So, he accepted an employee's suggestion that they hire unemployed locals. They rented a van, went to a low-income area of Grand Rapids, Michigan and – with the eight men they identified – started Cascade's welfare-to-career programme.

Their first attempt failed completely. Not one of the people hired remained after a few weeks: the men they hired weren't prepared or equipped for the requirements of regular work, and Cascade wasn't prepared to help them succeed. 'We didn't know what we didn't know,' recalls one of the managers involved, so they resorted to 'tough love' that just didn't work.

For most leaders, this inauspicious beginning would likely have also been the end. It seemed to confirm the common sentiment that helping people get out of intergenerational poverty isn't a role business can or should try to play. But not to Keller. For him, the initial outcome was simply data – the first attempt hadn't worked so, clearly, there were things to learn before taking another step.

The second attempt – which involved a partnership wherein potential Cascade employees first learned basic job skills and accountability at a local Burger King – failed, too. Cascade's managers still didn't really understand what it took to help this type of employee, and were frustrated with the additional effort 'Fred's programme' took. Leaders of other businesses thought it proved Keller was naive to think companies could address this type of social problem.

Amid this internal and external criticism, Keller persevered. He, and then everyone in a managerial position at Cascade, underwent focused training on intergenerational poverty.

He continued to be a cheerleader, encouraging managers to embrace the broader purpose they were serving. And he stepped further outside the box and convinced the state of Michigan to – for the first time – place a public social worker onsite at a for-profit business.

With those supports in place and a never-give-up, continuous learning culture infused from the top, the programme slowly found solid footing. Managers pushed through the hard times – iterating towards new processes that facilitated employee–social worker interaction without being too cumbersome, overcoming perceptions that there were two sets of standards, refusing to bow to employee threats to leave, and eventually letting go some employees whose attitude got in the way of their performance – because they believed in what they were trying to do and in Fred Keller.

If Keller had been hung up on old-fashioned notions of how to lead, none of this would have happened. He would have blamed others, given up, and tried to focus others on the company's success on traditional business metrics. He certainly wouldn't have been willing to be vulnerable by acknowledging that initial attempts hadn't worked or that he didn't know how to solve a problem. He wouldn't have gone first in asking for help, or repeatedly publicly apologised for mistakes along the way.

Conclusion

See Toolkit D to put these insights into practice.

Notes

1 Edelman Trust Barometer, available at: https://www.edelman.com/sites/g/files/aatuss191/files/2025-01/2025%20Edelman%20Trust%20Barometer%20Global%20Report_01.23.25.pdf.
2 See: https://wid.world/world/#ghweal_p0p100_z/WO;US;GB;CN;DE;SE/last/eu/k/p/yearly/g/false/0.522815/1/curve/false/country.
3 See: https://www.imf.org/external/pubs/ft/sdn/2011/sdn1108.pdf.
4 Carney, M. (2021) *Value(s)*. William Collins, p.125.
5 See: https://commercial.allianz.com/news-and-insights/reports/political-violence-and-civil-unrest-trends.html.
6 See: https://www.ohchr.org/en/what-are-human-rights/international-bill-human-rights.
7 See: https://unglobalcompact.org/compactjournal/25-years-un-global-compact-legacy-impact-and-call-bold-action#:~:text=On%2026%20July%202000%2C%20then,environmental%20stewardship%20and%20anti%2Dcorruption
8 See: https://www.ohchr.org/sites/default/files/documents/publications/guidingprinciplesbusinesshr_en.pdf.
9 Taylor, A. (2024) *Higher Ground: How Business Can Do the Right Thing in a Turbulent World*, p. 109.
10 See: https://www.worldbenchmarkingalliance.org/news/social-benchmark-press-release-2024/#:~:text=Alarmingly%2C%2090%25%20of%20the%20assessed,of%2020%20total%20possible%20points.
11 See: https://www.mckinsey.com/featured-insights/diversity-and-inclusion/diversity-matters-even-more-the-case-for-holistic-impact.
12 See: https://www.forbes.com/sites/forbesinsights/2020/01/15/diversity-confirmed-to-boost-innovation-and-financial-results/.
13 See: https://www.accenture.com/content/dam/accenture/final/accenture-com/document-2/Disability-Inclusion-Report-Business-Imperative.pdf.
14 See: https://on.ft.com/427sjCO.
15 See: https://www.forbes.com/sites/juliekratz/2024/12/29/history-of-dei-why-it-matters-for-the-future/.
16 82% of business executives think diversity initiatives are critical to their business strategies.
17 Peter Cheese, CEO, CIPD, February 2025. See https://www.linkedin.com/posts/cipd_inclusion-cipd-activity-7288582168803475456-SjIi/?utm_source=share&utm_medium=member_desktop.
18 Author's interview with Judy Hadden, entrepreneur.
19 Author's interview with 1 of the 50 leaders.
20 Extract from a *Harvard Business Review* article by James R. Detert, author of *Choosing Courage*, HBR Press, 2021. See: https://karrikinsgroup.com/wp-content/uploads/2023/08/What-courageous-leaders-do-differently.pdf.

Toolkit D: Social equity

What is your organisation's responsibility for social equity?

This toolkit enables you to create or test your organisation's plans. You should adapt it to complement your organisation's policies and processes.

How to use the toolkit

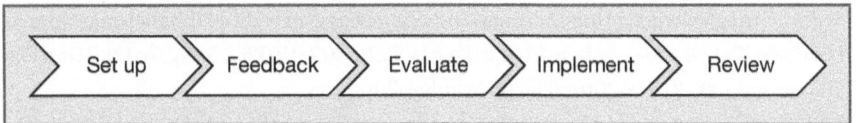

- **Set up with colleagues:**
  - Discuss the toolkit with a cross-section of colleagues, ideally at a time when you are planning next year's priorities or the long-term strategy.
  - Work out how this toolkit can benefit the business, for example reinforcement of values, stakeholder trust and risk reduction.
- **Gather feedback:**
  - Ask a group of colleagues to complete the toolkit including examples and evidence to back up their answers. If you think colleagues will answer more honestly by completing it anonymously, then set up an online poll to collect anonymous answers.
  - If the feedback identifies key risks 'that are hard to discuss', consider creating an independent review. It may need to report to a governance director or senior independent non-executive director to ensure objectivity.

- **Evaluate actions:**
  - Review the feedback as a group and identify strengths and areas to improve, looking at case studies in this book for inspiration, if necessary.
  - Identify actions to make improvements.
  - Evaluate each action against potential benefits, costs and risks, then rank the actions in order of net benefit. Decide which actions to take forward and which to drop or defer.

  Note: use your organisation's normal project evaluation process; if you do not have one, use the *Benefits Scoring Matrix* below.

- **Implement:**
  - Identify risks and enablers and who needs to be consulted and directly involved to achieve the benefits, reduce risks and unlock the resources to deliver the changes.
  - Secure commitment to make changes based on the actions that achieve greatest benefit.
  - If costs and investment are required, secure the budget required.
  - Assign responsibilities and follow through.

- **Review the impact:**
  - Revisit the impact of your actions.
  - Take action to improve further.

Benefits Scoring Matrix (if needed)

Heading	Ethical	Financial	Total
Benefits (e.g. Low = 1)	1–4	1–4	2–8
Costs and risks (e.g. Low = 4)	1–4	1–4	2–8
Total	2–8	2–8	4–16

- Use judgement to decide criteria for 'very high', 'high', 'medium' and 'low'.
- Use your stated purpose (or mission), values and behaviours as criteria for the ethical column. If you do not have these, use 'stakeholder trust' as a proxy.
- Score 'Benefits' as very high 4, high 3, medium 2, low 1.
- Score 'Costs and risks' as low 4, medium 3, high 2, very high 1.
- Add up total scores in the right-hand column, out of a maximum of 16.

- Rank the highest scoring action at the top and the lowest scoring at the bottom.

Note: the effectiveness of the toolkit depends on how rigorously you apply it and follow through.

Social equity Ratings: 4 very high, 3 high, 2 medium, 1 low	Priority Rate 1–4	Current effectiveness Rate 1–4	Actions to improve effectiveness
Process			
Strategy and planning • Set social equity strategy and principles. • Evaluate benefits, ethics, costs, risks and impact. • Prioritise against overall purpose and values. • Set targets. • Regularly review against best practice.			
Governance and compliance • Agree governance and oversight process. • Understand and comply with regulations. • Determine external review or audit process. • Report against benefits, costs, risks and impact.			
Management and reporting • Assign responsibilities, targets and resources. • Set operational processes and controls. • Manage performance and risks. • Track and report benefits, costs, risks and impact. • Learn and improve against best practice.			
Engagement and training • Consult with employees and communities. • Develop regular dialogue and feedback. • Inform and train managers and employees. • Publish plans, targets and performance.			

5 CORPORATE RESPONSIBILITY FOR SOCIAL EQUITY

Social equity Ratings: 4 very high, 3 high, 2 medium, 1 low	Priority Rate 1–4	Current effectiveness Rate 1–4	Actions to improve effectiveness
Actions – diversity, equity and inclusion of …			
Employees … hiring of new employees … pay and incentives … promotions … support and development of skills and health … access for disabled.			
Communities … engagement with relevant.[Note 1] communities.			
Customers … adaptation of products and services.			
Supply chain and distribution channels … procurement and partnering criteria … performance incentives and standards … performance and risks.			
Note 1: 'relevant' means local or related to the sector in which the business operates.			

chapter 6

Corporate responsibility for emerging technology

'As more and more artificial intelligence is entering into the world, more and more emotional intelligence must enter into leadership.'

Amit Ray

In this chapter you will learn:

- Why emerging technology is becoming one of the key challenges
- How ethical guide rails are being developed
- The role that business can play, illustrated by two case studies
- How to use a toolkit to guide ethical use of emerging technology in your business

Why is emerging technology an ethical challenge?

Adam Smith, the pioneer of free market economics, was writing at the start of the first industrial revolution 250 years ago. It moved society from an agricultural age to an industrial age, harnessing the new technologies of mechanisation and steam.

We are now at the beginning of another industrial revolution[1] driven by our new technologies of global connectivity, artificial intelligence, large data, bio-engineering and clean energy.

While there are risks in new technologies, the leaders I spoke to agreed they present an exceptional opportunity to take another positive leap but only if we apply the right guide rails.

As an example, cryptocurrency has grown to a $3 trillion market, creating an alternative to the traditional banking system, feeding off falling institutional trust after the 2008 financial crash.

Sitting outside the main regulatory systems, however, it has also created a safe haven for money laundering.[2] Even established technologies carry risks when trust is misplaced, as happened with the UK Post Office's Horizon system.[3]

The last two decades have already highlighted the importance of cybersecurity and data privacy, with regulations gradually catching up to protect users from exploitation, inaccuracy and bias.[4] There is also speculation about the 'Frankenstein' risk, creating a system of intelligence that is so powerful that we cannot control it[5] and the environmental cost of generative AI systems.[6]

According to the Markkula Center for Applied Ethics,[7] 86% of Americans believe that technology companies should be regulated and 51% do not trust the companies that are creating AI.

Even AI knows its own limitations: 'AI itself doesn't have an ethical conscience – it lacks consciousness, emotions, and the ability to truly understand right or wrong.'[8]

Who is setting the ethical bar?

Sean Williams is the founder and CEO of AutogenAI. His business uses natural language processing technology to help companies compete through tenders, proposals and marketing copy.

Sean sees human empathy and intelligence as essential to provide the ethical component of AI, which AI cannot do for itself. He compares our position today to the development and regulation of radioactivity, developed in the 1890s but not regulated until the 1940s, in the aftermath of its use in the Second World War. He sees greater complexity today because international technology companies own most of the intellectual property. That means one sovereign nation, or block of nations, has limited regulatory influence. Businesses, and global businesses in particular, can therefore choose to take more responsibility or leave ethical questions to the wisdom of markets.

Businesses are starting to publish self-regulatory principles and the World Economic Fund has created a Digital Trust Framework. It is designed to ensure security, accountability and responsible use from new technological developments. It includes avoidance of biased or discriminatory data, protection of privacy and ethical oversight aimed at businesses that prioritise long-term trust over short-term self-interest. Some businesses are making a virtue of their ethical credentials.[9]

The world's first comprehensive AI regulations have come from the EU, with the Artificial Intelligence Act of 2024.[10] It creates a governance framework for AI systems according to risk, prohibiting the highest risk systems including manipulation, which causes harm, exploiting vulnerabilities, discriminatory profiling and unauthorised use of biometrics.

Globally, self-regulation by businesses remains the principal guide rail.

What positive change can businesses create?

The following two case studies illustrate:

- the opportunity to find hidden potential, while overcoming data bias risks
- achieving major medical breakthroughs.

In this first case study, Arctic Shores has created new ways of finding hidden potential, while removing bias inherent in historic data sets.

> ## Case study – Arctic Shores[11]
>
> Robert Newry founded Arctic Shores in 2014 to revolutionise the field of psychometric assessment by focusing on what a person does rather than what they say they might do. Combining behavioural science, cognitive neuroscience, game design and data analytics, Arctic Shores created a task-based approach to screening candidates, helping organisations uncover potential and see more in people. In the 10 years since it was founded, it has worked with 350+ organisations in 45 countries and assessed over 3 million candidates for 75,000 roles.
>
> When it comes to using data (including AI), Robert emphasises the difference between social science, which actively looks for, and checks against, any adverse impact, as opposed to data science where the focus is just on statistical techniques irrespective of their social context or impact. This is especially relevant in the emerging world of AI where new techniques are being developed to match jobs to candidates and vice versa. For example, in a data science-led approach, key words are matched between job descriptions and candidates who have listed the relevant skills. Yet, a social science-led approach would know of research that shows women tend to under-declare skills compared to men so would question the appropriateness of the data-science word-matching approach. This is why Arctic Shores methods are designed and tested to avoid any adverse impact while still leveraging statistical methods.
>
> This is not a new problem or revelation. Robert refers to an early effort by Amazon to automate reviewing of job applications in 2015, when the rating of candidates for software developer jobs and other technical posts was found not to be gender neutral.[12]
>
> As a result, he broadly supports the intentions and framework of the new EU AI Act,[13] which categorises the risks to society of different AI uses and requires stricter measurement of impact (and penalties) the greater the risk.
>
> Ethical principles go beyond just the product for Robert, who sees ethical behaviour as an essential feature of his business practice, where one of the company's core values is 'making a difference' whether to DEI for its clients or in the community generally.

In this next example, Google DeepMind has demonstrated the power of artificial intelligence to transform medical research, shared openly for others to build on.

Case study – Google DeepMind[14]

DeepMind started in 2010 and was acquired by Google in 2014. It has since grown into one of the world's foremost artificial intelligence research and development labs.

In 2024, its chief executive and co-founder Sir Demis Hassabis was one of three joint recipients of the Nobel Prize in chemistry for unlocking a 50-year-old problem: predicting the structure of every known protein using AI software known as AlphaFold. The findings have been shared on a public database for other researchers to build on, with structures of 200 million proteins now being used by more than 1 million biologists around the world.

Decoding a protein used to take years and is the basis for a wide range of medical drug testing. DeepMind was founded with the mission of 'solving' intelligence – designing artificial intelligence systems that could mimic and even supersede human cognitive capabilities. In recent years, the technology has become increasingly powerful and ubiquitous and is now embedded in industries ranging from healthcare and education to financial and government services.

Despite its commercial underpinnings, Google DeepMind has remained focused on complex and fundamental problems in science and engineering, making it one of the most consequential projects in AI globally.

Interviewed by the *FT*'s Madhumita Murgia in October 2024, Sir Dennis Hassabis said '… what goals, what values and so on … that's more of a UN or geopolitical question. I think we need a broad discussion on that, with governments, with civil society, and academia, all parts of society – and social science and philosophy, even, as well.'

Conclusion

See Toolkit E to put these insights into practice.

Notes

1. Klaus Schwab (2016) World Economic Forum, https://www.weforum.org/about/the-fourth-industrial-revolution-by-klaus-schwab/.
2. See: https://www.ft.com/content/31b9053f-343e-4c47-ace9-2b0080ec8799.
3. See: https://www.ft.com/content/edcd12fc-6452-4cac-ae12-e8d220793e58.
4. See: https://www.science.org/doi/10.1126/sciadv.adu9368.
5. See: https://www.ineteconomics.org/perspectives/blog/can-we-avoid-a-franken-future-with-ai.
6. See: https://arxiv.org/abs/2311.16863.
7. See: https://www.scu.edu/ethics/about-the-center/press--media-hub/press-releases/ethics-in-the-age-of-ai/.
8. Copilot 18 March 2025.
9. See: https://www.weforum.org/stories/2024/11/tech-strategy-leaders-inclusivity-ethics-responsibility/.
10. See: https://artificialintelligenceact.eu/.
11. Author's interview with Robert Newry, founder of Arctic Shores.
12. See: https://www.reuters.com/article/world/insight-amazon-scraps-secret-ai-recruiting-tool-that-showed-bias-against-women-idUSKCN1MK0AG/.
13. See: https://digital-strategy.ec.europa.eu/en/policies/regulatory-framework-ai.
14. Extracted from Murgia, M. ((2024) 'Google DeepMind's Demis Hassabis on his Nobel Prize: "It feels like a watershed moment for AI"'. *Financial Times*, 21 October. Available at: https://www.ft.com/content/72d2c2b1-493b-4520-ae10-41c1a7f3b7e4.

Toolkit E: Emerging technology

What is your organisation's responsibility for applying emerging technology?

This toolkit enables you to create or test your organisation's plans. You should adapt it to complement your organisation's policies and processes.

How to use the toolkit

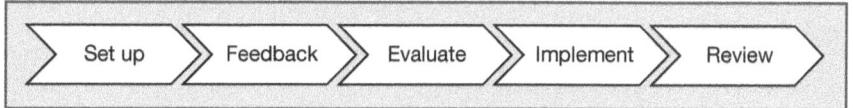

- **Set up with colleagues:**
  - Discuss the toolkit with a cross-section of colleagues, ideally at a time when you are planning next year's priorities or the long-term strategy.
  - Work out how this toolkit can benefit the business, for example reinforcement of values, stakeholder trust and risk reduction.
- **Gather feedback:**
  - Ask a group of colleagues to complete the toolkit including examples and evidence to back up their answers. If you think colleagues will answer more honestly by completing it anonymously, then set up an online poll to collect anonymous answers.
  - If the feedback identifies key risks 'that are hard to discuss', consider creating an independent review. It may need to report to a governance director or senior independent non-executive director to ensure objectivity.

- **Evaluate actions:**
    - Review the feedback as a group and identify strengths and areas to improve, looking at case studies in this book for inspiration, if necessary.
    - Identify actions to make improvements.
    - Evaluate each action against potential benefits, costs and risks, then rank the actions in order of net benefit. Decide which actions to take forward and which to drop or defer.
    - Note: use your organisation's normal project evaluation process; if you do not have one, use the *Benefits Scoring Matrix* below.
- **Implement:**
    - Identify risks and enablers and who needs to be consulted and directly involved to achieve the benefits, reduce risks and unlock the resources to deliver the changes.
    - Secure commitment to make changes based on the actions that achieve greatest benefit.
    - If costs and investment are required, secure the budget required.
    - Assign responsibilities and follow through.
- **Review the impact:**
    - Revisit the impact of your actions.
    - Take action to improve further.

Benefits Scoring Matrix (if needed)

Heading	Ethical	Financial	Total
Benefits (e.g. Low = 1)	1–4	1–4	2–8
Costs and risks (e.g. Low = 4)	1–4	1–4	2–8
Total	2–8	2–8	4–16

- Use judgement to decide criteria for 'very high', 'high', 'medium' and 'low'.
- Use your stated purpose (or mission), values and behaviours as criteria for the ethical column. If you do not have these, use 'stakeholder trust' as a proxy.
- Score 'Benefits' as very high 4, high 3, medium 2, low 1.

- Score 'Costs and risks' as low 4, medium 3, high 2, very high 1.
- Add up total scores in the right-hand column, out of a maximum of 16.
- Rank the highest scoring action at the top and the lowest scoring at the bottom.

Note: the effectiveness of the toolkit depends on how rigorously you apply it and follow through.

Emerging technology Ratings: 4 very high, 3 high, 2 medium, 1 low	Priority Rate 1–4	Current effectiveness Rate 1–4	Actions to improve effectiveness
Process			
Strategy and planning • Set technology strategy and principles. • Evaluate benefits, ethics, costs, risks and impact. • Prioritise against overall purpose and values. • Set targets. • Regularly review against best practice.			
Governance and compliance • Agree governance and oversight process. • Understand regulatory obligations. • Determine external review or audit process. • Report against benefits, costs, risks and impact.			
Management and reporting • Assign responsibilities, targets and resources. • Set operational processes and controls. • Manage performance and risks. • Track and report benefits, costs, risks and impact. • Learn and improve against best practice.			
Engagement and training • Consult and communicate with stakeholders. • Inform and train employees, suppliers and partners.			

Emerging technology Ratings: 4 very high, 3 high, 2 medium, 1 low	Priority Rate 1–4	Current effectiveness Rate 1–4	Actions to improve effectiveness
Actions			
Purpose and impact • Define purpose, ethics and benefits of each application. • Communicate benefits and ethics to stakeholders. • Test impact on employees and customers and adjust.			
Accuracy and fairness • Ensure outputs are accurate and consistent. • Risk-assess limitations[Note 1]. • Test outputs for bias and adjust. • Ensure 'human in the loop' where necessary.			
Accountability and transparency • Visibly label use of technology to users. • Openly report limitations of accuracy. • Ensure human accountability for decisions. • Provide clear channels for feedback and concerns.			
Privacy and safety • Set ethical standards. • Comply with privacy, safety and mis-use standards. • Test, report and improve compliance.			
Note 1: 'Model cards' are an example of a framework for providing transparent information about AI and machine learning models.[1]			

Note

1 See: https://www.techtarget.com/whatis/definition/model-card-in-machine-learning.

Part 1 Ethics in action: Quick read summary

Chapters 1–6 are summarised here in bullet points.

Chapter 1 The four key ethical principles

- The four principles most relevant to business ethics are:
  - **Integrity** – honesty, self-control and accountability.
  - **Duty** – commitment to the common good.
  - **Fairness** – compassion, care and justice.
  - **Freedom** – autonomy, enlightened self-interest and imagination.

Chapter 2 The purpose of business

- The East India Company, founded in 1600, was the pioneer of the joint stock company, separating the roles of investor and worker.
- Adam Smith was a moral philosopher and economist who laid foundations for the free market at the start of the first industrial revolution when he published *The Wealth of Nations* in 1776. Adam Smith saw a free market and specialisation as the ways of creating greater prosperity for both investors and society at large.
- Limited liability companies are now directly responsible for about 60% of employment in the UK and USA.
- Two broad schools of thought evolved in the 1970s and 1980s:
  - 'Shareholder primacy' was promoted by the Chicago School of Economics and Milton Friedman who said, 'The only social responsibility of business is to increase its profits.'
  - The Stanford Research Institute and Edward Freeman advocated 'stakeholder' value, taking a wider view of stakeholders, balancing the needs of employees, communities and the environment as priorities alongside shareholders.
- A broad view of stakeholder value, or corporate responsibility, has now taken root in the world's major markets.

- More recent concerns about over-regulation have started moving the regulatory pendulum the other way in the USA on climate change, diversity, equity and inclusion and enforcement of anti-corruption laws.

Chapters 3–6 Putting ethics into practice

- Successive studies have shown clear correlations between ethics, trust and competitive advantage.
- 25–30% of employees in the UK and USA work for publicly listed companies, the rest work for private companies, government bodies, charities and social enterprises. Some private companies resist having external shareholders so they can prioritise ethical health over short-term profits.
- Organisations balance the interests of all stakeholders, including customers, employees, investors, communities, suppliers and the natural environment, through clear purpose, values and follow-up actions.
- Some non-profits measure and report non-financial value through 'impact statements'. This is also seen in listed companies' ESG-related disclosures.
- People born between 1996 and 2012, known as Generation Z, have more demanding ethical expectations than previous generations. They are now 25% of the world population and set to be the highest spending cohort in the next decade.
- Conversations with 50 leaders highlighted ethical business behaviour in three broad categories.
    - Consistency – complying with commitments and regulations.
    - Conscience – going beyond obligations to do what is right.
    - Cause – pursuing system change for a cause beyond the organisation.
- The three key challenges of wider corporate responsibility are:
    - the natural environment
    - social equity
    - emerging technology.

part 2

Ethical leadership

chapter 7

The ethical compass

'Ethics used to be an important part of my work as a leader, now my leadership is all about ethics.'

Sarah Walker-Smith

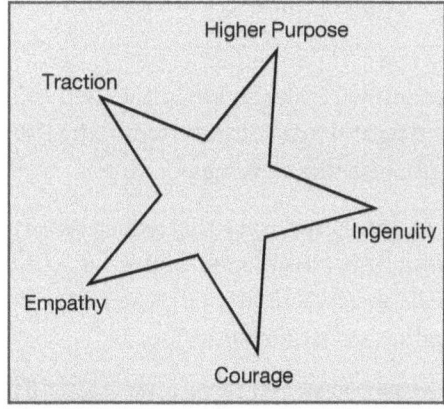

In this chapter you will learn:

- Insights into the motivation of leaders I interviewed
- How the public's trust in business leaders is falling
- The importance of leadership to build and maintain business ethics
- How the 'Ethical Compass' was developed from interviews with 50 leaders

Introduction

The next six chapters are derived from interviews with 50 leaders. About a third work in founder-led businesses, a third in charities or social enterprises and a third in large and listed businesses.

What motivates you?

When the next generations of your family ask you what you did to make the world a better place, what will you say? Is your work part of the answer?

One leader I spoke to said, 'I don't see myself as ethical, I just do what's best for the business and try and respect my customers and be kind to my teams. It seems to work. We make a decent profit most years and most people seem to enjoy working here.' Most of the leaders I spoke to were 'purpose-led' – they wanted to improve the world around them as part of their working life.

They all used similar language and rarely used the word 'ethics'. One said, 'Ethics sounds like an impossibly high bar.' They mostly talked about 'being responsible', 'being principled', 'doing the right thing' and 'personal and organisational values'.

The challenge is more complex for larger businesses with external shareholders. When leaders come and go and sub-cultures sprout, the risk is that bureaucracy takes over at the expense of ethics or values.

Charles Conn, chair of Patagonia, said that effectiveness and ethics do not always go hand in hand: 'It is possible to be effective without being ethical ... but ethical leaders are driven by a higher purpose and committed to a core set of uncompromising values, consistently applied.'

Michael Davis, CEO of The National Centre for Social Research, saw ethical leadership as a conscious choice '... a decision to follow the harder path, to meet charlatans on the way who may make more money than you. But none of that dissuades you that it is still the right thing to do.'

One leader I spoke to described a successful sales team he took over which routinely stole each other's client data to improve their individual sales performance. When he disciplined a team member for doing this, the rest of the team had to learn the new rule 'no stealing other people's data'. He had to learn that his conscience was not the same as his team's.

Sarah Walker-Smith, Group CEO of professional services group Ampa, said, 'Ethical leadership is synonymous with leadership ... doing the same thing whether anyone is watching or not.'

For most of the leaders I spoke to, 'doing the right thing' is both a moral and business imperative. Living out ethical principles with colleagues, customers, investors and the wider community supports long-term business success. In that sense, it is enlightened self-interest.

Are business leaders trusted?

Public trust is falling and leaders have to work harder to be and be seen to be trustworthy. The 2025 Trust Barometer is an annual survey across 28 countries with 33,000 respondents, revealing:[1]

- a significant fall in employees' trust that their employer will 'do what is right' and reduced trust in CEOs – more than two-thirds of the public fear that business leaders 'purposely mislead'
- more than half of 18–34-year-olds agree that hostile action (e.g. attacking on social media) is a viable way of achieving positive change.

While business remains more trusted than non-governmental organisations (NGOs), Government and media, the bar is low and the pressure from the public on those who hold power and authority is rising.

How do leaders affect business ethics?

From my conversations, and my experience, leadership and culture are the two largest influences on the ethical health of an organisation.

In work by business professor Celia Moore and others, they demonstrated the link between the behaviour of a leader and the behaviour of employees in that organisation, both positive and negative:[2]

> '... ethical leadership decreases employees' propensity to morally disengage, with ultimate effects on employees' unethical decisions and deviant behavior and leaders will shape their subordinate's moral cognitions, ultimately affecting the extent to which they engage in deviant and unethical behavior.'

Ronan Dunne, the former CEO of Verizon Wireless and O2, goes further, explaining that leadership should stretch what other people do: *'Ethical leadership is taking people to places they wouldn't otherwise have gone, in pursuit of the greater good.'*

The consistent insight from leaders it that actions, not words, make the difference.

How can leaders develop their ethical influence?

The chapters that follow are built on examples[a] of ethical challenges faced by leaders, how they arrived at decisions and the resulting impact and insights.

The interviews revealed a pattern of challenges used by leaders to lead both ethical and commercial performance. The result is the Ethical Compass with five challenges. It is a compass, not a map, and does not attempt to define right and wrong but helps you and your team set an ethical direction. The labels spell out the acronym ETHIC:

1 Empathy – how do you build trustful relationships with stakeholders?
2 Traction – how do you take an organisation with you?
3 Higher purpose – how do you create an ethical direction?
4 Ingenuity – how do you find ethical answers to business questions?
5 Courage – how do you find the courage to follow your conscience?

Business ethics at its best is a team activity, fuelled by challenge, diversity of thought and ingenuity.

Conclusion

The chapters that follow describe the five challenges in more detail. The focus is a leader's view supported by examples that illustrate each driver along with a wider set of practical leadership behaviours and challenges.

---

a   Each example has either been approved for publication by the interviewee or taken from the public domain, appropriately referenced.

Your approach to working with ETHIC will vary depending on your leadership experience and repertoire, Toolkit F shows you how to apply ETHIC in practice.

Questions

- What motivates you as a leader or colleague?
- How do your actions affect the ethical behaviour of colleagues around you?

Notes

1 Edelman Trust Barometer, available at: https://www.edelman.com/sites/g/files/aatuss191/files/2025-01/2025%20Edelman%20Trust%20Barometer%20Global%20Report_01.23.25.pdf.
2 Based on findings from *Leaders Matter Morally: The Role of Ethical Leadership in Shaping Employee Moral Cognition and Misconduct* by Celia Moore (Imperial College Business School), David M. Mayer (University of Michigan), Flora F.T. Chiang (China Europe International Business School), Craig Crossley (University of Central Florida), Matthew J. Karlesky (University of South Florida Sarasota-Manatee) and Thomas A. Birtch (University of Exeter Business School).

chapter 8

Empathy

How do you build trustful relationships with stakeholders?

> 'Business success depends on looking after your people and being fair to your customers.'
>
> Brian Harpur

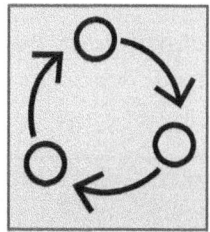

In this chapter you will learn:

- How leaders build productive and trustful relationships
- The role of empathy and compassion in meeting stakeholders' needs.
- How leaders take a long-term view to balance empathy with commercial judgement

Who are the key stakeholders?

They will vary for each organisation but, typically, they are:

- customers
- employees
- communities
- shareholders
- suppliers
- the environment.

Every leader has to balance the priority given to each stakeholder. The business and ethical strategy should determine the priority and a leader with integrity will be clear, transparent and accountable to do what they say they are going to do.

Simon Rogerson, founder and CEO of Octopus Group, said: '90% of businesses are sociopaths, self-interested, unkind and unimaginative, they should be judged as we judge a good friend ... great business is how you make people feel.' Octopus chooses to make a virtue of kindness to the extent that it is a competitive advantage in the same way that Patagonia competes through its environmental credentials.

The insights from my discussions time and again highlighted the importance of employees as stakeholders. Aside from physical and intellectual property, they are the business and will amplify whatever the real values are.

The challenge is to earn and maintain trust. Two key insights are compassion, or 'empathy in action', and balance.

1 Compassion

This case study describes a leader who drew on his conscience and instinct to change the organisation's priorities during and following an extraordinary crisis. It is also an example where the codified corporate values were influential and applied with grace and empathy.

Case study – Mark Malcomson[1]

Mark Malcomson CBE is principal and chief executive of City Lit, a London-based college providing classroom and online courses for adults. Mark previously held senior roles at London Business School and Pearson Group.

On 11 September 2001, Mark was president of The New York Institute of Finance, part of the Pearson Group. He was responsible for a team of 50 people based in the World Trade Centre, also known as the Twin Towers. Their office was on the seventeenth floor of Tower Two.

After the first plane exploded on impact with Tower One, a general message was given to all workers in Tower Two to remain where they were and not to go outside. Mark decided that staying on the seventeenth floor was risky, so took the decision to ignore the general advice and lead his team down to the ground floor.

In the walk down the stairs, one senior employee said how scared she was and asked to hold Mark's hand on the way down. They all eventually made it to the ground floor as debris from Tower One fell outside. By this time, it was becoming clear that it was more than an accident and people were talking about a plane crashing into Tower One. It was a beautifully clear day, and it was unlikely it was pilot error. Another English colleague, who had worked in the military, said if it was an attack that there was often a second attack. At that point, Mark decided to encourage his colleagues to leave the building through a passage under the complex to avoid the falling debris. Once outside, they witnessed the shocking sight of people jumping from higher floors of Tower One to their death and, as they were reeling from that, the second plane, seemingly appearing from nowhere, crashed into their building showering people with debris.

In the chaos, Mark could not keep track of all his team and had to trust that they would find their way to safety. He walked back to his flat in downtown Manhattan, looking back to see Tower Two and then Tower One fall. He arrived home to find a number of his team waiting on his doorstep. His flat became 'mission control' wo where more staff made their way and, with support from the team in London, the process of tracking everyone down carried on for the next 24 hours until everyone was found to be safe.

The business he led was a very small part of the huge Pearson Group. There was nothing left apart from the people, every part of the business had been destroyed when the Tower fell. From the beginning, the senior leadership of Pearson, CEO Dame Marjorie Scardino, director for people Sir David Bell and John Fallon, who went on to be Pearson's CEO after Scardino, offered consistent moral and financial support to the business and the staff.

In the days that followed, and the team reassembled in alternative offices provided by Pearson, it was clear to Mark that many of his colleagues had suffered significant trauma. For example, several people told him they were frightened every day getting the bus through the Mid-Town to Manhattan Island from New Jersey. Counselling support was provided but many in the team were deeply affected, and Mark was aware that many of them did not want to continue to work near the site of their trauma.

He called on two insights for his next step. One was from UK employment practice, where an employer can offer a voluntary redundancy scheme that gives support for colleagues to leave if they want to and bridge the financial gap until they find another job. The other was the values that Marjorie Scardino, CEO of Pearson Group, espoused, calling on the Pearson employees to be 'brave, imaginative and decent'. He took her at her word and recommended to Pearson that they offer a voluntary scheme to allow anyone in his team to leave with a financial package, if they wanted it. This would be costly and apply to everyone, even staff with critical skills. Pearson Group backed his judgement based on values, not on money.

A quarter of his team took up the offer and took the opportunity for a fresh start, which they were hugely grateful for. He was left with the challenge of rebuilding the team and the business. Those who chose to stay worked over the next year to re-invent the business in time for the Institute's 80th birthday in May 2022.

Over 20 years later, he remains close friends with many of his former colleagues, with texts called the 'glad we are here' messages shared every 11 September between them.

2 Balance

This next case study also deals with a crisis, the COVID-19 pandemic. It shows how shareholders' and employees' viewpoints had to be balanced with empathy and commercial judgement, thinking beyond the immediate costs and benefits.

Case study – Peter Marks[2]

Peter Marks is a leader in the late-night entertainment industry. He is chair of NEOS and previously chief executive of the UK's largest focused late-night operator of clubs and bars in the UK.

Going through the COVID-19 epidemic was one of the most severe business challenges he has faced.

He was CEO and one of the shareholders of the Deltic Group, a profitable, £100 million turnover in 56 nightclubs and bars, making around £10 million cash a year. It was a business with 500 full-time and 2,500 part-time staff. It was obliged to close at short notice in the UK's first lockdown in March 2020. Some of his investors and board wanted to cut their losses, close the business and make staff redundant, but they had £10 million of bank debt and Peter, as a member of the board of the trade body UK Hospitality, was aware of the possibility of government support. He persuaded the board to keep the company going in a kind of suspended animation state in readiness for reopening which, at the time, was predicted to be up to six months. The government 'furlough' scheme, subsidising the payroll of affected businesses, allowed them to pay 80% of staff salaries up to £30,000 but recognised that those paid more had higher fixed bills such as rent and mortgages so, as a business, they chose to pay the same proportion to higher paid staff even though it was only partly subsidised. Few in the sector did this. In fact, some companies, including some sizeable private equity owned businesses, made all their staff redundant only to have to reemploy them days later to process furlough payments.

Despite the £1 million monthly cost of trading with no income, Peter had one goal: to ensure the business was ready to re-open as soon as restrictions were lifted by retaining the loyalty and engagement of staff. He made a point of issuing a weekly online video blog (vlog) to staff throughout lockdown periods to keep them updated so they knew what he knew.

Throughout this, he helped the trade body lobby government ministers, seeking parity of treatment with pubs. Nightclubs were incorrectly seen as higher risk, even though they had tighter requirements on airflow in venues, far more air changes per hour than nearly all pubs. Peter thought this was far more to do with messaging than science.

Despite pubs being able to open in the summer of 2020, the late-night club and live music sector remained closed. They spent thousands of pounds preparing for a reopening, but events around Autumn of that year meant they had to remain closed and pubs had to close too.

By September 2020, the business was running out of cash reserves and was no longer viable and the main investor had fallen critically ill. It was also a huge risk to continue to support a business that had no opening date and £1 million cash burn per month. But the belief was that, once reopened, the business would return to the profitable business that it was previously. By this stage, their main legal obligation was to creditors, so Peter and his team had no choice but to put themselves second and to run an auction which resulted in the sale to a Danish business REKOM, crystalising a loss of shareholders' investment including his own. Importantly, the company and some 44 of its venues and their staff were saved.

By the time restrictions were lifted some 15 months after lockdown, all but 4 of the 500 full-time staff stayed on.

As REKOM UK, the business flourished after restrictions were lifted in July 2021 but started to shrink in Q3 2022 as the UK's cost-of-living crisis heavily reduced expenditure on late-night entertainment. By early 2024, it had to go through another administration, losing many of the large clubs with high fixed rents that had become no longer economically viable. Prior to this, he found buyers for eight of the smaller clubs that were facing an uncertain future, something that he did not have to do. However, the moral case to save the businesses and jobs were at the fore of his mind. The insolvency lawyers subsequently commented that this was most unusual as he was under no legal obligation to do so.

The business is now a lot smaller with 20 venues, but now profitable, stable and can look forward to a bright future with its new owners.

His leadership experience has taught him that being open and honest is the difference between success and failure, and the simple act of communicating every week when the business was closed was the way that trust was maintained and almost all staff returned to work when it was safe to do so.

Although shareholders, including Peter, lost their investment, this would have happened anyway. His principled approach at least allowed the business and the employees a chance to restart after the lockdowns.

This next example demonstrates a balance of commercial and ethical factors played out in discussion with a leadership team.

> ## Case study – Peter Beeby[3]
>
> Peter Beeby, CEO of Prospectus, described a dilemma about a campaign started in 2020 to improve fairness in pay by putting pressure on recruiters and employers to disclose salaries of all advertised jobs. He was unsure whether to sign up to it or not because in his words, 'It's not about the badge, it's showing the true action you are taking.' The company had previously chosen to apply for B Corp status because the standards reflected its existing approach but pushed for continuous improvement in a supportive way. He was less sure about the new salary-focused campaign, which had a fast-growing and strong profile but was short on a considered approach.
>
> Peter initiated a conversation among his leadership team where there were divergent views ranging from:
>
> (a) "We have to do it because it's ethical and we will lose competitive advantage if we don't join in", to
> (b) "It's just a social media campaign, and with no sight of who was behind the campaign, it's risky to join".
>
> Initially Prospectus did not sign up so it could take soundings from clients and weigh up the ethical and commercial impact. Eventually they did make a commitment on ethical grounds, but with the ability to exclude certain jobs which had a legitimate reason not to publish salaries.

Conclusion

Empathy, more than any other driver, builds trust between an organisation and its stakeholders and crucially rests on the leaders' actions more than their words.

The relationship with employees is particularly influential because they amplify the organisation's values with other stakeholders.

Toolkit F shows you how to apply the Ethical Compass.

Notes

1. Author's interview with Mark Malcomson, CEO City Lit.
2. Author's interview with Peter Marks, Chair, NEOS.
3. Author's interview with Peter Beeby, CEO, Prospectus.

chapter 9

Traction

How do you take an organisation with you?

> '**Vision without execution is hallucination.**'
>
> Thomas Edison

In this chapter you will learn:

- How leaders get traction, converting ethical purpose into action
- The importance of autonomy, high expectations and storytelling
- The importance of rules to ensure due process

What is traction?

Traction is about the basic leadership challenge of converting ideas, principles and strategies into targets and action. I consistently heard from leaders that business ethics often fail when rules, incentives and attitudes are not aligned. It is easy to lose perspective when 'the wrong thing' is rewarded by the organisation or short-term financial performance is over-prioritised, even when 'the right thing' is obvious.

The conversations focused, once again, on employees, understanding that this amplified the relationships with other stakeholders. Board support was also flagged up to ensure support for changes in strategy.

Traction is about getting the balance right between individual autonomy and adherence to rules. Rules do not usually build trust and can stifle innovation but are valuable to handle complexity and shift habits.

Traction is not about value statements. Most organisations attempt to set out high-level values, principles or ways of working that they expect of employees. High-level statements make a difference if actions follow the words, as in a previous case study (see Chapter 8) where Pearson's values of 'brave, imaginative and decent' were put to good use. However, reference to publicly stated values was a rare event in my conversations.

Traction is about applying the right balance of leadership behaviours, illustrated by Sheppard Moscow's influencing model of convincing, requiring, connecting and inspiring.[1] The insights from my discussions put it more simply – once ambition and targets are understood, it is down to balancing autonomy and rules.

1 Autonomy

In my conversations, this was part of a broader commitment by a leader to expect high performance from their teams but to place trust in how they achieved it, including their ethical judgement. Training was also mentioned by several leaders to help employees exercise effective judgement.

In short, enabling autonomy creates an emotional bond between the organisation and the individual.

In this case study, the CEO saw a correlation between positive ethical behaviour and reduction of rules in everyday questions about dress code and expenses.

Case study – Sarah Walker-Smith[2]

Sarah Walker-Smith is the Group CEO of Ampa, a group of legal and professional services businesses and certified B Corp. Sarah describes herself as 'being all about fairness and freedom'.

Sarah is mindful that ethics can imply perfection in some people's minds. However, this prevents progress and dialogue to hear different views, so a degree of pragmatism is required. Her advice is not to over-prescribe what is right and wrong.

An example was her decision to remove the prescribed dress code, trusting in colleagues' professional judgement which, in the event, proved to be reliable.

Another example was the expenses code which, aside from obligations required by tax authorities, was changed to 'spend in a way where anyone could see and understand why you chose to spend in the way you decided'.

Over five years, colleagues gradually started to put all the rules back in because they find it easier to deal with rules rather than principles. Sarah had to intervene again recently to reset this and explain why it's important to treat colleagues as adults. Sarah's learning is that this is never a finished job and a drift back to rules needs regular attention.

In both cases, transparency was the key test.

Storytelling is sometimes underrated as a leadership skill but is both powerful and empowering in developing an ethical culture.

Case study – Ronan Dunne[3]

Ronan Dunne is the former CEO of Verizon Wireless and O2. He focused on storytelling as a key feature of his leadership and the emotional connections in an organisation. In his words, *'I attribute it to the great Irish tradition in which I was raised. It is an inspirational tool, as long as it is tangible and actionable.'*

> ### Case study – Simon Rogerson[4]
>
> Simon Rogerson, CEO and founder of Octopus Group, says: 'Humans remember stories not spreadsheets.' He sends an all-employee update every Friday, retelling stories that demonstrate positive behaviour, for example: the engineer who was installing a smart-meter and found the elderly customer on the floor after a heavy fall; she didn't need permission to cancel her next visit so she could take the customer to hospital and probably saved their life; the salesperson who spent their weekend making a voice recording of a brochure for a sight-impaired customer.
>
> This is described in more detail in Chapter 14.

2 Rules

When challenges are complex and risks are high, rules and processes are effective at judging risk, balancing decisions and demonstrating fairness to stakeholders. Here are two examples of ethics committees that consider specific questions to protect professional standards and police grey areas so that the duty does not rest on one individual and due process is seen to be followed.

> ### Case study – Justin Rix[5]
>
> Justin Rix is a former partner in Grant Thornton's business consulting practice in the UK. He said: 'Professional credibility relies on a set of robust and transparent processes for deciding what organisations they work with and the nature of the work that they will undertake ... we therefore have a rigorous process applied consistently and with independence to decide whether to accept work from any potential clients which raise any "flags", whether actual or perceived. Decisions like this are not left to any one individual.'
>
> He added that leaders' decisions should have long-term resilience but, in practice, a longer-term view means more unpredictability: '... looking longer term means there are more "unknowables" to weigh up compared to short-term impact and therefore a greater need for leadership judgement based on a clear set of principles.'

Case study – Alastair Da Costa[6]

Alastair Da Costa CBE is the chair and pro-chancellor of the University of Leeds and a former partner and managing director at international law firm DLA Piper.

He sees organisational values as broad guidelines that require leadership to interpret them in particular cases. He emphasised the need for a process that does not rely on just one individual's interpretation. He pointed to the university's ethics committee which ensures that processes are observed, draws in stakeholders' views and guards against reliance on the judgement of one individual.

At the University of Leeds, the ethics committee has a broad remit determined by the university's Council, including questions about freedom of speech, donations and equity, diversity and inclusion. It uses a decision-making framework that includes collecting input from students and other stakeholders. In the past, it has considered the appropriateness of accepting donations from organisations in the tobacco and defence sectors. In each case, ethical considerations are weighed up and stakeholders are consulted with a view to protect the long-term reputation of the university.

Alastair described one of their key challenges as *'fluidity'*, i.e. what is ethical today may be different in 20 years' time. The greatest change he has noticed during recent years is the focus on mental health, reflecting a societal change from self-reliance towards greater openness in expressing vulnerability and the need for and expectation of support.

The Israel–Gaza conflict requires universities, on the one hand, to allow freedom of speech and, on the other, to protect the safety and well-being of students and staff who are attacked or offended.

At University of Leeds, the ethics committee has a framework to help them guide institutions on policies, freedoms and restrictions. However, they also have to make clear practical decisions that have an immediate effect on what is allowed and disallowed.

In this case, Alastair pointed out that, as chair of the institution and member of the ethics committee, his personal sympathies for one side of the debate or the other must be set aside. The leadership responsibility is to ensure fairness by listening to all stakeholders' views, including views he doesn't personally agree with, not shirking clear decisions and taking accountability to stand by those decisions. He emphasised empathy in listening to stakeholders, including the effort to understand *why* they held their views.

Conclusion

In conclusion, these insights bring out the balance of 'hard and soft landscaping'. The hard landscaping of processes and rules and the soft landscaping of autonomy and storytelling are both needed to create ethical resilience.

The ability of leaders to achieve an expectation of high ethical standards in formal and less formal methods is the key to gaining traction in the hearts, heads and hands of their teams.

Toolkit F shows you how to apply the Ethical Compass.

Notes

1 See: https://leadershipandprofessionalpractice.leeds.ac.uk/wp-content/uploads/sites/3/2022/05/Influencing-positively-around-hybrid-working.pdf.
2 Author's interview with Sarah Walker-Smith, Group CEO, Ampa.
3 Author's interview with Ronan Dunne, former CEO of Verizon Wireless and O2.
4 Author's interview with Simon Rogerson, CEO and Founder, Octopus Group.
5 Author's interview with Justin Rix, former partner at Grant Thornton.
6 Author's interview with Alastair Da Costa, chair and pro-chancellor, University of Leeds.

chapter 10

Higher purpose

How do you inspire an ethical purpose?

'High performing companies that are purposeful, profitable and socially aware are catalysing new ways of working.'

Sarah Rozenthuler[1]

In this chapter you will learn:

- How leaders inspire an ethical purpose beyond profit
- The role of authentic motivation
- The importance of teamwork to align stakeholders

Creating a purpose (or mission), values, strategies, targets and budgets are embedded in most organisation's business cycles. The role of the leader is to establish a purpose and supporting values that live and breathe in day-to-day activities.

Two key insights from my discussions with leaders are under the headings of authenticity and teamwork.

1 Authenticity

In this example, the CEO of Corps Security faced an urgent challenge turn around profitability. Referring back to its origins, he created an authentic, higher purpose for his board, staff and customers which turned around performance.

Case study – Mike Bullock[2]

Mike Bullock is the CEO of Corps Security, provider of specialist security services. He originally joined from a commercial facilities management provider and was promoted internally.

The organisation was founded as the 'Corps of Commissionaires' in 1859 by Captain Sir Edward Walter as a way of helping veterans from the Crimean War. It was a time when medical support in the battlefield was improving and many who would previously have died from their wounds returned to their parishes with disabilities. At one stage, Florence Nightingale was one of the governors.

It started by helping eight war veterans to find paid jobs as 'commissionaires', a term re-purposed by Edward Walter to give greater status to the role of providing security at the doors of buildings. It went on to become a UK business owned by a trust, where the profits are reinvested in military charities. A similar organisation was established in Canada in 1925. Since 1901, its patron has been the UK's reigning monarch, currently King Charles III.

When Mike became CEO, the business was not generating profit for the trust. Mike had been appointed to bring commercial rigour and return the business to profit. His first challenge was to reduce costs, but he negotiated with the board, representing the trust as a shareholder, not to cut too deeply so the business could become more efficient 'in the right way'. He went on to:

- remove the term 'not for profit' from the organisation's language, being clear that profit is used to provide more help for veterans

- register as an accredited social enterprise (he looked at B-Corp accreditation but saw social enterprise as more appropriate)
- increase pay to frontline staff to provide a 'living wage' above the UK's minimum wage
- introduce a social welfare fund to help employees in need
- introduce a death-in-service benefit to support colleagues' families
- further invest in technology – developing intruder and fire alarms and CCTV monitoring
- introduce charitable fundraising among staff, with each colleague given one paid day a year to raise funds for a military charity (Combat Stress), and another day to support another charity of their own choice; some clients also pay a 1% supplement to contribute to Combat Stress.

Impact

After a year, a small number of clients left because of the higher cost of security staff; however, over four years, turnover rose by more than 50% from £70 million to £115 million and the business returned to profit with resulting benefits to the charities it supports.

The trust is now able consistently to support charities including Combat Stress, ABF The Soldiers Charity, RAF Benevolent Fund, Royal Navy and Royal Marines Charity and other charities supporting veterans in need.

As the organisation has grown, it now employs around 3,500 people. It is no longer just service veterans because of staff transferring through contracts taken over from competitors.

Mike is clear that clients see two differentiators for Corps Security in the market:

1. It is an accredited social enterprise.
2. 99% of frontline staff are paid a living wage.

Their service quality also benchmarks well with a high-net promoter score.

Higher purpose

Mike explains their clarity of purpose: 'To make a difference, improving lives and protecting the things that matter to us all.'

As a social enterprise owned by a trust, Corps Security has the advantage of not having to meet shareholder pressure for quarterly earnings growth. The board can

> focus on the long-term purpose, as long as the organisation is economically viable in the short term. By paying more to staff, they can attract and retain a competent and loyal workforce and compete on quality instead of cost.
>
> Mike reflects on his previous experience as a manager in the commercial sector. He accepts that decisions to compromise quality or staff loyalty for short-term profit are difficult to challenge in a culture focused on the short term. His advice to managers in this position is to recognise that saying 'yes' all the time is not necessarily valued and that solutions that protect both values and profit may not be obvious but can be found.
>
> Mike talks about *'solid values'* and explains a *'circle of care'* at Corps where colleagues come first, they take care of customers, customers pay the business and, in turn, the business can pay a fair living wage.

The leader's personal motivation should both be and be seen to be authentic. In this case study, the CEO of Twin Group builds a business where the higher purpose is deeply connected to her own early experiences.

Case study – Caroline Fox[3]

Caroline Fox is CEO of Twin Group, which she founded with her twin sister Jacqui Fox in 1995. It now supports thousands of people every year with training, education and employability.

Caroline had a modest start in life, did not excel at school and did not get the opportunity to go to university. Family expectations of her were low.

When training to be a secretary, she became interested in the training process and secured her first job with the business that trained her. Her abilities led to quick promotions but, after seven years, she took maternity leave and was told, 'You will never be as committed after maternity.'

She decided to leave to set up her own business. The first high-street bank she approached for a loan would not lend her money despite the strength of the business case, her experience and the bank's marketing messages about supporting new businesses. The second bank she approached did make the loan and she has since built up a successful business which now employs 300 people.

Her commercial expertise, sense of fairness, competitiveness and instinct for doing the right thing have driven her company's success. What it stands for is an authentic reflection of her personal values.

Mark Huxley describes the 'missionary versus mercenary' model, but warns that the original sense of purpose is a muscle that needs exercise when external shareholders join a small and growing business.

> ### Case study – Mark Huxley[4]
>
> Mark Huxley is an entrepreneur, advisor and non-executive and Past Master of the Worshipful Company of Entrepreneurs, a City Livery Company.
>
> Mark refers to venture capitalist John Doerr, who coined the phrase, 'mercenary versus missionary' where mercenaries are 'all about the pitch and the deal' whereas missionaries are 'strategic', understanding that 'this business of innovation is something that takes a long time'.[5]
>
> Mark uses this model to decide which businesses to work with. According to Mark: 'I sit nearer the "missionary purpose" end of the spectrum and will only work with clients who share that bias', but it is a muscle that needs exercise. He continues, 'While small companies often start with a long-term, mission-driven culture, it is hard to keep that going through growth and introduction of external shareholders which pull towards a short-term, mercenary-driven culture. It can be done if the business finds an emotional alignment with customers in the way, for example, that Virgin Airlines successfully competed with the established corporate culture of British Airways.'

2 Teamwork

As previously noted, it is actions not words that influence how an organisation operates. In the next example, the CEO of APSCo chooses not to take ownership of the organisation she has founded and to assert rigorous standards.

It is an unusual model because the organisation is a trade body that has created a kitemark for the recruitment industry. Its focus is therefore to earn trust in the eyes of end users, the clients of recruitment businesses, while its revenue is from recruitment businesses themselves who are also the owners.

The CEO's choices about ownership and standards have created alignment to its purpose and a strong sense of teamwork between external stakeholders and employees.

Case study – Ann Swain[6]

Ann Swain is founder and CEO of APSCo Global, an international trade body for the recruitment sector, which is owned by its 1,100 members and has run for 25 years.

The recruitment sector is built on a brokerage model. If there is no deal, there is either no fee or a much-reduced fee. Like other brokerage models, it can lead to an aggressive sales and deal-making culture at the expense of service quality. APSCo is one of the organisations that is guarding against that by promoting professional standards.

As a trade body, APSCo relies on building trust with its members through honesty and quality. That is why Ann founded it without taking ownership, instead giving members ownership control.

For a business to be accepted as a member, it must be endorsed on its integrity and delivery of customer service by at least 20 clients. Applications are overseen by a committee of representative members, and about a quarter of applicants are rejected and receive transparent feedback on their application. APSCo also has 'trusted partners', who can market their services to members; they too must provide endorsements from at least 10 clients. Trusted partners pay a fee but not commission to APSCo, so the focus remains on quality. Members and trusted partners must maintain their standards. This is policed by a complaints process, where clients can lodge a complaint that goes through independent legal review. This can result in fines or expulsion. Members operating in regulated sectors (healthcare, education and welfare) have to meet additional standards to meet safeguarding and compliance obligations.

There are other business models for trade bodies that focus on networking, more like a club, than professional standards. Ann is clear that she is raising standards for a sector that changes people's lives by helping them find jobs and careers.

APSCo also supports charitable causes, having partnered with NSPCC and Childline for over 20 years.

Staff at APSCo also go through a rigorous selection process including psychometrics and assessment of emotional intelligence. In other words, members, trusted partners and staff are all vetted to ensure professional standards and trust are at the core of their work together.

Conclusion

Purpose is not an answer in isolation. As Stefan Stern has written in the *Financial Times*: 'Purpose ... can be a concept that is hard to pin down ... it is a more personal sense of purpose that counts.'[7] My discussions showed that a higher purpose that is authentic and aligned across stakeholders drives ethical and commercial value.

Toolkit F shows you how to apply the Ethical Compass.

Notes

1. Rozenthuler, S. (2020) *Powered by Purpose: Energise Your People to do Great Work*, p. 4.
2. Author's interview with Mike Bullock, CEO, Corps Security.
3. Author's interview with Caroline Fox, CEO, Twin Group.
4. Author's interview with Mark Huxley, entrepreneur.
5. See: https://hbr.org/2016/04/what-separates-high-impact-entrepreneurs-from-those-who-dont-make-a-big-difference.
6. Author's interview with Ann Swain, CEO, APSCo.
7. See: https://www.ft.com/content/ed0fb762-5407-4e7f-a1d9-a4ae1d67aa66, Stefan Stern, visiting Professor, Bayes Business School.

chapter 11

Ingenuity

How do you find ethical answers to business questions?

'Don't leave your business brain at the door when making ethical decisions.'

Ronan Dunne

In this chapter you will learn:

- How leaders use ingenuity to apply ethical principles to business decisions
- The role and risk of incentives
- How both ethical and economic objectives can be achieved with imagination

Some leaders talked about trade-offs between ethics and business performance, and there are sometimes short-term costs when an organisation is uncompromising on its values. However, the leaders who successfully achieved ethical competitive advantage are consistent in rejecting the idea of trade-offs overall.

My conversations highlighted two key insights about leadership ingenuity: incentives and imagination.

Incentives

The recruitment industry is known for paying commission to employees for successful placements. One agency, which works with not-for-profit clients, chooses not to pay commission because it discourages teamwork.

Case study – Peter Beeby[1]

Peter Beeby is CEO of Prospectus, a London-based recruitment agency with 50 staff, finding staff for not-for-profit clients. Unusually for the sector, it does not pay commission to its staff, choosing to encourage collaboration on client assignments. It is also a registered B Corp, the first in its sector.

Another sales-driven business shares profits using 'Marxist' principles.

Case study – Simon Biltcliffe[2]

Dr Simon Biltcliffe is founder and CEO of print services agency Webmart, which now has a £30 million turnover and 44 employees. He created an unconventional business model and aimed at maximising everyone's 'intellectual, emotional and financial return'. He uses capitalist principles to generate the wealth and Marxist principles to redistribute that wealth back to the company and the wider community.

He uses a formula, transparent to employees and shareholders, to share the value created by the business. The result is a profitable business that has run for 25 years with unusually high sales per employee.

Measurement, simplicity and good relationships are at the heart of the business. For example, the aim is to 'outcollaborate' competitors by creating positive relationships with customers and suppliers and between colleagues; the business defines its goals every year in simple visible steps.

> The pay and incentives are a key part of his success:
>
> - Pay is good and above market rates but 'not excessive'.
> - A minimum profit level is retained in the business, everything above that is distributed to colleagues.
> - Everyone's performance is measured in three ways:
>
>   1. *Intellectual return:* are you realising your potential?
>   2. *Emotional return:* how happy are you in your work?
>   3. *Financial return:* what financial impact are you having?
>
> The focus is on recruiting carefully, involving peers in selection and feedback, and promoting to more senior roles from inside the business.

Imagination

As business founders, entrepreneurs have a strong appetite for the risks inherent in start-ups. Successful entrepreneurs feed off their imagination and this is where I found valuable insights in bringing together ethical standards with business performance. There were also warnings about misplaced confidence if a team does not have the required competence.

> ### Case study – Ben Rowland[3]
>
> Ben Rowland is CEO of the Association of Employment and Learning Providers, a UK trade association, and previously an entrepreneur bringing new businesses and products to market.
>
> He warns against conventional thinking that might stifle innovation. Entrepreneurship can challenge ethical boundaries, for example selling a 'future truth' – a service or product that is not yet ready or tested. His ethical borderline is whether he is being honest with himself and with customers about potential and risks.
>
> Many small technology businesses have grown into successful large corporations in recent decades, for example Microsoft's experimental software of the 1980s has evolved into one of the global standards. Others have failed, for example the health diagnostic business Theranos which raised $700 million but never developed a viable product and eventually failed in 2018, 15 years after it was founded.

> Ben sees a strong connection between 'competence' and 'ethics', i.e. a highly competent team may claim 'future truths' with integrity and transparency based on their expertise, in contrast with teams that over-rate their competence.

Case study – Sean Williams[4]

Sean Williams is an experienced entrepreneur with a strong social conscience in the field of technology-enabled businesses. He is currently the founder and CEO of AutogenAI, built on natural language processing technology.

At a system level, Sean sees innovation as a driver of common good that must be protected. Monopolistic or anti-competitive behaviour by large businesses is an example of practices that must be avoided.

He also sees visionary entrepreneurs mostly as a force for good because they see the world 'as an improvement on what it is today' and 'beyond current possibilities'. He appreciates there is a gap between the vision and the reality.

Selling the vision to investors is one step, ensuring it is implemented is another. For him, an ethical boundary is crossed when the entrepreneur pretends they have both the vision and the solution when all they have is the vision.

His current business sets prices to help small- and medium-sized businesses (SMEs) compete more effectively against larger businesses, i.e. SMEs can access the same level of service at a lower price. This is both values driven, levelling the playing field to an extent between larger and smaller businesses, and good commercial sense because it maximises total revenue and supports the ultimate customer (the government) in its policy of encouraging smaller businesses to bid.

Conclusion

Ingenuity is a key skill for any successful leader and their organisation, whether it is applied to strategy, financing, product development, marketing, operations, development of people or a combination. These examples show how it can be applied as much to business ethics as any other part of the business.

Toolkit F shows you how to apply the Ethical Compass.

Notes

1 Author's interview with Peter Beeby, CEO, Prospectus.
2 See: https://www.cranfield.ac.uk/som/research-centres/bettany-centre-for-entrepreneurship/events-and-networking/simon-biltcliffe-the-radical-entrepreneur.
3 Author's interview with Ben Rowland, CEO, AELP.
4 Author's interview with Sean Williams, CEO, AutogenAI.

chapter 12

Courage

How do you find the courage to follow your conscience?

'We need braver leaders and more courageous cultures.'

Brené Brown[1]

In this chapter you will learn:

- How leaders find or avoid the courage to do what they see is right
- How leaders use and challenge power
- How leaders deal with temptation

A company is a person at law, with all the basic rights and responsibilities that people have, but it has no conscience. Its ethics depend entirely on the conscience of its people, particularly its leader.

When a leader takes a bold action and acts with their conscience, this heavily influences the next stage of the organisation's direction. This is an example of 'actions not words', where a leader's visible decision has a marked effect on the behaviour of colleagues around them and on the whole culture.

Courage is a reaction to risk. The level of risk varies according to the culture of the region, the organisation and the status of the individual within it.

In my conversation with Sean Vernell, an elected trade union official, he defined leadership as *'... having the courage to explore alternatives and listen, not follow the crowd, then finding the strongest argument to make positive change'.*

These were some of the more sensitive conversations I had, presented anonymously but with the interviewees' permission.

The key insights were about temptation and power.

Power

I heard several examples of speaking out with courage. In one instance, an individual was placing her power and reputation behind a colleague's freedom of speech, in another the individual risked their entire livelihood.

> ### Case study[2]
>
> One leader I spoke to is prepared to speak out publicly on potentially controversial issues. They are aware that, in social media, views can get misunderstood very quickly because the quality of dialogue is more superficial than in a face-to-face discussion.
>
> Nevertheless, they stood up for a colleague who had expressed a view about the Israel–Gaza conflict on social media. The leader's intention was to support them personally and their right to express a view, not to 'take sides'. However, it was interpreted by a trade publication that the business was taking a biased position.
>
> The leader learned from that experience that taking a bolder public role in speaking out has unintended consequences. In any case, they are clear that they acted from sound ethical intention and would do so again rather than doing nothing. They also appreciate that being 'authentic' also means taking the risk of being misinterpreted but that often engaging with those who misinterpret you can result in a better outcome and shared learning.

Case study[3]

A senior HR professional described his firm belief that the essence of leadership is to 'do the right thing' even at personal cost. He defines ethical leadership as setting ethical standards and then acting on them. He refers to the teaching of Aristotle when he says, 'It is only ethical if you act on it.'

He was aware of persistent bullying and lying by a senior colleague. When he challenged the behaviour, his employer did not support him so he resigned on principle with immediate effect. At a time when he was responsible for a young family, he was left without income for nearly a year while he fought a legal dispute with his employer which he eventually won.

Temptation

In my conversations, some leaders described the temptation to do the wrong thing, and how they faced risks that were sometimes too much to take on.

I heard several examples of misogyny and other forms of discrimination, where the temptation to conform was too great for colleagues to speak out. Abuse of power is common; the challenge is for witnesses to take a stand, which I will examine in Chapter 16 on speaking up and whistleblowing.

The first three examples are about bribery.

A large bribe was a temptation that was resisted, but the risk of following through and exposing the individual offering the bribe was too great.

Case study[4]

One of the leaders I spoke to described the temptation of bribery early in their career. They were offered a life-changing amount of money by their line manager to influence a family relative, a decision maker in a related business, to place a valuable contract 'with the right supplier'.

The person being offered the bribe had to weigh up the size of the bribe, the impact on their career of saying 'no' to their boss and their relative who would be an accomplice.

They were tempted but turned it down. However, they did not blow the whistle on the person offering the bribe because it was too risky without written proof.

Here are two examples from two leaders in the education sector, operating in countries where bribery was relatively common.

In both cases, they used their power to take a principled position.

Case study[5]

A leader I spoke to was responsible for an educational institution and resisted attempts to give or receive what he saw as bribes. Persistent parents of a student at the institution tried to give a substantial sum to the leader in an envelope, which he turned down. They then gave it to a more junior employee who declared it to the leader. He rang the parents to ask them to take it back, but they were offended that this 'gift' was being rebuffed. His solution was to treat the sum as sponsorship, purchase equipment for the institution, tracking receipts as evidence of its use and thank the parents publicly for their generosity. By turning it from a covert to an overt act, he was able to redefine the transaction and signal to other 'enthusiastic' parents that covert payments would not be tolerated and would benefit the institution as a whole, not an individual student.

Case study[6]

Another example of bribery was about the supply of water for students and staff in an educational institution in a country where, at the time, bribery was relatively common. The leader discovered that an employee was arranging for the college to pay a premium for water and personally receiving half the premium as 'commission' from the supplier. She knew that 'commission' payments like this were not seen as major transgressions and were previously dealt with through an informal warning. On the other hand, the institution had a legal right to dismiss the employee. A warning fitted in with the local custom; dismissal fitted with the leader's ethical instinct but could prevent continuing supply of water to the college.

The leader consulted with colleagues and turned to the purpose of the institution, which was to deliver an education to 'British standards'. On this basis, she decided not to go with local custom and dismissed the employee, making it clear to all stakeholders that it was about standards not pragmatism.

In this example, a 'white lie' was justified in the mind of the decision maker.

> ## Case study[7]
>
> One of the leaders I interviewed described the temptation of a 'white lie' to help build an individual's confidence. The leader was overseeing an assessment of an individual's performance which initially met the standard required to be publicly recognised. However, an error in the process had slightly inflated the score and, at the last minute, the leader was asked to decide whether to mark it back or leave it be. It would not affect anyone else's score. The leader chose to let it go because, although it did not meet transparent standards, it served the higher purpose of building confidence and was within the margin of error of the scoring system.

This final example illustrates the common problem of prioritising loyalty to a colleague above the needs of the organisation.

> ## Case study[8]
>
> One of the leaders I interviewed described a business where the CEO was the founder and technical brains behind the product. Although the market potential was clear, the CEO's financial decisions were proving ineffective and the board decided to move the CEO to become CTO in order to make best use of their skills.
>
> It is a common story in technical start-ups: the 'white coat vs grey suit' dilemma. The 'white coat' founder who may have taken a technical product to its minimum viable stage is usually not the person best placed to the 'grey suit' tasks of securing funding, managing shareholders and making scale-up decisions. That is why many venture investors prefer investing in teams rather than individuals.
>
> The dilemma for a board is to judge the time to make the change of leadership and to motivate a founder who remains crucial to the business and may own substantial equity but must relinquish power to an incoming CEO. The challenge for the board is to get the founder to prioritise the success of the business above their own prestige. Loyalty and emotion do not always give way to hard-nosed economics and inevitable decisions often take too long to deliver.
>
> It also highlights the fact that a non-executive board has limited power. Its single biggest decision is usually the choice of CEO. The temptation is to prioritise loyalty and short-term risk above the long-term health of the organisation.

Conclusion

Acts of courage set the ethical culture of an organisation. However, conformism, personal risk or short-term business risk can obstruct ethical decision making.

Toolkit F shows you how to apply the Ethical Compass.

Notes

1. Brown, B. (2018) *Dare to Lead*. Vermilion.
2. Author's interview with one of the 50 leaders.
3. Author's interview with one of the 50 leaders.
4. Author's interview with one of the 50 leaders.
5. Author's interview with one of the 50 leaders.
6. Author's interview with one of the 50 leaders.
7. Author's interview with one of the 50 leaders.
8. Author's interview with one of the 50 leaders.

Toolkit F: The Ethical Compass (ETHIC)

How do you apply the Ethical Compass?

Background

The 'Ethical Compass' is derived from the experience and insights of 50 leaders. It does not attempt to define right and wrong but supports and challenges an individual or team to develop an ethical direction. You should adapt it to complement your organisation's policies and processes.

The labels for the five challenges spell out the acronym ETHIC:

1. Empathy – how do you build trustful relationships with stakeholders?
2. Traction – how do you take an organisation with you and deliver?
3. Higher purpose – how do you create an ethical direction?
4. Ingenuity – how do you find ethical answers to business questions?
5. Courage – how do you find the courage to follow your conscience?

The five challenges help you build ethical practice into day-to-day actions. Each challenge relies on your leadership competence which can be learned and developed. It recognises that business ethics at its best is a team activity, fuelled by challenge, diversity of thought and ingenuity.

The following preparation is recommended to use this toolkit effectively:

- Complete Toolkit B (Ethical health).
- Read Chapters 7–12.

The toolkit is in two sections.

- Section 1, Ethical visibility, is for individuals to understand the visibility of your ethics as a leader.
- Section 2, The Ethical Compass, is a group exercise to help you work with your team on five challenges to make a greater impact as an organisation.

In both sections you are invited to test your scores with colleagues, look for evidence of impact and identify areas to develop further.

Section 1 Ethical visibility (as a leader)

Most of the leaders I have spoken to see themselves striving to be 'ethical'. However, the examples they give show that it is often a tightrope between pressures of business performance and principles or, more subtly, competing principles.

Many businesses have ethical codes, often with regulatory obligations. This toolkit does not replace those codes but focuses on leadership behaviour and visibility of ethics in day-to-day work.

How to use the toolkit

The group who will work together on Section 2 should also complete this 10-point questionnaire individually to establish the visibility of your ethics (or values or principles) as a leader. To get a rigorous result, look for evidence or validation from colleagues for each of your scores.

Section 1 Ethical visibility (as a leader) Ratings: 4 consistently/always, 3 often, 2 sometimes, 1 rarely/never	Rating 1–4	Evidence
1 Do you consider the ethical impact you make as a leader?		
2 Do colleagues see you as a values-driven leader?		
3 Do you prioritise values above short-term profit when necessary?		
4 Do you share stories of other people putting values into action?		
5 Do you formally recognise colleagues who demonstrate values?		
6 Do you discuss and debate values with key stakeholders?		
7 Do you call out colleagues who do not meet your values?		
8 Do you include values in hiring decisions and appraisals?		
9 Do you learn about better ways of applying values?		
10 Do you apply values in the same way whether in or out of work?		
Total score	**Max 40**	
Note: for these purposes, 'ethics', 'values' or 'principles' can be used interchangeably.		

Total score	How to make your values (or ethics or principles) more visible
30–40	Your values have high visibility. Consider whether there are any areas to improve and how you can support colleagues in their ethical development.
20–30	You can improve the visibility of your values from a sound starting point. Use Section 2 of this toolkit to identify specific areas to work on and consider pairing up with a colleague to encourage each other.
Below 20	You can improve the visibility of your values from a low starting point. Use Section 2 this toolkit to identify specific areas to work on and consider working with a mentor or coach to develop this aspect of your leadership.

Section 2 How to apply the Ethical Compass (as an organisation)

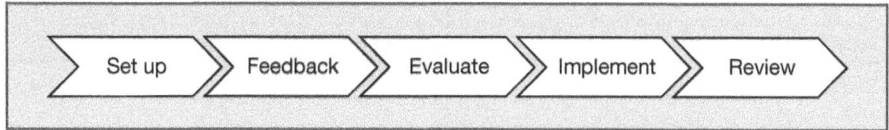

- **Set up with colleagues:**
  - Discuss the toolkit with your team, ideally at a time when you are planning next year's priorities or the long-term strategy.
  - Work out how this toolkit can benefit the business, for example reinforcement of values, stakeholder trust and risk reduction.
- **Gather feedback:**
  - Ask your team to complete the toolkit including examples and evidence to back up their answers. If you think colleagues will answer more honestly by completing it anonymously, then set up an online poll to collect anonymous answers.
- **Evaluate actions:**
  - Review the feedback as a team and identify strengths and areas to improve, looking at case studies in this book for inspiration, if necessary.
  - Identify actions to make improvements.
  - Evaluate each action against potential benefits, costs and risks, then rank the actions in order of net benefit. Decide which actions to take forward and which to drop or defer.
  - Note: use your organisation's normal project evaluation process; if you do not have one, use the *Benefits Scoring Matrix* below.

- **Implement:**
  - Identify risks and enablers and who needs to be consulted and directly involved to achieve the benefits, reduce risks and unlock the resources to deliver the changes.
  - Secure commitment to make changes based on the actions that achieve greatest benefit.
  - If costs and investment are required, secure the budget required.
  - Assign responsibilities and follow through.
- **Review the impact:**
  - Revisit the impact of your actions.
  - Take action to improve further.

Benefits Scoring Matrix (if needed)

Heading	Ethical	Financial	Total
Benefits (e.g. Low = 1)	1–4	1–4	2–8
Costs and risks (e.g. Low = 4)	1–4	1–4	2–8
Total	2–8	2–8	4–16

- Use judgement to decide criteria for 'very high', 'high', 'medium' and 'low'.
  - Use your stated purpose (or mission), values and behaviours as criteria for the ethical column. If you do not have these, use 'stakeholder trust' as a proxy.
- Score 'Benefits' as very high 4, high 3, medium 2, low 1.
- Score 'Costs and risks' as low 4, medium 3, high 2, very high 1.
- Add up total scores in the right-hand column, out of a maximum of 16.
- Rank the highest scoring action at the top and the lowest scoring at the bottom.

Note: the effectiveness of the toolkit depends on how rigorously you apply it and follow through.

Section 2 The Ethical Compass (ETHIC)			
Challenge and features (refer to Chapters 7–12)	Questions Ratings: 4 very high, 3 high, 2 medium, 1 low (refer to Toolkit B)	Rating 1–4	Potential actions

Section 2 The Ethical Compass (ETHIC)			
Empathy Compassion Balance	How much trust and loyalty do our customers, employees, suppliers, shareholders and communities demonstrate?		
Traction Autonomy Rules	How consistent is our ethical and financial health across the organisation?		
Higher purpose Authenticity Teamwork	How well is our purpose embedded in our products and services and what is our impact beyond the organisation?		
Ingenuity Incentives Imagination	How well do we find ingenious solutions to business problems that are both ethically and commercially sound?		
Courage Power Temptation	How well do we stand out as an ethically courageous and collaborative organisation?		
Total score		Max 20	

Total score	How to improve
15–20	Your leadership as a team is delivering effective ethical and business performance. Consider any areas that are inconsistent and need improving.
10–15	You can improve from a sound starting point. Identify and rank potential actions to make improvements.
Below 10	You can improve from a low starting point. Identify and rank potential actions to make improvements and consider systemic changes.

Part 2 – Ethical leadership: Quick read summary

Chapters 7–12 are summarised here in bullet points.

- The insights on ethical leadership are derived from interviews with 50 leaders. About a third work in founder-led businesses, a third in charities or social enterprises and a third in large and listed businesses.
- The leaders are mostly 'purpose-led', i.e. seeking to improve the world as part of their working life.
- The challenge is more complex for larger businesses with external shareholders.
- Public trust is falling and leaders have to work harder to be seen to be trustworthy.
- Leadership and culture are the two largest influences on the ethical health of an organisation.
- Leadership actions, not words, make the difference.
- The interviews revealed a pattern of challenges used by leaders to lead both ethical and commercial performance. The resulting tool is a compass, not a map, and does not attempt to define right and wrong but helps you and your team set an ethical direction. The five challenges are under the acronym ETHIC:
    1. Empathy – how do you build trustful relationships with stakeholders?
    2. Traction – how do you take an organisation with you?
    3. Higher purpose – how do you create an ethical direction?
    4. Ingenuity – how do you find ethical answers to business questions?
    5. Courage – how do you find the courage to follow your conscience?
- Business ethics at its best is a team activity, fuelled by challenge, diversity of thought and ingenuity.

part 3

Organisational culture

chapter 13

Moral psychology

'There are shared and permanent values arising from the nature of humanity itself.'

Mary Warnock

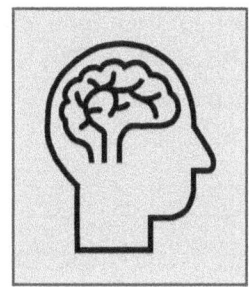

In this chapter you will learn:

- Where morals come from
- What psychological studies tell us about our underlying motivations
- The extent to which they are shaped by intuition and reasoning
- How an organisational culture enhances or undermines ethical behaviour

Introduction

Alongside leadership, culture is the key influential factor in the ethical health of a business.[1]

I will use the simple definition of culture:[2] 'The way things get done around here.' In other words, the habits, norms and rituals beyond written codes and policies that distinguish one organisation from another.

This chapter explores moral psychology at an individual and group level. Because it focuses more on personal choice, it refers to 'morals', whereas 'ethics' focus on organisational standards which feature in later chapters.

Where do morals come from?

This is an ancient question with many contending answers: from religions that ascribe moral authority to a higher being to philosophers like Immanuel Kant who apply reasoning to define frameworks as we saw in an earlier chapter. More recently, biologists and psychologists have studied both human and animal behaviour to understand the mystery of instincts and emotion.

There are broadly two schools of thought. The 'intuitionist' (or nativist) view is that morals have evolved as an intuitive trait, with a common set of patterns for all humans which then develop for each individual through family, cultural, religious and other communal experiences. The 'empiricist' view is that morals are learned more as a cognitive process.

Empiricist view

Psychologist Lawrence Kohlberg was an empiricist who identified developmental steps of 'moral reasoning', first published in 1969. He proposed that morals are mainly a learned behaviour. He observed children making moral decisions based on avoiding punishment, young people learning a sense of duty and a small minority of mature adults developing personal and strongly held principles.[3]

He developed and tested a theory with three levels, each demonstrating learned behaviour and increased moral reasoning:

1 **Preconventional reasoning**

   Usually developed as children who learn that 'bad' behaviour leads to punishment and 'good' behaviour leads to rewards.

2 **Conventional reasoning**

   Usually developed as young people who learn to meet social expectations, respect authority and maintain social order.

3 **Postconventional reasoning**

Sometimes developed as mature adults, or precocious young people, who build the confidence to promote rights and responsibilities and challenge authority.

According to Kohlberg, only 10–15% of people reach the postconventional level of moral reasoning, as it requires an advanced capacity for abstract thinking.

Psychologist Carol Gilligan, who had worked with Kohlberg and accepted much of the findings, was critical of the exclusive focus on males, arguing that women place more value on interpersonal connections. She conducted new studies interviewing both men and women, finding women more often emphasised care and relationships over rules. Gilligan argued that Kohlberg's theory overlooked this 'different voice' in morality and was influential in later work by social intuitionists.[4]

Intuitionist view

The Moral Foundations Theory is a social intuitionist view developed by psychologist Jonathan Haidt from 2004 onwards. He observed that there are moral instincts that are present in all cultures. The theory does not claim this list is exhaustive but so far has identified six common instincts:[5]

- **Care/harm:** showing kindness or compassion and avoiding harm or cruelty.
- **Justice/cheating:** upholding fairness or justice and avoiding cheating or exploitation.
- **Loyalty/betrayal:** being loyal or showing allegiance and avoiding betrayal.
- **Hierarchy/subversion:** respecting authority and avoiding defiance.
- **Sanctity/degradation:** seeking purity and avoiding taboos and disgust.
- **Liberty/oppression:** upholding freedom and avoiding oppression and coercion.

Subsequent work by anthropologist Oliver Curry, published in 2019, examined 'morality as co-operation'.[6] It looked at 60 diverse societies across the world to look for behaviours that all societies regarded as morally good. The results show remarkable consistency under seven headings: family, group, reciprocity, bravery, respect, fairness and property.

This shows further evidence of intuitively moral behaviour that supports cooperation within a wide range of communities.

These theories are broadly defined and allow for significant variation of specific moral judgements, for example a taboo in one culture may be a freedom in another. They also highlight unavoidable moral dilemmas, for example sharing resources with the community may reduce resources for the family.

Overall, they help us understand how communities and cultures cooperate, how families and small groups draw out 'the better angels of our nature'[7] and how we can develop our moral courage as individuals.

As Michael Sandel said: 'Altruism, generosity, solidarity and civic spirit are not like commodities that are depleted with use. They are more like muscles that develop and grow stronger with exercise.'[8]

How rational are we?

'Confirmation bias' is well-known as a tendency to focus on evidence that supports existing beliefs, giving less weight to evidence that contradicts them.

Haidt's research also shows that we use intuition to make moral decisions but use reasoning to explain them afterwards, sometimes convincing ourselves we are more rational than we really are.

Work by psychologist David DeSteno also showed that we consistently exaggerate the ethically positive aspects of our own behaviour. We do the same for people belonging to our social group.[9]

Among all the qualities of good leaders, self-awareness is both critical and elusive. As Charles Conn, chair of Patagonia, said to me: 'We often apply hindsight to over-determine the cause of success.' For some leaders, reflective practice, such as Theory U,[10] Kolb's or Gibb's reflective cycles,[11] is worth considering.

Overall, we over-estimate the rationality of our ethics.

How altruistic are we?

A way of answering the question was developed by Daniel Kahneman, the economist and Nobel Prize winner, and Amos Tversky when they developed 'prospect theory' using the 'ultimatum' or 'dictator' game.[12]

In the game, an individual is given the power to share a financial windfall with someone else, with discretion on how much to keep and how much to give away.

What would you do?

Variants on this game have found that players tend to give away a significant minority (on average 28%) of their windfall, giving more if they know the other person and less if they do not. In this analysis, the range is broad: 36% keep it all, 17% split it evenly and 5% give it all away.[13]

Another insight came from the 'dropped wallet' experiment carried out over two years, led by behavioural economist Alain Cohn and published in 2019. 17,000 wallets, containing varying amounts of money and sometimes just a key, were deliberately dropped in 355 cities across 40 countries to see how many would be returned by strangers who found them.

Would you take the trouble to return a wallet you found in the street?

The result was that empty wallets had the lowest return rate below 50%, whereas over 60% of those with money were returned. Return rates varied by country, with Demark, Sweden and New Zealand at the top and China, Peru, Kazakhstan and Kenya at the bottom. Every country with a significant sample showed higher return rates for wallets with more money.

In the follow-up to the experiment, researchers found that altruism was not the dominant motivation. 'People want to see themselves as an honest person, not as a thief. Keeping a found wallet means having to adapt one's self-image, which comes with psychological costs,' said economist Michel Maréchal and a co-author. 'The psychological forces ... can be stronger than the financial ones.'

Economist Dan Ariely commented, 'The study shows in a very natural, experimental way our decisions about dishonesty are not about a rational cost-benefit analysis but about what we feel comfortable with from a social norm perspective and how much we can rationalize our decisions.'[14]

Evolutionary biologists have proposed that kindness serves an evolutionary purpose. 'Hamilton's Rule' was developed by W.D. Hamilton in 1964 and later developed and explained by Richard Dawkins in his book *The Selfish Gene* in 1976. The rule is that altruism or kindness, i.e. where an individual benefits someone else at their own cost, follows evolutionary logic if the two individuals are related. On the other hand, philosopher Mary Midgley saw this as reductionist and wrote in her book *Beast and Man* (1978): 'The motivation of living creatures does not boil down to any single basic force.'

In any case, we know that doing good is often intrinsically motivated, with no reward other than feeling good.[15]

Whatever the underlying motivation, altruism fuels effective communities and organisations.

Does power change our ethics?

Have you ever taken advantage of your power over someone else?

In my interviews, I found several examples of leaders abusing power. This example shows a powerful client exercising self-interest in failing to honour an agreement and the supplier feeling forced to follow self-interest to retain the revenue and the relationship, with patience rewarded in the end.

Case study – Veronica Heaven[16]

Veronica Heaven is the MD of The Heaven Company, a sustainability and communications consultancy. The Heaven Company's stated values are integrity, understanding, collaboration and positive behaviour which mirror Veronica's own strongly held principles.

She was working with a large client that provided a significant source of revenue. The client stood to profit from the joint work but the client used their power to claim full credit, treating Veronica's business as a 'white label' supplier, which was not the agreement.

The client's size and resources were much greater than The Heaven Company and the working relationship was too important to lose. In practice, the choice was to stop working with the client, and lose the revenue, or continue working with them in the hope that the credit for the partnership would eventually become clear.

Veronica decided to continue working with them because the loss of a major partner would have been too great. However, she also kept a log of the actions so there was a record of the problem.

Her approach paid off when a new person was appointed as the key contact. Veronica laid out the history and they agreed to change the way they operated, giving due prominence to the role of her business.

David DeSteno writes in his article 'Who Can You Trust?' that 'wrong' behaviour often results from analysing costs and benefits and almost all of us do it if we think we won't get caught: '... we need to abandon the notion that people wrestle with "good" and "evil" impulses ... the mind focuses on two types of gains: short-term and long-term. And it's the trade-off between them that typically dictates integrity at any given moment.' He goes on to observe, '90% of people, most of whom identify themselves as morally upstanding, will act dishonestly to benefit themselves if they believe they won't get caught.'[17]

Psychologist Jessica Kennedy also found that senior leaders are less likely to raise questions about ethics than less senior colleagues.[18]

This reminds us that power and self-deception are a dangerous cocktail.

Two studies were carried out several decades ago to test how far authority would influence ordinary people to harm others. The studies became well-known for their alarming results. Both studies used controversial methods and questions were subsequently raised over their conclusions. However, they are relevant for understanding the significant influence of authority.

In 1961, a series of experiments were conducted by psychologist Stanley Milgram at Yale University. The aim was to see how far participants would obey instructions to administer electric shocks to another person, the 'learner'. Participants thought it was real, but in fact the learner was acting and the shocks were fake. The result was that 65% of participants administered what they thought was the maximum 450-volt shock, which, if real, would have been fatal. They were prompted and encouraged by a supervisor who assured them that no harm would come to the learner but that delivering the shock was 'essential'. Some of the findings were subsequently challenged,[19] but the willingness of many participants to defer to authority was clear.

The Stanford Prison Experiment was a psychological experiment performed in 1971 by psychologist Philip Zimbardo at Stanford University.[20] It was meant to test the effects on participants of playing roles of prisoners and guards. The experiment involved 24 students who were paid to participate for two weeks. Each was randomly assigned the role of prisoner or guard, with the guards asked to ensure the prisoners did not escape. It was ended after only six days following escalating abuse by guards. The validity of the experiment was later questioned,[21] particularly the coaching of guards to continue to escalate their abusive behaviour, but aspects of the findings showed how easily 'good' people could abuse power to harm others.

The studies may have over-reached in their conclusions, but they remind us of the uncomfortable truth that authority is readily misused and moral courage does not easily hold out against authority.

It means that individuals will often conform to unethical behaviour despite their conscience.

How well do we judge long-term versus short-term benefits?

Would you wait for two marshmallows, or eat the one in front of you?

From a very early age, we are taught to value patience. The 1970 'marshmallow experiment' at Stanford University asked three- to five-year olds to exercise self-control by choosing not to eat a single marshmallow straight away, on the promise of receiving two marshmallows later on. The children were very creative in distracting themselves from the single marshmallow on offer, one even lulled herself to sleep.[22]

However, follow-up studies to this experiment showed mixed results when trying to correlate willpower as a child with adult life outcomes.[23] Despite our efforts to develop patient habits, it seems that 'impatience bias' is a powerful instinct.

Time and again, studies have shown that we favour impatient decisions, i.e. those that appear to create a short-term impact. In financial analysis, benefits are discounted to favour the short-term, but our minds apply much heavier discounting.[24]

The economist and philosopher John Maynard Keynes described it in this way: 'Most, probably, of our decisions to do something positive ... can only be taken as a result of animal spirits – of a spontaneous urge to action rather than inaction, and not as the outcome of a weighted average of quantitative benefits multiplied by quantitative probabilities.'[25]

Our bias towards impatience leads us to poor decision making, missing out on long-term gains and putting too much weight on short-term solutions.

Is there a need to adjust for regional, national and class differences?

Understanding and adapting to regional, national and class differences is critical to any international or multi-cultural organisation.

The World Values Survey (WVS)[26] has been conducted in close to 100 countries since 1981 and compares cultures in two ways:

1 **'Traditional' versus 'secular-rational':**
   - Traditional values emphasise religion, family, deference to authority and national pride.
   - Secular-rational values place less emphasis on collectivist views.

2 **'Survival' versus 'self-expression':**
   - Survival values emphasise economic and physical security, with lower levels of trust and tolerance.
   - Self-expression values emphasise environmental protection, tolerance of difference and rising demands in decision making in economic and political life.

Work by psychologist John Snarey (1995)[27] found that the emphasis of more 'collectivist' or 'traditional' societies and social classes to duty and obligations to family had a marked impact on moral choices. It also showed less evidence of Kohlberg's post-conventional mindset.

It emphasises the need for context-sensitive policies and leadership where centrally set rules may have less influence than cultural norms.

How does culture affect our behaviour?

Culture significantly affects our moral judgements, for example:

1 **The Bystander Effect.** This shows that people will tend to feel less moral responsibility in a group than they do as individuals. Psychologist Peter Fischer and others in 2011[28] showed that context is influential, and groups can both inhibit and enhance moral judgements.
2 **The Majority Must be Right.** Research by psychologist Solomon Asch in the 1950s[29] and subsequent studies show that individuals often conform to the majority opinion, even when they do not really agree.[30]
3 **Stereotyping.** According to the work on prejudice by psychologist Henri Tajfel (1970),[31] we tend to think about people in terms of the groups they belong to and to create inaccurate stereotypes of people we do not know.

Psychologist Merete Wedell-Wedellsborg puts this in a business context when she summarises key behaviours that create unethical cultures.[32]

- **Omnipotence:** when someone feels so aggrandised and entitled that they believe the rules of decent behaviour don't apply to them.
- **Cultural numbness:** when others play along and gradually begin to accept and embody deviant norms.
- **Justified neglect:** when people don't speak up about ethical breaches because they are thinking of more immediate rewards such as staying on a good footing with the powerful.

When the stakes are low, returning a lost wallet or sharing a small windfall, kindness is a common behaviour. However, when the stakes are higher or we are under pressure to conform, integrity and fairness have less influence. As professors of organisational behaviour and ethics, Linda Trevino and Michael Brown say: 'Most people are the product of the context they find themselves in. They tend to "look up and look around", and they do what others around them do or expect them to do.'[33]

Conclusion

As psychologist, leadership adviser and novelist Kevin McKee said to me: 'Values are not universal, they are entwined with your personality.'

Self-awareness as an individual and as a team requires an understanding of our human bias:

- We over-estimate the rationality of our ethics.
- Authority is readily misused.
- We tend to conform to the behaviour around us.
- We are too impatient for short-term benefits.
- There are important cultural differences in regions across the world.

Working in groups and teams is the essence of our cooperative success and, under the right conditions, can help us avoid the pitfalls of self-deception, impatience and misuse of power.

Questions

- Do you set high ethical expectations?
- Do you make it safe for colleagues to speak up?
- Do you listen to and act on what they say?
- Do you give enough weight to the long-term benefits and consequences of your decisions?

Notes

1 See: https://psycnet.apa.org/doiLanding?doi=10.1037%2Fh0093718.
2 Deal, T.E. and Kennedy, A.A. (1982) *Corporate Cultures: The Rites and Rituals of Corporate Life*. Addison-Wesley Publishing Company.
3 See: https://www.researchgate.net/publication/387751558_Kohlberg's_Stages_of_Moral_Development.
4 Gilligan, C. (1982) *In a Different Voice*. Harvard University Press; Gilligan, C. (1995) *Hearing the Difference: Theorizing Connection*. Hypatia, 10(2), pp. 120–7.
5 Haidt, J. and Joseph, C. 'Intuitive ethics: how innately prepared intuitions generate culturally variable virtues'. Available at: https://web.archive.org/web/20160909124829/http://faculty.virginia.edu/haidtlab/articles/haidt.joseph.2004.intuitive-ethics.pub035.pdf; https://web.archive.org/web/20170731065520/http://www-bcf.usc.edu/~jessegra/papers/GHKMIWD.inpress.MFT.AESP.pdf.
6 See: https://www.journals.uchicago.edu/doi/full/10.1086/701478.
7 Abraham Lincoln, 1861.
8 Sandel, M.J. (2013) *What Money Can't Buy: The Moral Limits of Markets*. Penguin, p. 130.
9 David DeSteno, see: https://static1.squarespace.com/static/52853b8ae4b0a6c35d3f8e9d/t/528d2625e4b059766439b916/1384982053230/moral-hypocrisy-social-groups-and-the-flexibility-of-virtue.pdf.
10 Otto Scharmer, https://ottoscharmer.com.
11 See: https://libguides.cam.ac.uk/reflectivepracticetoolkit/models.
12 See: https://www.investopedia.com/terms/p/prospecttheory.asp.
13 See: https://homepage.coll.mpg.de/pdf_dat/2010_07online.pdf.
14 See: https://www.npr.org/2019/06/20/734141432/what-dropping-17-000-wallets-around-the-globe-can-teach-us-about-honesty.
15 See: https://www.psychologytoday.com/gb/blog/social-instincts/202105/happiness-comes-making-others-feel-good.
16 Author's interview with Veronica Heaven, MF, The Heaven Company.

17 DeSteno, D. (2014) 'Who Can You Trust?' *Harvard Business Review*. Reprint R1403K, Managing Your Professional Growth, March, hbr.org.
18 Kennedy, J.A. (2021) 'Does Getting Promoted Alter Your Moral Compass?' *Harvard Business Review*, 9 February. Available at: https://hbr.org/2021/02/does-getting-promoted-alter-your-moral-compass.
19 See: https://psycnet.apa.org/record/1964-03472-001.
20 See: https://pubmed.ncbi.nlm.nih.gov/32250143/.
21 See: https://pubmed.ncbi.nlm.nih.gov/32250145/.
22 See: https://psycnet.apa.org/record/1971-02138-001.
23 See: https://srcd.onlinelibrary.wiley.com/doi/10.1111/cdev.14129.
24 Berns, G.S., Laibson, D. and Loewenstein, G. (2007) 'Intertemporal choice: toward and integrative framework'. National Library of Medicine. Available at: https://pubmed.ncbi.nlm.nih.gov/17980645/.
25 Keynes, J.M. (1936) *The General Theory of Employment Interest and Money*. Atlantic Publishers, p. 144. ISBN 978-81-269-0591-1.
26 See: https://www.worldvaluessurvey.org/wvs.jsp.
27 See: https://www.researchgate.net/publication/283422380_In_a_Communitarian_Voice_The_Sociological_Expasion_of_Kohlbergian_Theory_Research_and_Practice.
28 See: https://pubmed.ncbi.nlm.nih.gov/21534650/.
29 See: https://doi.org/10.1037/h0093718.
30 See: https://rips-irsp.com/articles/10.5334/irsp.874#results.
31 See: http://www.holah.karoo.net/tajfestudy.htm.
32 See: https://hbr.org/2019/04/the-psychology-behind-unethical-behavior.
33 Trevino, L.K. and Brown, M.E. (2004) 'Managing to be ethical: Debunking five business ethics myths'. *Academy of Management Perspectives*, 18(2), 69–81.

chapter 14

Learning from responsible cultures

'We must be wary of any individual's ability to reason ... but if you put individuals together in the right way ... you can create a group that ends up producing good reasoning.'

Jonathan Haidt[1]

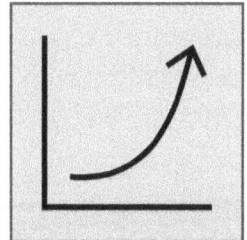

In this chapter you will learn:

- Examples of responsible cultures
- The importance of the relationship with employees

Introduction

Moral psychology shows us that culture, i.e. the habits and norms of a group, heavily influence ethical behaviour.

There is always the risk of a 'bad apple', an individual doing the wrong thing. A positive culture encourages everyone else to do the right thing, to put their conscience to work and challenge wrongdoing, especially when the bad apple is in a position of authority.

My discussions have provided insights into a range of positive cultures. They sometimes rely on the focus and drive of a founder, but they also feature in organisations that have chosen to evolve as CEOs come and go. In all cases, the aim is not perfection but ethical ambition, fuelled by stories, dialogue and decisive action.

Does your organisation have a responsible culture?

The Institute of Business Ethics (IBE) regularly reports on trends and risks that show that a significant minority of employees are aware of misconduct or illegal activity that is overlooked.

The 2024 report was based on a survey of 12,000 individuals across 16 countries,[2] compared to previous results in 2021, 2018 and 2012.

Overall, 71% of employees believe their organisations take ethics seriously, 84% report that honesty is always or frequently practised at work. There are positive trends in awareness of four key building blocks of an ethics programme as defined by the IBE:

1 Written standards of business conduct (increased to 71%).
2 Confidential 'speak up' mechanisms (increased to 61%).
3 Ethical standards training (increased to 60%).
4 Access to advice or a helpline (increased to 53%).

Other positive trends were willingness to speak up (increased to 64%) and satisfaction with speak up outcomes (increased to 71%).

On the other hand, a growing proportion (25% up from 18%) report that they had been aware of misconduct or illegal activity at work, 15% feel pressured to compromise ethical standards and 46% of those that spoke up experienced retaliation or personal disadvantage.

This study shows how extensively organisational cultures prevent people from speaking up, leaving ethical risks to simmer and grow. According to Lauren Branston: 'The reasons people don't speak up are either fear or futility – the fear of retaliation or the futility of nothing being done as a result.'

The following examples illustrate how ethically positive cultures encourage speaking.

What are examples of ethically positive cultures?

These are three examples in founder-led businesses in a large, medium-sized and smaller organisation. Examples of listed companies are in Chapters 18 and 19.

Case study – Octopus Group[3]

Octopus Group is a £12 billion turnover business, focused on provision of affordable green energy as well as investment, financial and educational activities. In discussion with Simon Rogerson, its founder and CEO, his aspiration is that, 'If Octopus Group was a person, it would be a good friend.'

Simon is an entrepreneur who has built up the organisation over 25 years on his strongly held principles:

- Entrepreneurs are the agents of positive social change, government sets tramlines, business delivers.
- There is no trade-off between kindness and business performance, kindness creates loyal customers and employees.
- Businesses should be judged as we judge a good friend. Great business is how you make people feel, more with kindness and stories than rules and spreadsheets.
- Businesses should not try and be the parent in a parent–child relationship with employees and customers. This also applies in the group structure. Each new business is founded as a separate entity, taking what it needs from the group but without centrally imposed rules.
- The world is changing so quickly that a business built today needs to work very differently to a business built five years ago. Part of Simon's role is to protect new businesses in the group from 'the mothership' so they can adapt effectively.

The environment is one of the key stakeholders alongside customers, employees, communities and shareholders.

Octopus is a certified B Corp which Simon describes as 'shorthand for what we hold dear' and has ethical accreditation as one of the top 200 ethical businesses in the Good Shopping Guide.[4]

Simon does not think public ownership would support these principles. He sees institutional investment managers focus too much on the short term, typically managing a stock for less than a year, then moving to another job. Octopus is therefore privately held and has created a closed market for the 20% of the business that is owned by employees.

He believes the world is more transparent than before; we can see not just what businesses do but how they do it. He talks about Octopus 'outbehaving' competitors because the alternatives (outpricing, outsmarting or outmanoeuvring) are too short term.

Culture

Simon personally interviewed the first 600 employees. Looking for emotional intelligence, his questions included:

- Which business do you like being a customer of?
- Which business do you feel is a friend to you?
- What makes you feel embarrassed?
- What vulnerability would you normally not share in an interview?

Now with over 11,000 employees, the principles still translate into the relationship with colleagues:

- He sends an all-employee update every Friday, retelling stories of colleagues taking the initiative to be positive and kind.
- There is a regular 'Grand Tentacle' prize of £1,000 for the best example of positive behaviour.
- There is no central record of holiday; teams and individuals manage their own leave.
- Employees are assessed on a nine-box grid – A, B, C (brilliant, on target or off target) on how they deliver, 1, 2, 3 on what they achieve.
- Achievement delivered the wrong way (C1, 2 or 3) leads to a serious conversation, intentional poor behaviour normally leads to dismissal, unintentional poor behaviour leads to learning.

Case study – Richer Sounds[5]

Richer Sounds is a UK home entertainment retailer founded by Julian Richer in 1978. It now has over 50 stores and 500 employees who, since 2019, own 60% of the business.

Julian says, *'I do think that businesses are important in society and their contribution is not recognised enough, but I also think that businesses have social responsibilities ... one of the most important roles you can perform today is providing jobs ... businesses are also doing something worthwhile if they give better value than the competition ... Richer Sounds also regularly donates 15% of profits to a charitable foundation that supports several organisations including The Good Business Charter.'*

In his book *The Richer Way* (2017),[6] Julian spells out the practical methods that the business uses to deliver its mission:

1. To provide second-to-none service and value for money to customers.
2. To provide colleagues with secure, well-paid jobs, working in a stimulating, equal-opportunities environment.
3. To be profitable to ensure long-term growth and survival.

Julian uses straightforward and carefully chosen language, referring to 'responsible' not 'ethical' or 'purpose-led' business, so as not to imply moral superiority. The mission of the business is deliberately targeted at colleagues, the term preferred to 'employees' or 'staff'.

1% of profits go into 'A Helping Hand' hardship fund to provide grants or interest-free loans to colleagues suffering hardship. Over 30% of profits go on profit-sharing or to charity.

The following extracts from *The Richer Way* illustrate the balance between measurement, recognition and the 'buzz' of working in a retail business.

Culture

'You cannot separate culture from motivation. The culture has to come from the heart.'

'The primary measure of a business's success should be customer and staff satisfaction, not profits.'

'Culture is more important than image. It is not about how you look, but what you do.'

▶

'If your prices are too high that is not good service. If your product is unreliable, that is not good service. You are selling integrity as well as a product.'

Procedures

'Control means clear standards and robust procedures. Control means there is a firm framework within which everyone works. All organisations must have rules because people must know what is expected of them.'

'When it comes to sorting out a customer's problem, there are no rules ... rely on treating the customer as you would like to be treated.'

'If a rule isn't really necessary, strip it away.'

Suggestion scheme

'How to run an effective suggestion scheme

- *The most senior person in the organisation must be involved with the scheme.*
- *Make it easy for people to enter their suggestions.*
- *Answer all the suggestions.*
- *Answer suggestions quickly.*
- *Encourage people to meet in small groups.*
- *Reward little and often. Nearly everyone who makes a suggestion gets a small prize.*
- *Measure and publish the results.*
- *Use the ideas.*

If colleagues have an idea, they are not only empowered to tell us about it, they have a responsibility to do so.'

'The number of ideas generated per employee ... is around 20 [per year].'

'Only 1% of customer ideas can be taken up, whereas 20% of staff suggestions are worthy of further consideration.'

Recruitment

- *'Hire for attitude, train for skills.*
- *Look for people who are either exceptional or exceptionally dedicated.*
- *The most important quality we look for is friendliness.*
- *There is a constant flow of applicants, 25–50% do well in a phone interview and they then join a shortlist for future vacancies.*

- Use group interviews including a wide range of colleagues.
- There is a trial day, week or two weeks, until we are happy that they can make the grade.'

Performance

- 'Each store's and department's performance is measured weekly. For stores it includes: sales, oldest repair, customer service, telephone answer rates, overtime and team morale and is discussed every Monday. People only work a six-day week or overtime if there is an exceptional reason for it.
- The mistake is to equate long hours with working hard.
- Mystery shopper checks lead to £100 reward for a high score on the mystery shopper report.
- Shrinkage [loss of stock through theft, errors and breakages] and absenteeism are significantly better than typical retail performance.'

Benefits

- 'Pay is at the top of market benchmarks.
- Private healthcare is provided at a subsidised rate.
- Colleagues receive discounts on home entertainment products.
- Profit share is paid monthly for store colleagues on store performance and annually for everyone on company performance.
- All colleagues have use of the company's 13 holiday homes and 1 motor home, across the UK and Europe.
- Health and fitness memberships are subsidised at 50%.'

Recognition

- 'There is a wide range of recognition schemes for good performance and loyalty, together with a sense of fun.
- "High-flyers" receive a "golden aeroplane" badge for exceptional customer service or a brilliant idea.
- The five-year club is for colleagues with five years' service, a silver lapel badge and a holiday every year after that.
- After ten years' service they receive £500 and after twenty years £1000.
- Every birthday, an additional paid day off and a cake to share with colleagues.'

Training and Development

- 'Every new recruit receives 6 months training with an experienced colleague shadow, plus a 3-day in person welcome seminar.
- There is a product update, technical training from suppliers and team huddle every morning, stores open to customers at 12 noon.
- Annual seminar for all colleagues.
- Every colleague receives career counselling after 6 months and then any time the colleagues wants it, with anyone they want, not necessarily their manager.
- Promotion is from within unless a specialist skill is required eg Finance Director.
- The business is quick to promote and unafraid to demote.
- There are dual roles to enrich roles of people who are not promoted but earn extra, for example, as store inspectors, or helping recruitment, training and buying.'

Feedback

- 'Feedback is regularly collected through Colleagues' Representatives, question time sessions, the suggestion scheme and career counselling.
- All directors work on the shop floor at least two days a year.
- An annual anonymous staff colleague survey is carried out.'

Carrots and Sticks

- 'Up to £10 is paid for each instance of good customer service, using various forms of customer feedback. About 1800 good customer reviews are received each month.
- Any colleague that causes avoidable complaints is investigated.
- Theft and dishonesty usually lead to dismissal, including staff who aware of other staff committing theft. Integrity is at the core of the culture, there is no sitting on the fence, colleagues are either preventing fraud or assisting it.'

Role of managers

- 'Management's job is to keep the excitement going ... there needs to be a drip-feed of new incentives.
- Managers cannot manage more than 10 people effectively.'

Case study – GRP Solutions[7]

Brian Harpur is the owner of GRP Solutions, a composites solutions and services business in Portsmouth, which he set up in 2015.

Brian had previously run another business in the same market in Portsmouth. When it was taken over by an individual investor who was overly focused on profit and not the people, Brian left to join an employee-owned business in Wales. When he was offered the opportunity to set up and own a business back in Portsmouth, he had a point to prove – that a business could be successful by looking after its people and being fair to its customers.

GRP Solutions is simply based on doing the right thing because, as Brian puts it, 'It is the right thing to do.' They have a reputation built on happy employees who care about the quality of service and fair dealing with customers. Brian has proved his point with a 'virtuous circle', caring about proper customer service, taking care of employees, contributing to the community which all comes round to growth and profitability. He sees a company like a person and wants GRP Solutions to be a good friend to its employees and customers, fair and compassionate.

The business has grown from nothing to £32 million turnover, with higher profitability than competitors.

Examples of how they do it:

- It is a sales-driven business but focuses on solutions for customers.
- Sales managers are not paid commission because all business is a team effort.
- They hold ISO9001, errors are treated as lessons not mistakes.
- He keeps all 32 staff involved in what is happening with the business; they are all on the website.
- They meet every month; the first items on the agenda are welcoming new staff and health and safety.
- Sales and finance are fifth on the agenda.
- Everyone gets a percentage of profits as a bonus.
- The business supports six charities with which they have a long-term relationship not just giving money (about £50,000 per year) but helping them with operational challenges, volunteering and further fundraising by employees.
- Brian asks candidates at job interviews what they do outside of work to help other people, e.g. charity work, caring, sports coaching.

- If there are disagreements between employees, Brian will personally get involved to resolve them.
- Occasionally, new employees don't fit in and are let go; fairness has to work both ways, e.g. they parted company with a senior employee who did not fit with the company values, lost some business as a result but, in the long run, their reputation improved.
- Brian prefers to allow his team flexibility as life has a habit of throwing up challenges that a strict rule-based system is not good at addressing.
- Living by 'doing the right thing' – Brian believes that it empowers individuals to make the best decisions.
- If employees need time for personal challenges, to work from home or help furnish a new flat, the business sees that its responsibility is to help them; e.g. an employee was seriously ill for two years and got paid in full; they are now back full-time.

Founders can still leave their mark as external shareholders take over. In the case of Virgin Atlantic and Disney, the founders' broader visions of the business continue to have a direct impact on day-to-day practice.

Case studies – Virgin Atlantic and Disney[8]

These case studies came from a discussion with Sharon Saxton, an experienced non-executive director and coach, with a corporate career as an HR director in the education, media, retail and airline sectors, including Virgin Airlines and Disney.

Because she has worked in several sectors, Sharon has unusual insight into the way that values and culture can become an organisational strength in a way that is relevant to that sector.

Virgin Atlantic

Sharon was head of HR during the first 10 years of the business start-up. Entrepreneur Richard Branson remained closely involved while external shareholders were brought in. The business was established to disrupt the sector with customer service designed to meet individual customer needs in more exciting and bespoke ways. A culture of 'pioneering' was established and Sharon was required to develop an HR strategy, including a leadership development programme that balanced the pioneering culture with the need for core policies and systems.

There was also flexibility guided by one of Virgin Atlantic's core values of 'providing experiences that make people feel safe, cared for and listened to'.

For example, when they first opened a route to Japan, they were initially unable to recruit Japanese nationals because of UK visa restrictions. It was clear that the experience of Japanese customers would not meet Virgin's core values unless at least some of the cabin crew had a deep understanding of Japanese culture. As a result, the business changed its recruitment criteria and was eventually able to negotiate a dispensation to allow recruitment of Japanese nationals.

Disney

Disney was founded by brothers Walt and Roy Oliver Disney in the 1920s.

Sharon was VP of human resources and global lead for the international TV businesses 80 years later and many years after the death of the founders. She saw how the purpose and values of Disney were put into practice.

Disney's vision is to 'create happiness for others' and, to achieve this, there was a sharp focus on developing creative and authentic leadership. All leaders were encouraged to have a creative vision aligned to Disney's values and to develop their personal brand to deliver this. For example, in the sales training for the teams responsible to win new business, the teams were explicitly shown how to walk away from deals where the values were not aligned and the quality of customer experience would not meet Disney's creative standards.

For Sharon and her direct experience in these organisations, she saw cultures focused on a purpose beyond profit – creativity in the case of Disney and customer experience in the case of Virgin Atlantic.

How do cultures change?

Shifting a culture is one of the most challenging roles of a leader or leadership team. This is explored further in Chapter 15 and Toolkit G.

At this stage, this is a case study is about a professional services firm that chose to appoint a CEO with strong ethical credentials to transform the culture. It required significant changes in systems, policies and the method of sharing profits, using B Corp principles as a key tool.

Case study – Ampa[9]

Ampa is a group of professional services firms. Under Sarah Walker-Smith's leadership over six years, it is now among the top 100 UK companies to work for[10] and is a certified B Corp.

She describes the need for the purpose (including vision and a set of values) of a business 'directly affecting how you make moral decisions and how you behave with each other'.

Her organisation demonstrates this as follows:

- Ampa has developed a 'culture code', published on their website,[11] explaining each of their four values: authentic, collaborative, trusted and brave followed by 19 commitments. It also explains that 'Our culture is underpinned by our positivity and passion for what we do. We take ownership and responsibility to tackle behaviour or actions that hinder our purpose or progress.'
- Their shadow board then developed a 'client service charter' that translates the code into service commitments to clients.
- Their operating procedures must meet five criteria: simple, empowered, accountable, transparent and agile.
- Members are senior staff who also own the business and receive a share of profits every year. Ampa introduced a new membership remuneration approach that includes a personal scorecard to determine the profit share of each member. The scorecard is partly determined by personal adherence to the culture code, not just financial and client satisfaction measures.

Introducing the culture code and new remuneration methods took two years to implement fully. It was driven by her personal commitment to fairness which meant that a balance of purpose and sustainable profitability became the key driver for the business. Indeed, Sarah believes the two are interrelated not a choice. A key test of this change was whether Ampa would satisfy B Corp regulations, which require profit, people and planet to be prioritised together.

B Corp status

Sarah is an advocate of B Corp status to ensure focus on purpose and values, which drive sustainable profitability as long as the measure is long-term and not just one year.

As Group CEO of Ampa, she saw B Corp status as a way of holding themselves to account. First, they developed the culture code and the scorecard system in order to change the remuneration process. Second, they rewrote the membership agreement two years later in order to become a B Corp.

The change to the membership agreement also brought internal governance in line with the changes to section 172 of the UK Companies Act, as prescribed by the Better Business Act. The requirement is to make sure all stakeholders, including the planet and not just shareholders, are taken into account in decision making.

Ampa was one of the first professional service firms to take this approach.

Sarah was clear that B Corp was a challenging set of regulations, particularly on their governance and commitment to sustainability targets. However, aside from being an ethical commitment, Sarah described four clear commercial benefits:

1. Clients are attracted by it. Indeed, many larger clients now require evidence of ESG credentials.
2. Employees, particularly those in their 20s, are attracted by it.
3. It reduces costs, for example in use of paper, travel and other consumables.
4. It gives her business an external profile, because B Corps are unusual in the professional services sector, although many are now following.

How can a business be an activist?

If a business stands for an ethical cause, it can collaborate with others and work through a third party, such as the Better Business Act,[12] a coalition of organisations seeking amendments to the UK Companies Act so that 'the purpose' of the company is prioritised over 'success'.

It can also be an 'activist', i.e. be publicly active at three levels:

1. Encouraging and supporting employees to champion one or more social causes.
2. The CEO or other figurehead personally championing one or more social causes.
3. The whole business standing for a cause as part of its purpose, values and communications.

Douglas Lamont is CEO of the privately owned Dutch chocolate business Tony's Chocolonely. He says, 'We've got a strong point of view on something really important: ending exploitation in cocoa, millions of farmers living in poverty ... child labour. That's a big societal issue.' However, he adds: 'I don't have to have an opinion on every single political event going on around the world.'[13]

Ben & Jerry's social mission 'seeks to eliminate injustices in our communities by integrating these concerns into our day-to-day business activities'.[14] even to the extent of creating legal protection for its activist agenda when it was acquired by Unilever in 2000.

This is now creating tensions with its parent company,[15] illustrating the challenge of being an ethical activist as a publicly listed company.

Conclusion

Businesses with an 'organisational conscience' are marked by their positive relationship with employees, their openness to dialogue and their clarity of purpose.

It is easier for privately held businesses to stand for an ethical cause than those that are publicly listed.

Questions

- Do your employee relationships support and encourage open dialogue?
- Do you have a way of improving your culture, e.g. through an externally assessed standard?
- Is there a positive way you could pursue an ethical cause, e.g. by joining a collaborative network?

Toolkit G, at the end of Chapter 15, provides a way of improving your organisation's culture more broadly.

See also Chapter 19 for further suggestions.

Notes

1 Haidt, J. (2012) *The Righteous Mind*, p. 105.
2 See: https://www.ibe.org.uk/ethicsatwork2024.html.
3 Author's interview with Simon Rogerson, CEO, Octopus Group.

14 LEARNING FROM RESPONSIBLE CULTURES

4 See: https://thegoodshoppingguide.com/top-200-ethical-businesses/.
5 Author's interview with Julian Richer, founder, Richer Sounds.
6 Extracts reproduced here with Julian Richer's permission.
7 Author's interview with Brian Harpur, CEO, GRP Solutions.
8 Author's interview with Sharon Saxton, non-executive director and coach.
9 Author's interview with Sarah Walker-Smith, CEO, Ampa.
10 See: https://ampa.co.uk/media/ampa-brand-named-one-of-the-best-places-to-work-in-the-uk/.
11 See: https://ampa.co.uk/wp-content/uploads/2022/02/0038-Group-Culture-Code-2022_compressed.pdf.
12 See: https://betterbusinessact.org.
13 See: https://www.ft.com/content/00936eab-291d-4bae-95b1-cbac761a5cd3, December 2024.
14 See: https://www.benjerry.co.uk/values/issues-we-care-about.
15 See: https://www.ft.com/content/67eefa32-9284-4a25-9aa8-db200a3ee19d.

chapter 15

Learning from ethical failures

'There are times when moral conscience comes ahead of the duty to protect your organisation.'

Kevin McKee

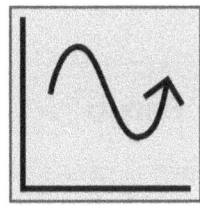

In this chapter you will learn:

- How six respected organisations did not notice the heat until it was too late
- How some of them learned and recovered

Introduction

If you put a frog into boiling water, it jumps straight out. If you put it into warm water and slowly turn up the heat, it falls asleep and dies.

It is an old story but untrue. It is more likely that that frogs are cleverer than humans in working out when it is time to leave an unhealthy environment.

This chapter is followed by a toolkit to help you improve your culture.

What are the risks of prioritising sales targets over ethics?

The first two examples, Wells Fargo's cross-selling and the Siemens' bribery scandals, describe cultures where senior executives created pressure to perform at the expense of ethical standards. Senior executives deceived themselves that their actions were serving the organisation's interest, in Wells Fargo's case setting unrealistic sales targets, in Siemens' case enabling systematic bribery.

Both organisations endured heavy financial and reputational costs, but they survived and eventually recovered.

Case study – Wells Fargo[1]

In 2016, Wells Fargo was one of the largest banks in the USA, claiming: 'Our vision has nothing to do with transactions, pushing products, or getting bigger for the sake of bigness. It's about building lifelong relationships one customer at a time.'

However, branch employees were incentivised to meet aggressive sales targets by cross-selling to customers without customers' consent. This contrasted with corporate initiatives including an ethics programme, a whistleblower hotline and executive level incentives that emphasised integrity.

In September 2016, the bank settled a $185 million lawsuit with regulators, admitting to as many as two million accounts opened by employees over five years without customers' authorisation. Initially, the bank used the 'bad apples' excuse. Over 5,000 employees lost their jobs: '99% of the people were getting it right ... the 1% that did it wrong ... we fired.' Soon afterwards the CEO resigned.

The board later commissioned an independent investigation report. It concluded that the failure was systemic including:

- **Sales pressure:** the sales targets were so high that they created pressure to open new accounts without the customers' agreement.
- **Risk evaluation:** central audit and risk functions were discouraged from identifying the root cause of emerging risks.
- **Leadership:** a bias among key leaders to avoid negative feedback, in particular the CEO 'was not perceived within Wells Fargo as someone who wanted to hear bad news or deal with conflict'.

The bank subsequently clawed back benefits paid to senior executives, who had left after the problems were exposed, and made a $3 billion[2] settlement 'to resolve ... potential criminal and civil liability stemming from a practice between 2002 and 2016 of pressuring employees to meet unrealistic sales goals'.

Wells Fargo survived and recovered. It remains one of the largest banks in the USA.

Case study – Siemens[3]

In 2006, Siemens, the global engineering business with 400,000 staff in 170 countries, was raided by German authorities on suspicion of corruption.

After initial denials by senior executives and the departure of the chair and CEO, the new CEO, Peter Löscher, called an amnesty for whistleblowers to come forward. It revealed bribes worth several hundred billion dollars, systematically used to win contracts, supported throughout the business with reporting designed to mask the bribery.

It was culturally embedded. Reinhard Siekaczek, who was responsible for the bribery budget of the telecommunications division, said, 'We thought we had to do it, otherwise we'd ruin the company.' Uwe Dolata from the Association of Federal Criminal Investigators in Germany said, 'Bribery was Siemens' business model. Siemens has institutionalised corruption.'

As a result, Siemens carried out root-and-branch reform including:

- new anti-corruption rules
- strengthened investigation and compliance units, with 500 additional compliance officers

- comprehensive anti-corruption training and education
- 900 internal disciplinary actions
- voluntary withdrawal from World Bank funding for two years
- withdrawal from regions where corruption was deeply entrenched in business transactions.

Prosecutions in Germany and the USA resulted in penalties of $1.6 billion with additional investigations in 10 other countries. Together with internal investigations, the total cost was estimated at $2.5 billion.

It set the business back but did not break it. Turnover in 2006 of €80 billion dropped significantly but, over 18 years, steadily recovered back to its original level. Transparency, patience and resolute principles have been key in rebuilding trust in Siemens.

What are the risks of cover-ups?

The collapse of Enron and Barings also prioritised profits over principles. However, in these examples, the profits were illusions, covered up by the executive team of Enron and by a senior trader in Barings. Both pointed to cultures that resisted challenge inside the organisation and could have prevented the ultimate failure. Neither business survived.

Case study – Enron[4]

According to the FBI's Supervisory Special Agent, 'Enron was a company where it was OK to lie; it was OK to cheat as long as you were making money for the company. And that attitude was permissible up to the top levels of the company. Both Skilling and Lay [the former CEOs of Enron], they agreed with that, and they allowed employees, they tolerated transgressions as long as employees were making money for the company.'

Enron was formed through a merger of energy companies in 1985. Its aim was to take advantage of changes in regulations that allowed energy companies to speculate on future energy prices. Its stated values were 'integrity, communication, respect and excellence'.

Over the next 16 years, it diversified into other markets and used complex structures and accounting methods to inflate the value of its balance sheet. When the value of technology market stocks fell in the 'dotcom bubble' of 2000, it was heavily exposed but was able to hide losses from investors. The conflict of interest built into its corporate structures were approved by the board and not disclosed externally. Its balance sheet and share price were increasingly over-stated.

There was growing internal discomfort. A whistleblower formally raised concerns with the CEO a few months before problems became public. A limited investigation revealed nothing and the whistleblower did not take it further. One of the non-executive board members was asked why they agreed to bypass conflict-of-interest rules. Their reasoning was, 'Well, no one else said anything.'[5]

However, concerns were growing externally over the transparency of Enron's accounts. They led to a Securities and Exchange Commission (SEC) investigation in 2001 and the company filed for bankruptcy soon afterwards. Shareholders lost an estimated £74 billion and employee pensions were also depleted. At the time, it was the largest bankruptcy on record.

Several senior executives were later convicted of fraud and other charges.

This deception of shareholders by Enron, WorldCom and others led to significant regulatory reform. The main effect was the introduction of The Sarbanes-Oxley Act of 2002 in the USA, increasing the obligations on executives, non-executives and auditors to report honestly to shareholders, with heavier penalties for non-compliance and greater protection for whistleblowers.

Enron's external auditor was Arthur Andersen LLP, one of the 'big 5' global audit firms. It was initially convicted of obstructing justice by destroying key evidence. Although the conviction was later overturned on appeal, the reputational damage led to its loss of licence to practise in the USA and the firm all but collapsed in 2002.

Case study – Barings[6]

In 1995, half-way between the 'Big Bang', which deregulated banking in the City of London in the 1980s, and the global financial crisis of 2008, an extraordinary corporate failure took place.

Baring Brothers & Co, known as Barings, was founded in 1762 as the world's first merchant bank. It had already had one narrow escape in 1890, when investments it had made in Argentina failed. It was considered 'too big to fail' and a large loan by the Bank of England and other institutions kept it afloat until it could trade its way out of trouble and repay its debts. For another hundred years it was seen as a prestigious institution with the British Royal Family among its customers. In 1985, the Baring family transferred its shares to a charity, The Baring Foundation, which shared ownership of the bank with the executive team. The Baring Foundation, which supports a range of cultural, health and social initiatives, continues to this day.

Like many of its competitors during the 1980s, Barings diversified its activities from the relational world of corporate finance deal-making to the transactional world of trading, taking on more risk and, initially, making more profit. Barings bought a small brokerage firm which specialised in Far Eastern markets and allowed it to operate with very limited controls. By 1992, eight years after its acquisition, it had achieved mixed results. The bank made the unusual move of appointing a relatively inexperienced employee, Nick Leeson, who had failed his maths exams at school, to lead both its trading and back-office activities in Singapore. He soon built a reputation for bold and seemingly profitable trading, as well as reckless behaviour outside of work.

After a series of small losses, he started to manipulate the accounts and tried to trade his way out of trouble with ever larger risks. An earthquake in Japan in 1995 and consequent fall in Japanese stock prices brought the problem to a head. Early signs of growing risks and regulatory breaches were under-estimated by the board. The cost to the bank of over £800 million put it out of business altogether, this time with no bail-out from City institutions.

The lack of controls, misplaced confidence in a colleague and drive for profits all created the conditions for one reckless individual to bring down an institution and some of its executives.[7]

It was an early signal of the much larger global financial crisis that would hit the financial system in 2008.

How should an organisation view its responsibility?

When a risk turns into a crisis, it is often the time that the ethical character of a business is tested. In the case of the UK Post Office 'Horizon Scandal', The Court of Appeal judgement of 2021 found that 'there was a culture ... of seeking to avoid legal obligations …'.[8] In these two examples, the oil company BP and healthcare business Johnson & Johnson took two different routes. BP's challenge was admittedly more complex but, by taking responsibility for something that was not their fault, Johnson & Johnson were able to show what they really stood for.

Case study – BP PLC[9]

In 2010, 11 oil workers died when the Deepwater Horizon oil rig exploded in the Gulf of Mexico. An estimated four million barrels of oil then poured into the Gulf of Mexico for three months, while engineers worked out how to stop and cap the spillage. It is the largest accidental oil spill on record.

The initial reaction from BP, which operated the rig, placed responsibility on another company, Transocean, which owned the rig. BP's CEO downplayed the wider impact, 'The overall environmental impact of this will be very, very modest' and, later, inflamed the growing criticism by saying, 'There's no one who wants this over more than I do. I would like to have my life back.'

The oil slick grew to 50,000 square miles and the environmental costs in the sea and the shoreline were extensive. The initial financial effect was to halve BP's share price and subsequent legal processes found BP to be predominantly responsible. It paid an estimated $65 billion in fines, compensation and clean-up costs. The CEO was replaced within six months of the spillage and BP's stock market value took many years to recover.

There was a lesson in BP's own history 20 years earlier, when BP had been involved in another oil spillage. On that occasion, chair of BP America, James Ross, took a similar approach to Johnson & Johnson when he said, 'Our lawyers tell us it's not our fault. But we feel like it's our fault, and we're going to act like it's our fault.'

Overall, this highlighted the risks of deep-water drilling and led to tighter regulations.

By 2020, BP had become a leading voice in the switch to renewable energy, becoming 'a force for good as well as a provider of competitive returns', according to its CEO at the time. In 2025, under pressure from shareholders to increase financial returns,[10] it decided to revert to its more traditional focus on oil and gas, demonstrating the challenge of pursuing long-term goals as a listed company.

It is worth contrasting BP's approach to the crisis faced by global healthcare business Johnson & Johnson in 1982.

> ### Case study – Johnson & Johnson[11]
>
> Following malicious tampering of one of Johnson & Johnson's market-leading products, Extra Strength TYLENOL®, seven people in the Chicago area died after taking pills laced with cyanide. It was established that the contamination took place after the pills were on the shelves and that Johnson & Johnson's production process was not responsible.
>
> Even though the contamination was local to the Chicago area, the manufacturing process was not at fault and Tylenol was 17% of total turnover, Johnson & Johnson immediately chose to make a blanket recall. Citing the company's stated priority that, 'We believe our first responsibility is to the doctors, nurses, and patients, to mothers and fathers, and all others who use our products and services', it stopped production and replaced sales promotion with a campaign to recall over 30 million bottles. The company was not responsible for the contamination but chose to give financial and counselling support to the bereaved families.
>
> The recall and replacement with other pain and symptom-relief products cost an estimated $100 million. Within a few weeks, the business introduced tamper-proof packaging, the first in its sector to do so. Initially, Tylenol lost 80% of its market share, but this was all but recovered within a year and Johnson & Johnson's reputation was, if anything, enhanced by its response.

How does an organisation hit the target but miss the point?

The final example is Volkswagen (VW) and other car manufacturers' 'Dieselgate' scandal. Once again, it illustrates the trade-off between profits and principles. In this case, it also draws out a culture so focused on the target (to reduce car emissions when they are tested) that it missed the point (to reduce car emissions in normal driving conditions). Although VW was the first to be found out, many other car manufacturers were also manipulating test data. The short-term cost to VW was very significant, but its responsible approach to the crisis eventually worked in its favour.

Case study – Volkswagen (VW) and other car manufacturers[12]

In 2015, the US Environmental Protection Agency (EPA) exposed the 'Dieselgate' scandal. It found that emissions tests on diesel cars were being manipulated by VW using software known as a 'defeat device'. It could suppress accurate readings by a multiple of up to 40 when the car was being tested. Having previously said these were 'technical issues', VW later admitted that 11 million cars worldwide were using the defeat device.

The head of VW America said, 'We've totally screwed up.' The chairman of the management board initially blamed 'the terrible mistakes of a few people' but soon resigned and was subsequently charged with fraud. He was replaced by Matthias Mueller, who said, 'My most urgent task is to win back trust for the Volkswagen Group – by leaving no stone unturned.' The company initially set aside €7 billion to cover costs of recovery and recalled nearly 10 million cars, but the ultimate cost of fines and damages was €30 billion. The group suffered heavy losses as a result but survived.

According to George Kell, member of VW's Sustainability Council,[13] 'The Dieselgate scandal was the product of a corporate culture where financial targets had to be met and failure was not an option. Inability to meet emissions regulations at the target costs could not be reported to leadership – so it was necessary to cheat.' Business professor Luann Lynch identified three causes:[14]

- **Pressure from the top:** VW had a Code of Conduct on ethical behaviour, but this was overridden by a leadership style to succeed at any cost.
- **Opportunity to hide cheating:** cars typically have 100 million lines of software, making it an easy place to hide.
- **Rationalisation of impact:** VW had done something similar in the 1970s, resulting in a relatively small fine of $120,000. The risk and cost of being found out appeared small compared to the benefit to the business.

Over the subsequent four years, it emerged that many other car manufacturers were also manipulating results. By being the first to be exposed and taking assertive action, VW was able to play a leading role in its industry. Its reputation and sales growth recovered steadily after 2015. By 2019, VW was readmitted into the UN Global Compact, the voluntary agreement for companies prioritising environmental sustainability.

Conclusion

A study conducted in 2015 by Alison Taylor, professor of organisational culture, asked experts to identify common features of unethical cultures. She drew out five features:[15]

- **The ends justify the means:** this includes an urge to seek market dominance at any cost.
- **Autocratic command-and-control leaders:** making employees fearful and reluctant to share concerns and providing leaders with plausible deniability.
- **Lack of individual accountability:** diffusing personal responsibility, particularly at the top.
- **Badly designed incentives:** not accounting for market conditions and judging employees on targets not methods.
- **Culture of urgency and necessity:** undermining stated values, together with pressure to conform.

A key insight from these failures is that enabling employees to speak up can prevent unethical behaviour from taking root.

Questions

Does your organisation:

- create multiple channels and incentives for employees to raise concerns and psychological safety to raise sensitive questions without fear of retaliation?
- follow up and communicate actions, as far as obligations to confidentiality allow, so that justice is seen to be done?
- create an 'organisational conscience' so there is an expectation of doing what is right without the need for detailed rules?
- routinely share stories of positive ethical behaviour as well as guidelines for what is expected?
- set incentives that support the organisation's purpose beyond profit?
- establish systems of governance and oversight to guard against autocratic behaviour?

Further guidance for employers is available from the Institute of Business Ethics (IBE).[16]

Toolkit G, which follows, provides a way of improving your organisation's culture more broadly.

Chapter 16 considers speaking up from the employee's point of view.

Notes

1. See: https://corpgov.law.harvard.edu/2019/02/06/the-wells-fargo-cross-selling-scandal-2/.
2. See: https://www.justice.gov/archives/opa/pr/wells-fargo-agrees-pay-3-billion-resolve-criminal-and-civil-investigations-sales-practices.
3. See: https://www.ibe.org.uk/static/929d6dc3-5eca-4471-916ba15e617f7cb6/ibere-porttherecoveryoftrust.pdf.
4. See https://www.investopedia.com/updates/enron-scandal-summary/.
5. Taylor, A. (2014) *Higher Ground: How Business Can Do the Right Thing in a Turbulent World*. Harvard Business Review Press, p. 184.
6. See: https://baringarchive.org.uk/history/a-brief-history-of-barings/.
7. See: https://www.ft.com/content/94e473f4-804a-11d9-bd50-00000e2511c8.
8. Wallis, N. (2022) *The Great Post Office Scandal*, p. 493.
9. See: https://phillipskaiser.com/crucial-role-of-empathy-in-crisis-management/; https://www.theguardian.com/environment/2011/apr/20/deepwater-horizon-key-questions-answered; and https://www.britannica.com/event/Deepwater-Horizon-oil-spill/Legal-action.
10. See: https://www.ft.com/content/4dcb19c9-4c98-4564-a65d-efed7ff26472.
11. See: https://professional.dce.harvard.edu/blog/what-is-ethical-leadership-and-why-is-it-important/#Meeting-the-Ethical-Challenges-of-Leadership and https://online.hbs.edu/blog/post/examples-of-ethical-leadership.
12. See: https://www.bbc.co.uk/news/business-34324772.
13. See: https://www.forbes.com/sites/georgkell/2022/12/05/from-emissions-cheater-to-climate-leader-vws-journey-from-dieselgate-to-embracing-e-mobility/.
14. See: https://ideas.darden.virginia.edu/vw-emissions-and-the-3-factors-that-drive-ethical-breakdown.
15. See: https://hbr.org/2017/12/5-signs-your-organization-might-be-headed-for-an-ethics-scandal.
16. See: https://www.ibe.org.uk/knowledge-hub/ibe-business-ethics-framework/speak-up-processes.html.

Toolkit G: Ethical culture (employer viewpoint)

How can you improve your organisation's culture?

This toolkit helps you apply the lessons from responsible cultures and business failures. The toolkit highlights the features of ethical cultures that focus on building an 'organisational conscience' leading to long-term relationships. You should adapt it to complement your organisation's policies and processes.

How to use the toolkit

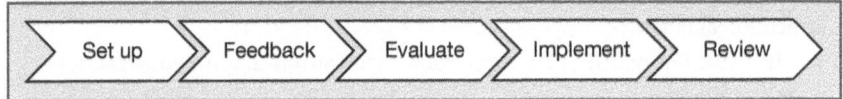

- **Set up with colleagues:**
  - Discuss the toolkit with a cross-section of colleagues, ideally at a time when you are planning next year's priorities or the long-term strategy.
  - Work out how this toolkit can benefit the business, for example reinforcement of values, stakeholder trust and risk reduction.
- **Gather feedback:**
  - Ask colleagues to propose potential improvements in the right-hand column, look at the examples given below and case studies in Chapter 14 for inspiration, if necessary.

- **Evaluate actions:**
  - Evaluate each proposed improvement against potential benefits, costs and risks, then rank the actions in order of net benefit. Decide which actions to take forward and which to drop or defer.
  - Note: use your organisation's normal project evaluation process; if you do not have one, use the *Benefits Scoring Matrix* below.
- **Implement:**
  - Identify risks and enablers and who needs to be consulted and directly involved to achieve the benefits, reduce risks and unlock the resources to deliver the changes.
  - Secure commitment to make changes based on the actions that achieve greatest benefit.
  - If costs and investment are required, secure the budget required.
  - Assign responsibilities and follow through.
- **Review the impact:**
  - Revisit the impact of your actions.
  - Take action to improve further.

Benefits Scoring Matrix (if needed)

Heading	Ethical	Financial	Total
Benefits (e.g. Low = 1)	1–4	1–4	2–8
Costs and risks (e.g. Low = 4)	1–4	1–4	2–8
Total	2–8	2–8	4–16

- Use judgement to decide criteria for 'very high', 'high', 'medium' and 'low'.
  - Use your stated purpose (or mission), values and behaviours as criteria for the ethical column. If you do not have these, use 'stakeholder trust' as a proxy.
- Score 'Benefits' as very high 4, high 3, medium 2, low 1.
- Score 'Costs and risks' as low 4, medium 3, high 2, very high 1.

- Add up total scores in the right-hand column, out of a maximum of 16.
- Rank the highest scoring action at the top and the lowest scoring at the bottom.

Note: the effectiveness of the toolkit depends on how rigorously you apply it and follow through.

Ethical culture (Employer viewpoint)

Feature	Leading with consistency	Leading with conscience	Improvements
1 Products and services	Reliable	… and considerate	
2 Suppliers and partners	Reliable	… and considerate	
3 Speaking up	Safe ways of reporting concerns	… and visible action on breaches of values	
4 Interaction with leaders	Regular communications	… and consult on key decisions	
5 Recruitment of employees	Test for competence	… and for potential and mindset	
6 Employee support and development	Focus on knowledge, skills and behaviour	… and well-being and career development	
7 Pay, terms and conditions	Clear and transparent	… and flexible	
8 Employee recognition and incentives	Based on personal performance	Based on team performance	
9 Ethical codes and procedures	Clear rules	… and autonomy to 'do the right thing'	
10 Support charitable causes	Limited	Paid time off	

Examples from cultures with an 'organisational conscience':

Feature	Example
1 Products and services	Free repairs on products returned, with no time limit
2 Suppliers and partners	Increasing prices paid to suppliers to enable payment of living wages to their employees
3 Speaking up	Paying rewards for valid concerns raised
4 Interaction with leaders	C-suite leaders hold a meaningful dialogue with all employees every month and meaningful union representation
5 Recruitment of employees	Example question: What do you do to support your local community or care for people in need?
6 Employee support and development	Employees have a regular review of their long-term ambitions, prospects and well-being
7 Pay, terms and conditions	Duration of sick pay is determined case by case with no upper limit
8 Employee recognition and incentives	No sales commission, profits shared among all employees
9 Ethical code and procedures	Do what is right and seek forgiveness not permission
10 Support charitable causes	All employees have two paid days off work every year to support a charitable cause

chapter 16

Speaking up (employee viewpoint)

'The more rules we have the less people will actually think about what is right.'

Roger Steare[1]

In this chapter you will learn:

- How to improve ethical practice, assuming the organisation is not corrupt
- How to call out corrupt, deceitful or illegal activity

In this chapter, I will examine how individuals inside an organisation can influence ethical change when they do not hold powerful positions.

How do you improve ethical practice?

You may be:

- a non-executive director who wants to influence a board and CEO
- a divisional head who wants to help a peer take a more ethical direction
- a trade union representative who wants to improve terms and conditions
- a less experienced employee who has an ethical point to make.

I will use the word 'influencer' to cover anyone who wants to improve ethical practice but does not hold decision-making authority. It assumes the goal is not just to make a proposal but to make a positive difference. This section assumes that the organisation is not conducting corrupt, deceitful or illegal activities.

This is a five-step model, under the acronym 'ILEAP', which starts with an idea and ends with successful persuasion that it should be implemented in some form. The steps in between, learning, evaluation and allies, may be a repeating cycle for more complex ideas.

Step 1: Idea – turn your idea into a proposal

You see something that could be improved and have an idea how to do it, but you do not have the power or authority to make the change.

At this stage, it may be ill-defined. An organisation that actively encourages feedback and ideas may be ready to consider it straight away, however it is more common that new ideas need some work before they are put in front of decision makers.

At this stage, develop it from 'idea' (the change you want to see) to 'proposal' (the change plus the impact it is likely to have). For example:

- Customers are complaining about coercion to buy a product.
- Your initial idea is to reduce targets in an incentive scheme for employees to sell that product.
- The proposal becomes 'change targets in the incentive scheme in order to eliminate customer complaints and rebuild customer trust'.

Step 2: Learning – test and improve the proposal

(a) **Test the proposal.** Test your proposal with people you trust to give you an objective and competent view, so you can learn how to improve it and what questions you will face. It may be a colleague who works in the same team or a friend who will understand the problem and help you think it through.

(b) **Your motivation.** Reflect on your own motivation so you can learn exactly why you want to propose this idea. Is it purely to give better customer service? Are you seeking recognition for being innovative? Do you have a target that you are worried about missing? All of these are legitimate but, as an influencer, it is particularly important to understand your personal motivation so that you can be honest with yourself and the people you are trying to influence so that you are earning trust.

Note that ethics are often driven by passionately held views leading to impulsive action. Reflecting and taking advice from a trusted source will help you judge risk and the likely 'chess moves' of your actions so you can achieve the greatest impact or avoid foreseeable setbacks.

(c) **Understand stakeholders' viewpoint.** Understand which stakeholders will be affected (what is in it for them?) so you can learn who is likely to support and prevent your idea from being developed. Stakeholders may include customers, shareholders, regulators, suppliers, employees, your line manager, communities and the environment.

Ensure you weigh up the decision makers' viewpoint as part of this. What benefits and risks does it present for them personally and professionally?

Note that Stephen Covery coined the powerful phrase, 'Seek first to understand, then to be understood.'[2]

(d) **Improve the proposal.** Keep improving the proposal so that it has a greater impact and becomes more persuasive.

Step 3: Evaluation – add rigour and ingenuity

(a) **Alignment and context.** Check how your proposal aligns with the organisation's purpose or mission and values and how it might work in the context of other organisational priorities. For example, if one of the values is 'trustworthiness', then the pricing of products should reflect that. If the organisation is going through a financial crisis, it is unlikely to be the right time to consider new investments.

Note: Ronan Dunne's advice is '... *speak up but consider context very carefully, i.e. do not assume you fully understand the context in which the decision maker has to balance decisions. The responsibility is then on the decision maker either to explain context or learn from new information they may have overlooked.*'

(b) **Benefits, costs and risks.** Work out the ethical and financial impact of your proposal and test it with a trusted source. The ethical effect is likely to be qualitative but, if your organisation measures stakeholder trust and environmental impact, an estimate of quantitative may also be possible. Compare the impact to the best alternative.

Note that reduction of regulatory risk or risk of complaints often carries significant weight.

(c) **Barriers and enablers.** Work out what will help and hinder your proposal. It may be that the annual planning cycle is about to begin, so it is likely to be an enabler because the organisation is looking for innovation. It may be that your line manager is risk averse because they will not help you develop and promote your proposal.

(d) **Ingenuity.** If your proposal has a negative financial effect or disadvantages some stakeholders, look at it again to work out how a more ingenious solution achieves the same ethical impact without any detriments. It may not be possible, but proposals that have no downside are an easy decision.

Note that the value in a proposal will be in its ingenuity, creating value for stakeholders and avoiding trade-offs. Businesses like Ampa, Patagonia and Octopus do not see a trade-off between values and business performance, it is part of their competitive advantage. It is easier in a culture that encourages feedback and dialogue throughout the organisation. At Citysearch, a business founded by Charles Conn, one of their colleagues was known as 'the minister of the interior' and his role was to challenge decisions by reminding them of their values. Charles' advice for people who are not decision makers, but want to make an ethical difference, is 'you catch more flies with honey than vinegar', i.e. advocate change positively not negatively.

Step 4: Allies – find supporting allies

(a) **Find allies.** It is rare for one person to make significant change on their own. Seek out advice from a colleague or mentor who is not necessarily a decision maker but has sympathy with your proposal and has more experience of making change happen. If the decision maker has an advisor, test out your proposal with them and see if they have suggestions to improve it. If at this stage there is a flaw in your proposal, it is better to find out before you take it through a decision-making process. If they see you taking on their advice, they are likely to become allies in the process.

(b) **Let go.** By discussing your proposal more widely, it may be that someone else is better placed to propose it or a related project would benefit from your proposal and together they help each other. As US President Harry Truman said, 'It is amazing what you can accomplish if you do not care who gets the credit.'

Note that when a new proposal is considered, tested and implemented it will change. That is why the Richer Sounds suggestion scheme rewards employees on initial consideration of their ideas, not their implementation which may evolve into something very different.

Step 5: Persuasion – apply leverage

(a) **Power of the argument.** The process so far has been building up the power of the argument, testing, adding rigour and comparing to the best alternatives. Repeat some or all of steps 1–4 if you think it will make a significant difference and is worth the extra time and effort.

(b) **Decision-makers' viewpoint.** Consider again the benefits and risks to decision makers, personally and professionally. Either address them directly in your proposal or expect to answer questions about them.

(c) **Processes.** Depending on the size and style of your organisation, the decision-making process may be a simple corridor conversation with a decision maker who is prepared to listen or a formal business case presentation to a board or committee. It is key to use the right processes. In any case, assume you have only 'one shot' so, be prepared, anticipate questions and make sure you follow due process. Impatience to cut corners rarely helps.

(d) **Call on allies.** If you have an influential set of allies, encourage them to speak in favour of your proposal formally and informally. The power of an argument is often not enough; allies are often the real source of influence, particularly if you are competing for time and resources against other key decisions.

Note that trade unions are an example of influencers who hold power as 'organised allies'.

Case study – Sean Vernell[3]

Sean Vernell is an elected trade union official in the UK's University and College Union (UCU). He distinguishes two types of power. 'Institutional power' is held by organisational leaders who hold authority to make decisions and implement change and are appointed by their employer. 'Representative power' is held by elected representatives who rely on the continuing support of their voting members to influence change.

In Sean's view, representative power relies on four components:

1 Leverage over those who hold institutional power.
2 Numbers of members who elect them, i.e. collective power.
3 Putting forward alternatives to proposed changes.
4 Eloquence by those advancing the arguments.

His role as a trade union official is to ensure his union colleagues are united behind sound arguments so that they can apply pressure to those with institutional power. His ability to influence relies on the unity of his union colleagues behind him. This gives him leverage and numbers, it is then up to him to advance the arguments as convincingly as possible.

What have you learnt?

After the initial celebration of success or disappointment of rejection, reflect calmly on these questions:

1 Exactly why did the proposal succeed or fail?

Were there other priorities that helped or hindered? How good was the presentation and the answers to questions raised? Was the proposal as good or better than I thought?

2 Did I choose the right advisors and allies? Were they objective and competent, did they stand up for the proposal when I needed them to?
3 In any case, what did I learn for the next time I make a proposal?

It may raise a deeper question, whether you share the same values as the organisation or the sector you work in.

Are your personal values being fulfilled?

Personal and organisational values do not always match but can still be compatible. As a colleague once said to me when discussing business values, 'Don't tell me what my values are' and, after further discussion, 'I'm happy to commit to the business values when I'm at work.'

Some employers have more than one ethical path within the same business. A leader I interviewed described a professional services firm that had secured a new large project for a client in the tobacco industry. The firm's leadership wanted to work with this client but understood that some colleagues would be uncomfortable. It offered its employees a choice to decline the assignment. One team declined, another was happy to go ahead. It did not impose a corporate view and allowed different views to co-exist in one firm.

In his book *Moral Ambition* (2025), Rutger Bregman encourages us to see our careers through a moral lens '... make the leap and the possibilities are endless. Because so many others waste their talents, people with moral ambition can make a world of difference'.

Ultimately, only you can answer the following questions:

- What ethical impact do I want to make through my work?
- What is the best sector or organisation to achieve that impact?
- What are my options for influencing where I am or moving elsewhere?

Toolkit H (ILEAP), at the end of this chapter, helps you make the case for positive change.

How do you call out unethical practice?

Unethical practice is widespread and on a rising trend. The Ethics & Compliance Initiative (ECI) conducts an annual Global Business Ethics Survey

(GBES®) across 42 countries. The 2023 survey showed that 28% of employees experienced pressure to compromise ethics and compliance standards and 65% had observed at least one breach of their organisation's standards in the previous 12 months.[4]

One positive trend identified by ECI is that a growing proportion of employees are reporting breaches, though nearly half (46% according to ECI) experience retaliation as a result. There are also trends to take collective action. According to Professor Alison Taylor, 'What we're seeing is a shift from individual employees calling the whistleblowing line and hoping someone does something about it, to a lot more collective action and a lot more use of tools like social media and going to the media.'[5]

The previous chapter looked at the actions that lead to an ethically healthy culture. It is more challenging from an employee's viewpoint.

I spoke to five people who had experienced being an actual or potential whistleblower.

- In one case, the organisation responded ethically, investigated the allegation, protected the whistleblower's anonymity and took quick action when the allegation was found to be accurate.
- In another case, the potential whistleblower asked a trusted source whether they should raise their concern. The risks to their career and livelihood were too high and they decided to say and do nothing.
- In three other cases, when they spoke up, it was rejected by the organisation and they later faced legal action, leading to lengthy legal processes that tested their resilience in every way. Two eventually won their cases and the third restored their professional reputation after initial legal setbacks.

Their insights were:

- **Understand your motivation.** The benefits of speaking up or being a whistleblower are usually down to the individual's conscience, i.e. standing up for integrity and fairness. However, the stakes can be high with risks to career, earnings and well-being.
- **Understand your risks.** An employee raising a serious concern with their employer can, in practice, take an employee outside the legal protection of the employer because the reputation of the employer is at risk. The human

resources and legal functions should focus on whether a legal line has been crossed, but they are also concerned with protecting the reputation of the employer. It can sometimes lead to suspension of the employee while investigations are carried out, for example.

- **Get professional support.** Depending on the jurisdiction and sector, regulators and courts can provide protection but they are also responsible for thorough investigations which can expose a whistleblower to lengthy legal proceedings and costs. They can also sometimes prevent whistleblowers from leaving the country pending investigations. Most countries protect whistleblowers, for example in the UK it is the Public Interest Disclosure Act 1998 (PIDA) and the EU has the Whistleblowing Directive 2019/1937.[6] If you are a member of a trade union or a professional body, they will usually provide confidential and impartial advice on your options.

Please note that there may be a financial upside. In some jurisdictions, including the USA, South Korea and Nigeria, a whistleblower who proves to be correct in law can be given a substantial reward by the court. In 2025, this is under review in the UK.[7]

If the risks are too high, speaking up may not be a reasonable option. Several interviewees described working in an organisation or sector that behaved legally but did not meet their personal ethical standards. As a result, they left to find or found a business that met a higher standard.

Conclusion

The barriers to speaking up are removed by ethically healthy employers, as we saw in Chapter 14. However, some businesses enable unethical practice by discouraging employees from speaking up and retaliating if they do.

It presents ethical employees with three options: tolerate the unethical practice, take the opportunity and potential risk of speaking up or leave for a more ethical culture. In any case, the first step should normally be to take advice from a trusted and competent source.

See Toolkit H, which follows, to help you make proposals to influence and improve ethical practice. It is *not* suitable for whistleblowing about potential corruption.

Notes

1 Steare, R. (2009) *Ethicability: How to Decide What's Right and Find the Courage to Do it.* Roger Steare Consulting Limited, p. 58.
2 Covey, S. (2020) *The 7 Habits of Highly Effective People.* Simon & Schuster UK.
3 Author's interview with Sean Vernell, UCU elected official.
4 See: https://www.navex.com/en-gb/blog/article/ecis-2023-global-business-ethics-survey-reveals-harsh-realities-about-ec-programs/.
5 See: https://www.ft.com/content/88e1801a-b3cd-4997-a928-e5b761583da1.
6 See: https://commission.europa.eu/aid-development-cooperation-fundamental-rights/your-fundamental-rights-eu/protection-whistleblowers_en.
7 See: https://www.ft.com/content/41355234-47b7-406a-87ae-fa151073bab0?shareType=nongift.

Toolkit H: Improving ethical practice (ILEAP – employee viewpoint)

How do you influence ethical practice as an employee?

This toolkit is a guide to help you make proposals to influence and improve ethical practice. It is *not* suitable for whistleblowing about potential corruption (see Chapter 16).

It does not attempt to define right and wrong but supports and challenges you to make a positive impact when you are not in a position of authority. It has five stages under the acronym ILEAP:

1 Idea – turn your idea into a proposal.
2 Learning – test and improve the proposal.
3 Evaluation – add rigour and ingenuity.
4 Allies – find supporting allies.
5 Persuasion – apply leverage.

How to use the toolkit

- Read Chapter 16 before applying the toolkit.
- Go through each step in turn.

- Repeat steps 1, 2, 3 and 4 if your proposal is complex or fails to attract support.
- Before committing to step 5, weigh up the risks and benefits of going ahead.
- Whether you are successful or not, reflect on what you have learnt at the end of the process.

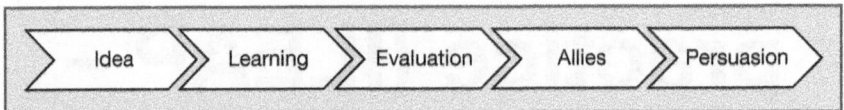

ILEAP	Improving ethical practice Note: *not* suitable for whistleblowing about potential corruption.	**Example** *Employees are incentivised to sell insurance to new customers. Customers are starting to complain because they feel coerced. You want to find a way to improve customer trust.*
Step	See Chapter 16.	
1 Idea Turn your idea into a proposal	Define the change you want to see and its impact.	*Your initial idea is to reduce incentive scheme targets so that customer complaints reduce and trust in the organisation increases.*
2 Learning Test and improve the proposal	Test the proposal with others. Understand your motivation. Work on stakeholders' viewpoint. Improve the proposal.	*You learn that the insurance product is profitable, some customers value the product, the emerging problem of customer complaints is not widely known. You change the proposal by keeping the incentive scheme but reducing the price to customers although less profitable for the business.*
3 Evaluation Add rigour and ingenuity	Understand the organisation's goals and where this fits. Work out benefits, costs, risks, barriers and enablers. Use imagination and ingenuity to improve further.	*You find that the cost of insurance from your suppliers is too high, so it is possible to renegotiate terms to reduce the price to your customers and maintain the margin for your organisation.*
4 Allies Find supporting allies	Find allies to test and support your proposal. Let your proposal become part of a bigger change if the opportunity arises.	*You find that another team is working on product structuring and pricing and agree to work together. By sharing your proposal, it is more likely to be agreed as part of a wider initiative to increase customer trust.*
5 Persuasion Apply leverage	Understand decision makers' viewpoint to make your case. Follow organisational processes if appropriate. Call on support from allies.	*The full proposal is put to the board, highlighting the organisation's value of 'being trustworthy'. Customer prices are reduced, supplier costs are reduced offset by higher volumes.*
What did you learn?		

Part 3 – Organisational culture: Quick read summary

Chapters 13–16 are summarised here in bullet points.

Chapter 13 Moral psychology

- Moral judgement changes as people mature in response to family, community and other cultural stimuli. Morals are a combination of intuition and reasoning, but we tend to over-estimate the influence of reasoning.
- Altruism is a key component of cooperation but is less evident when the stakes are high or when the beneficiary is a stranger.
- Authority is readily misused and most people conform to the behaviour around them. This highlights the importance of ethical leadership and ethically healthy cultures.
- There are important cultural differences in regions across the world.

Chapter 14 Learning from responsible cultures and Chapter 15 Learning from ethical failures

- 25% of employees report that they had been aware of misconduct or illegal activity at work, 15% feel pressured to compromise ethical standards and 46% of those that spoke up experienced retaliation or personal disadvantage.
- Ethically healthy cultures:
  - create multiple channels and incentives for employees to raise concerns and psychological safety to raise sensitive questions without fear of retaliation
  - follow up and communicate actions, as far as obligations to confidentiality allow, so that justice is seen to be done
  - create an 'organisational conscience' so there is an expectation of doing what is right without the need for detailed rules
  - routinely tell stories of positive ethical behaviour as well as guidelines for what is expected

- set incentives that support the organisation's purpose beyond profit
- establish systems of governance and oversight to guard against autocratic behaviour.
- Organisational cultures can be changed under assertive and resilient leadership. External standards can be a useful lever.
- Some organisations pursue an ethical cause beyond their business. It may include activism to raise awareness, lobbying for more rigorous regulation and collaborating on voluntary standards.

Chapter 16 Speaking up (employee viewpoint)

- If the organisation does not provide channels to raise concerns safely, employees should get support from a trusted and competent source before taking further steps.
- In any case, employees without decision-making authority can make a positive impact.

part 4

Regulations, standards and impact[a]

---

[a] Nothing in this book is intended, or should be taken, to constitute any form of professional advice. Particularly with regard to legal matters, you should obtain advice from appropriately qualified professionals.

part 4

Regulations, standards and impact

chapter 17

Directors' duties and anti-corruption laws[b]

'Those are my principles, and if you don't like them ... well I have others.'

Groucho Marx[1]

In this chapter you will learn:

- The general duties of directors and the fact that they vary depending on the jurisdiction
- The main differences in directors' duties in the UK and the USA
- How duties to stakeholders beyond shareholders are recognised
- Key anti-corruption laws and a case study of a business avoiding corruption

---

[b] Nothing in this book is intended, or should be taken, to constitute any form of professional advice. Particularly with regard to legal matters you should obtain advice from appropriately qualified professionals.

Introduction

The law plays an important part in enforcing and encouraging ethical behaviours.

Note that this book does not go into all the other types of law that codify ethical considerations, including environmental laws, laws of discrimination and employment law.

What is the legal context?

Certain laws are designed to protect individuals and businesses from unethical practices, essentially setting guardrails for dealing with a person or a business knowing that there are legal consequences if they fail to comply with their side of the transaction.

If a business has policies that expect or encourage employees to break the law, then the law will take precedence and the policies may be unlawful and should not be followed.

Generally, a company is a 'person' in law, able to own property, enter into contracts, sue and be sued. It has similar rights and obligations to individuals and acquires its rights when it is formed through a legal process. As a society, we therefore give companies a 'licence to operate' through the laws that govern creation and regulation of companies and the role and duties of directors.

There are many different forms of company, including statutory corporations, public companies (including listed companies), private companies and charities. They are mostly 'limited liability' entities. This means that individuals associated with the company, including shareholders and directors, are not personally liable for the company's obligations and debts, although there are exceptions to that general principle.

What are the general duties of directors?

A company has both legal and ethical responsibilities but has no conscience. That means the ethical responsibilities fall to the employees and the directors in particular. These ethical responsibilities are, to some extent, enshrined in law.

In most jurisdictions, directors broadly have a duty to act in the best interests of the company that employs them, although the details of their duties are not the same in all jurisdictions. Acting in the best interests of the company excludes breaking the law which takes precedence over the company's constitution or policies.

Acting in the best interests of the company means that directors have 'fiduciary duties'. They are based in the common law duties of loyalty, good faith, care and confidentiality:[2]

- Duty of loyalty means acting in the best interests of the company. This is the duty that prevents directors from using their role for personal gain or other conflicts of interest.
- Duty of good faith means directors must disclose material information and act on a reasonable basis that is within relevant laws and regulations.
- Duty of care means applying reasonable effort to make informed decisions and using appropriate skills and professional expertise.
- Duty of confidentiality means protecting and keeping company information confidential and not using it for personal gain.

Fiduciary duty underpins many jurisdictions' definitions of directors' duties. In the UK and some other countries, there also more specific responsibilities defined in law.

What are directors' duties in the UK?

Directors have seven general duties under the UK Companies Act 2006:[3]

1 To act within powers, defined by the company's constitution.
2 To promote the success of the company for the benefit of its members or shareholders as a whole. This is defined in Section 172 of the Companies Act.[4] In promoting the success of the company, directors must have regard to the following:
   - the likely consequences of any decision in the long term
   - the interests of the company's employees
   - the need to foster the company's business relationships with suppliers, customers and others

- the impact of the company's operations on the community and the environment
- the desirability of the company maintaining a reputation for high standard business conduct
- the need to act fairly as between members of the company.

If the purpose of a company is not for the benefit of its members, for example a charity, the directors' duty is to act in a way that is most likely to achieve the stated purpose. Larger companies, broadly those with turnover above £36 million, must publish an annual statement to demonstrate how directors have met their obligations.[5]

3 **To exercise independent judgement.** Directors are required to act independently, without subordinating their powers to the will of others. They may obtain advice but must exercise their own judgement on whether or not to act on it.

4 **To exercise reasonable care, skill and diligence.** In carrying out their responsibilities, directors must exercise reasonable care, skill and diligence.

5 **To avoid conflicts of interest.** Directors must generally avoid any situation in which they have, or can have, a direct or indirect interest that conflicts or may conflict with the interests of the company, for example an interest in a competing business. Companies will often have provisions for disclosing and agreeing to transactions that otherwise would be conflicts of interest.

6 **Not to accept benefits from third parties.**

This is a broad and strict duty that prevents a director from accepting a benefit from a third party conferred by reason of the director being a director or doing or omitting to do anything as director. It would include taking bribes as defined by the UK Bribery Act (see below).

7 **To declare interests in transactions or arrangements with the company.**

If a director is in any way directly or indirectly interested in a proposed transaction or arrangement with the company, the director must declare the nature and extent of the interest to the other directors and this declaration must be made before the company enters into the transaction or arrangement.

In addition, the UK Corporate Governance Code[6] applies to publicly listed and some other companies and sets standards to stimulate company boards' thinking on how they can carry out their role in governing effectively.

Note that The Better Business Act[7] is a coalition of 3,000 organisations seeking amendments to the UK Companies Act including Section 172 so that 'the purpose' of the company is prioritised over 'success', aligning social and environmental impact with shareholder returns.

What are the key differences between directors' duties in the UK and USA?[8]

- In the UK, 'directors' are responsible for day-to-day management of the company, with non-executive directors or trustees responsible for oversight.
- In the USA, 'directors' are responsible for oversight and 'officers' are responsible for day-to-day management.
- In the UK, responsibilities are determined by the Companies Act and directors' identities are publicly available through Companies House. This includes a responsibility to have regard to a broad range of stakeholders including employees, customers, suppliers and the environment.
- In the USA, each state has its own governing laws and responsibilities, broadly defined in terms of duty to loyalty, good faith and care. Few states disclose directors' or officers' identities. Directors also have 'Business Judgement Rule' protection which means that, if they have observed their duty of care, courts will not second-guess business judgements by directors even if the business has suffered as a result.
- In the UK, it is possible for individuals to be disqualified from being directors for misconduct.
- In the USA, it is in the hands of each company to decide if someone is fit to serve as a director or officer.

What are directors' duties in EU countries?

The UK, USA and EU share many principles including similar definitions of fiduciary duties. However, there are significant variations country by country.[9]

How do US directors recognise their duties to stakeholders beyond shareholders?

In US states, there is no duty in law to take account of the interests of stakeholders beyond shareholders, though directors may do so. The exceptions are Public Benefit Corporations (PBCs) which are for-profit companies that are formed 'to produce a public benefit ... and to operate in a responsible and sustainable manner'. Directors of PBCs are obliged to balance the interest of shareholders with those of the wider public.

There are over 10,000 PBCs of which some are publicly listed, including education business Coursera and farming business Vital Farms.[10] PBCs are not the same as B Corp certification, which I will explore in the next chapter, but some PBCs like Patagonia and Coursera are also B Corp certified.

As referred to earlier in the book, in 2019, The Business Roundtable, the association of CEOs of leading companies in the USA, published a revised definition of the purpose of a corporation, encompassing a broad range of stakeholders as follows:

> *Statement on the Purpose of a Corporation[11]*
>
> *'Americans deserve an economy that allows each person to succeed through hard work and creativity and to lead a life of meaning and dignity. We believe the free-market system is the best means of generating good jobs, a strong and sustainable economy, innovation, a healthy environment and economic opportunity for all.*
>
> *'Businesses play a vital role in the economy by creating jobs, fostering innovation and providing essential goods and services. Businesses make and sell consumer products; manufacture equipment and vehicles; support the national defense; grow and produce food; provide health care; generate and deliver energy; and offer financial, communications and other services that underpin economic growth.*

'While each of our individual companies serves its own corporate purpose, we share a fundamental commitment to all of our stakeholders. We commit to:

- *Delivering value to our customers. We will further the tradition of American companies leading the way in meeting or exceeding customer expectations.*
- *Investing in our employees. This starts with compensating them fairly and providing important benefits. It also includes supporting them through training and education that help develop new skills for a rapidly changing world. We foster diversity and inclusion, dignity and respect.*
- *Dealing fairly and ethically with our suppliers. We are dedicated to serving as good partners to the other companies, large and small, that help us meet our missions.*
- *Supporting the communities in which we work. We respect the people in our communities and protect the environment by embracing sustainable practices across our businesses.*
- *Generating long-term value for shareholders, who provide the capital that allows companies to invest, grow and innovate. We are committed to transparency and effective engagement with shareholders.*

'Each of our stakeholders is essential. We commit to deliver value to all of them, for the future success of our companies, our communities and our country.'

How widespread is corruption?

Despite decades of legal and ethical effort, corruption is more than 3% of the global economy[12] and aspects of anti-corruption enforcement in the USA have now been paused because 'it's going to mean a lot more business for America'.[13] 25% of employees[14] are aware of unethical practice in their workplace.

What are the key anti-corruption laws?

The UK's Bribery Act of 2010 is largely seen as the global benchmark because of its broad scope including:[15]

- both the private and public sector
- a wide range of corrupt practices, not just bribery of public officials

- global activities by any company or individual connected to the UK
- an obligation of private companies to prevent bribery.

The US Foreign and Corrupt Practices Act (FCPA) of 1977 (amended and strengthened in 1988 and 1998) had, until recently, been seen as robust legislation because of its global reach. Compared to the UK Bribery Act, FCPA primarily applies to bribery of public officials, with more limited application to private companies and no specific obligation to prevent bribery.

While there is a consistent trend of legislating to strengthen anti-corruption laws, there is one notable exception. Enforcement of FCPA was halted by an executive order of the US President in February 2025[16] with the intent of boosting US business interests.

In the EU, anti-corruption laws vary country by country, but a proposed directive is currently under consideration to strengthen and harmonise aspects of anti-corruption laws and strengthen accountability in the public sector.[17]

The failures of Enron and others led to enactment of the Sarbanes-Oxley Act in the USA in 2002,[18] which remains a key piece of US legislation on corporate accountability and financial transparency. It is enforced by the Securities and Exchange Commission, the agency responsible for regulating securities markets in the USA, and includes stronger regulation of record-keeping, disclosure, internal controls, personal accountability and criminal penalties.

Recent decades have also led to stronger regulations over disclosures and protection for consumers in financial services. The global financial crisis of 2008 led directly to a number of regulatory changes, increasing the stability and oversight of financial institutions, including:

- Basel III commitments, increasing the financial resilience of banks globally, with higher capital requirements and risk thresholds, with greater scrutiny by the Financial Stability Board (FSB).[19]
- The Dodd-Frank Wall Street Reform in the USA together with greater oversight of risks and greater protection for consumers under the Consumer Protection Act.[20]
- EU reforms giving the European Central Bank greater powers of supervision over banks operating in the EU through a 'Single Supervisory Mechanism' (SSM).[21]

How do you do business in a market that has a higher risk of corruption?

World Economics publishes a corruption perception index every year. It uses data from Transparency International which surveys perceived corruption.[22] The 2025 index shows Denmark, Finland and Singapore, New Zealand and Luxembourg at the top of 180 countries. Only 33 countries score above 60 on a scale of 0 to 100.

With bribery commonplace in many countries, robust leadership and systems are required to conduct business ethically.

Celtel International was a telecommunications service provider operating in sub-Saharan Africa from 1998. It built cellular phone systems that relied on winning government contracts. Siemens was not a direct competitor but was also bidding for government contracts in related markets. It later emerged that Siemens was involved in systemic bribery for which it paid heavy penalties, as we saw in a previous chapter. On the other hand, Celtel's founder Mo Ibrahim developed a successful approach to avoid bribery, including:[23]

- recruiting the right board
- being public about its ethical commitments
- being public about its transactions and payments
- funding communities, not individuals
- hiring local security staff
- making a public event of key imports to avoid customs corruption
- introducing local investors
- being patient and being prepared to walk away from government deals.

Celtel proved that it is possible to conduct successful ethical business in a corrupt environment. It was acquired by Zain Group in 2005 for $2.8 billion.

Conclusion

Corruption is a risk and a high risk in many regions.

Legal obligations vary by jurisdiction, and it is important to understand the legal obligations that apply to your business.

Ethical standards go beyond the law and the next two chapters explore this further.

Questions

- Do you and your directors understand your legal obligations?
- If you operate in several jurisdictions, do you understand the differences in obligations?
- Do you carry out due diligence or risk assessment of markets that have a higher risk of corruption?
- How do you ensure that you offset the risk so that you can conduct business both ethically and competitively?

Notes

1 *Monkey Business* (1931).
2 See: https://www.iod.com/resources/governance/fiduciary-duties-for-directors-a-comprehensive-guide/.
3 See: https://www.icaew.com/regulation/membership/icaews-guide-to-directors-responsibilities/general-duties-owed-to-the-company#7 and https://cms.law/en/int/expert-guides/cms-expert-guide-for-directors-of-companies/united-kingdom.
4 See: https://www.legislation.gov.uk/ukpga/2006/46/section/172.
5 See: https://www.icaew.com/technical/corporate-reporting/section-172-1-statement.
6 See: https://www.frc.org.uk/library/standards-codes-policy/corporate-governance/uk-corporate-governance-code/#uk-corporate-governance-code-2024-effective-2025-16c7508e.
7 See: https://betterbusinessact.org.
8 See: https://bouwen.us/resources/company-directors-in-the-us-and-the-uk and https://www.thecorporategovernanceinstitute.com/insights/news-analysis/difference-between-corporate-governance-uk-and-united-states/?srsltid=AfmBOoqu8PdTrWAzwR5U8C6rQ5ckdmH_mUw-5FtIdAT43HGMbup2MO9L.
9 See: https://www.squirepattonboggs.com/-/media/files/insights/publications/2021/12/quick-guides-to-directors-duties-across-europe/quick-guides-to-directors-duties-across-europe.pdf?rev=3fa266da4f92413c9dd8c228499d0725.

10 See: https://www.sup.org/books/business/becoming-public-benefit-corporation.
11 See: https://www.businessroundtable.org/business-roundtable-redefines-the-purpose-of-a-corporation-to-promote-an-economy-that-serves-all-americans.
12 See: https://www.weforum.org/stories/2018/12/the-global-economy-loses-3-6-trillion-to-corruption-each-year-says-u-n/.
13 See: https://www.ft.com/content/f880bfc3-6069-427b-9873-51255d4e0b8c.
14 See: https://www.ibe.org.uk/ethicsatwork2024.html.
15 See: https://www.legislation.gov.uk/ukpga/2010/23/contents.
16 See: https://www.ft.com/content/f880bfc3-6069-427b-9873-51255d4e0b8c.
17 See: https://baselgovernance.org/blog/eus-anti-corruption-directive-enters-critical-juncture.
18 See: https://www.investopedia.com/terms/s/sarbanesoxleyact.asp.
19 See: https://www.investopedia.com/terms/b/basell-iii.asp.
20 See: https://www.investopedia.com/terms/d/dodd-frank-financial-regulatory-reform-bill.asp.
21 See: https://www.sciencedirect.com/science/article/pii/S0261560623001249.
22 See: https://www.worldeconomics.com/Indicator-Data/Corruption/Corruption-Perceptions-Index.aspx.
23 See: https://www.london.edu/think/managing-ethically-in-corrupt-environments.

chapter 18

The UN global compact, ESG and SDGs

'Without regulation markets are not moral.'

Mark Carney[1]

In this chapter you will learn:

- The key UN initiatives to create standards and reporting frameworks
- The role of environment, social and governance (ESG)
- The role of sustainable development goals (SDGs)
- Key ESG regulations, frameworks and standards
- How a large listed company applies the frameworks and standards in practice

Introduction

Growing environmental concerns in the 1980s and 1990s were captured by the work of corporate responsibility pioneer, John Elkington. His book *Cannibals with Forks: The Triple Bottom Line of 21st Century Business*[2] promoted the role of business in economic prosperity, environmental quality and social justice, shortened to 'people, planet and profit'. He later replaced this with more a more challenging framework of 'responsibility, resilience and regeneration'.[3]

In the 2000s, the United Nations (UN) became heavily influential in working with businesses to create ethical standards.

What is the UN Global Compact?

The UN Global Compact was created in 2000 as a voluntary initiative, based on CEO commitments, to unite businesses in advancing human rights, labour standards, environmental stewardship and anti-corruption.[4]

It started with the support of 50 companies and has now grown to 20,000 businesses in 160 countries. It led to:

- Environmental, social and governance (ESG), which is now a global framework for evaluating business impact, described below.
- The launch of the Principles for Responsible Investment (PRI) to drive integration of ESG factors into global capital markets, influencing over $100 trillion in assets.
- Key initiatives in global water stewardship.
- The Women's Empowerment Principles (2010) setting a new standard for gender equality in the workplace.
- The Science-Based Targets Initiative (2015) helping companies align their climate commitments with the latest scientific data.
- The CFO Coalition for Strategic Development Goals (SDGs) in 2020, mobilising financial leaders to direct capital toward sustainable development. See SDGs summarised below.
- The Forward Faster initiative (2023) accelerating corporate action on the SDGs, reinforcing the urgent need for businesses to lead the charge in addressing global challenges.[5]

It is based on 10 principles for signatory businesses to follow.

UN Global Compact's Ten Principles[6]

Regarding human rights, businesses should:

1. support and respect the protection of internationally proclaimed human rights
2. make sure that they are not complicit in human rights abuses.

Regarding labour, businesses should:

3. uphold the freedom of association and the effective recognition of the right to collective bargaining
4. support the elimination of all forms of forced and compulsory labour
5. support the effective abolition of child labour
6. support the elimination of discrimination in respect of employment and occupation.

Regarding the environment, businesses should:

7. support a precautionary approach to environmental challenges
8. undertake initiatives to promote greater environmental responsibility
9. encourage the development and diffusion of environmentally friendly technologies.

Regarding anti-corruption, businesses should:

10. work against corruption in all its forms, including extortion and bribery.

What is ESG?

Environmental, social and governance (ESG) questions later became the shorthand for responsible business practice, putting pressure on businesses and regulators to raise their standards. Many businesses have increasingly spelt out their ethical credentials, in relation to human rights, employee welfare and the environment. Corporate failures have continued to be a reminder of the cost of unethical practice.

ESG has a broad scope, but in summary it includes the following:

- **Environmental** – energy consumption, waste management, pollution, emissions, water conservation and biodiversity.

- **Social** – observing human rights throughout the supply chain, employee relations, diversity, equity and inclusion, customer relations and community relations.
- **Governance** – processes, controls and resources to oversee and take accountability for ESG activity, measuring performance, transparency and rigour of reporting.

The term ESG was coined by a report, 'Who Cares Wins', commissioned by the United Nations (UN) in 2004. It emerged from the UN Global Compact, reflecting growing awareness of the responsibility of businesses to positively shape the world around them. The report recommended action by the whole ecosystem of companies, regulators and advisors:[7]

1 **Analysts** – to provide better environmental, social and governance (ESG) factors in their research, supported by academic institutions, business schools and other research organisations.
2 **Financial institutions** – to commit to integrating environmental, social and governance factors in a more systematic way.
3 **Companies** – to take a leadership role by implementing environmental, social and corporate governance principles and polices and to provide consistent and standardised information and reports on their performance.
4 **Investors** – to request and reward research that includes environmental, social and governance aspects and to reward well-managed companies.
5 **Pension fund trustees** – to consider environmental, social and governance issues in the formulation of investment mandates and the selection of investment managers, taking into account their fiduciary obligations to participants and beneficiaries.
6 **Consultants and financial advisers** – to create a greater and more stable demand for research in this area by combining and publishing research on environmental, social and governance aspects with industry-level research.
7 **Regulators** – to shape legal frameworks requiring a minimum degree of disclosure and accountability on environmental, social and governance issues from companies. The formulation of specific standards should rely on market-driven voluntary initiatives.
8 **Stock exchanges** – to include environmental, social and governance criteria in listing particulars for companies as this will ensure a minimum degree of disclosure. Other self-regulatory organisations, professional credential-granting

organisations, accounting standard-setting bodies and rating agencies to establish consistent standards and frameworks in relation to environmental, social and governance factors.

9 **Non-governmental organisations** (NGOs) – to contribute to better transparency by providing objective information on companies to the public and the financial community.

What are the UN Strategic Development Goals?

The United Nations (UN) and its member countries later developed 17 Strategic Development Goals, agreed in 2015.[8]

They are an urgent call for action by governments and businesses to achieve the goals by 2030. They recognise that ending poverty and other deprivations must go hand-in-hand with strategies that improve health and education, reduce inequality and spur economic growth – all while tackling climate change and working to preserve our oceans and forests. They are:

1 No poverty.
2 Zero hunger.
3 Good health and well-being.
4 Quality education.
5 Gender equality.
6 Clean water and sanitation.
7 Affordable and clean energy.
8 Decent work and economic growth.
9 Industry, innovation and infrastructure.
10 Reduced inequalities.
11 Sustainable cities and economies.
12 Responsible consumption and production.
13 Climate action.
14 Life below water.
15 Life on land.

16 Peace, justice and strong institutions.

17 Partnership for the goals.

What are the key ESG-related regulations?

The 20 years that followed the 'Who Cares Wins' report saw laws and regulations developing across the world, including the following:

- The UK Companies Act of 2006 raising the bar on governance.[9]
- The UK Equality Act of 2010 protecting people from discrimination.[10]
- The UK Corporate Governance Code for listed companies, requiring them to 'comply or explain' against a comprehensive set of governance and disclosure requirements.[11]
- The EU's Corporate Sustainability Due Diligence directive of 2024 requiring larger companies, i.e. those with turnover above EUR450m, to validate and report on human rights and environmental standards for their entire supply chain.[12]
- China embarking in 2024 on a national disclosure system to support lowering carbon emissions.[13]

The regulations are far from standardised and remain a contentious question in the USA where ESG questions have been downgraded by the US administration in 2025, including the following:

- The executive order banning diversity, equity and inclusion programmes.[14]
- The short-lived Securities and Exchange Commission (SEC) regulations on climate-related disclosures being shelved.[15]

What are the key ESG frameworks and standards?

There is no universal, mandatory reporting ESG framework. However, large and listed companies are obliged to report on a wide range of non-financial questions. ESG-related reporting is evolving into commonly accepted frameworks and standards and are at early stages of regulatory adoption, particularly in the EU.

These are the key frameworks and standards.

1. **The Global Reporting Initiative (GRI).**[16]

   GRI was founded in Boston (USA) in 1997 following on from the public outcry over the environmental damage of the Exxon Valdez oil spill, eight years previously. It has evolved into a comprehensive set of reporting frameworks and standards including sectoral guidance.

2. **The IFRS International Sustainability Standards Board (ISSB).**[17]

   ISSB has developed the first two global standards IFRS S1 and S2 for sustainability reporting, which are currently voluntary but being considered by individual country's regulators for mandatory adoption. This incorporates the SASB standards and starts to integrate sustainability reporting with financial reporting.

3. **The International Integrated Reporting Council (IIRC) framework.**[18]

   The IIRC seeks to fully integrate financial and sustainability reporting.

4. **The EU Corporate Social Reporting Directive (CSRD).**

   This came into force in 2023 and led to the European Sustainability Reporting Standards (ESRS). So far, there are 12 standards ready to be brought into force by EU member countries.[19]

   Note that the EU's Sustainable Financial Sustainable Disclosure Regulation (SFDR) of 2019[20] was designed to improve the rigour of ESG claims. It is now being enhanced to require stronger verification to prevent 'greenwashing', i.e. false claims of ethical credentials.[21]

5. **Science Based Targets Initiative (SBTi).**[22]

   SBTi helped companies align their climate commitments with the latest scientific data. It works with certification businesses including Planet Mark[23] and support organisations such as the Science Based Targets Network.[24]

6. **Principles for Responsible Investment.**

   A set of principles for responsible investors.[25]

As a large, listed company in a regulated industry, SSE plc is a good example of a business that has gone beyond its regulatory obligations to meet broader ESG challenges. It is also a signatory to the UN Global Compact.

The following is a summary of its approach to culture, transparency and collaboration for wider system change.

Case study – SSE plc[26]

SSE plc is an energy company based in Scotland with interests across Great Britain and Northern Ireland, Republic of Ireland, Japan, Spain, France, Denmark and Poland. It was formed after the privatisation of energy companies by the British Government in the early 1990s and is now listed on the London Stock Exchange as one of the largest 100 listed companies, the FTSE 100. It has a turnover of £10.1 billion and about 14,000 employees.

SSE is a leading generator of renewables and flexible energy in the British and Irish markets and one of the world's fastest growing electricity network companies. It develops, builds, operates and invests in low-carbon electricity infrastructure in support of the transition to net zero. This includes onshore and offshore wind, flexible generation such as hydro and efficient thermal, electricity transmission and distribution grids, alongside providing energy products and services for businesses and other customers.

According to its chair, Sir John Manzoni, 'SSE is leading the way when it comes to helping to deliver a cleaner, more affordable and secure energy system. In doing so, we create value for our shareholders as well as the society which we proudly serve.'

Values[27]

SSE's culture is based on its core values of safety, service, efficiency, sustainability, excellence and teamwork. Its public statements on culture include the following:

> 'Our number one value is safety. Whether we're fixing power lines, helping customers, or inventing the energy technologies of tomorrow, we work as a team, look out for one another, and keep each other safe.

> **Doing the right thing**

> 'We all want to work for a fair and ethical company and SSE is committed to doing business in the right way, ethically. While we know we must follow the legislative and regulatory rules set for us, at SSE, we consistently seek to go beyond these and set standards for the company that promote better outcomes for employees, shareholders and society as a whole. Examples include our commitments to the Fair Tax Mark, being a Real Living Wage, Hours and Pensions employer, meeting science-based carbon targets and empowering people to speak up against wrongdoing in our Whistleblowing Policy.

Preventing bribery and corruption

'Corruption and criminality, including bribery, fraud and other financial crime, are unacceptable in all circumstances. We take proactive steps to mitigate this risk occurring in our direct or supply chain operations. This includes a robust approach to governance, mandatory training and an established policy framework.

Speaking up

'Empowering people to speak up against wrongdoing is a central element of our approach to good business ethics and doing the right thing. Employees can raise concerns with their line manager or nominated internal Speak Up contacts throughout the business or this can be done through an independent whistleblowing channel, hosted by SafeCall, with the option to report anonymously.

Powered by our differences

'Inclusion is at the heart of our Teamwork value, so we don't pay lip service to our inclusion and diversity strategy. We put the principles of equality, fairness, diversity, and inclusion at the heart of everything we do. Because we believe everyone has a part to play in the journey to net zero.

'SSE's inclusion and diversity strategy, introduced in 2021 is about embedding inclusion for the long term, underpinned by four pillars:[28]

1. Ambition – setting measurable goals, ambitions and KPIs, and using external benchmarking.
2. Education and development – focusing on behaviours and building leadership confidence, raising awareness for all to create an inclusive workplace.
3. Inclusive processes – embedding best practice and ensuring policies and processes are inclusive to support everyone.[29]
4. Employee voice – actively listening and understanding what matters to inform and shape the improvements needed.[30]

'SSE has set four core 2030 business goals aligned to the four UN Sustainable Development Goals (SDGs) most material to its business. SSE's 2030 Goals address climate change at their core and provide important milestones on the journey to net zero, placing sustainability firmly at the heart of SSE's business strategy.'

As a large, listed and regulated business, SSE follows the UK Corporate Governance Code and has a comprehensive set of governance disclosures[31] as well as a 'culture dashboard'.[32] It regularly publishes a sustainability statement including its ESG scores according to rating agencies' indices.[33]

Just Transition Strategy

In November 2020, SSE became the first company to publish a 'Just Transition Strategy', the first of its kind globally. It includes a framework of 20 principles to guide how SSE influences greater fairness for those impacted by the changes the transition to net zero entails.[34]

Doing the right thing[35]

SSE also published a 32-page guide for employees on what 'doing the right thing' means, combining its six values with rules and policies in a comprehensive document. It shows how SSE goes beyond its regulatory obligations, for example living wage, living hours and living pensions commitments. It represents SSE's framework for doing business ethically and for maintaining a healthy business culture, comprising:

- *A decision-tree for navigating ethical dilemmas and guidance on how to speak up.*
- *Staying safe and secure – including health and safety, cyber security, data and safeguarding the environment.* This includes meeting the ISO 14001 standard for managing environmental impact in key parts of the business.
- *Trading fairly and transparently – including responsible procurement, fair competition, avoiding conflicts of interest and observing corruption and financial crime prevention policies. SSE requires its supply chain to commit to responsible practice, such as the Living Wage, and following a transparent sustainable procurement code.*[36] SSE has also joined the Initiative for Responsible Mining Assurance.[37]
- *Working together – including human rights and modern slavery legislation, SSE's Living Wage and Living Hours accreditation, their commitment to Living Pensions, observing inclusion, diversity, bullying, harassment and discrimination policies.*
- *Engaging with stakeholders – including tax transparency and providing accurate information externally.*

Conclusion

ESG is a good example of the challenge of finding a common language of ethical business.

If the term ESG becomes more contentious, it is worth remembering that, at its heart, it is a shorthand for ethical business. Whether called ESG or not, most of the leaders I spoke to appreciate external mandatory standards because they define the social licence and the baseline for competition. They also see regulation as a low bar that lags the market.

While standardisation of measurement and reporting may be some way off, the ethical and commercial case for acting responsibly remains strong.

In his paper from 2022, business professor Alex Edmans compares it to other business intangibles:[38]

> 'ESG ... shouldn't be put on a pedestal compared to other intangible assets that affect both financial and social value, such as management quality, corporate culture, and innovative capability. Like other intangibles, ESG mustn't be reduced to a set of numbers, and companies needn't be forced to report on matters that aren't value relevant…We can embrace differences of opinion about a company's ESG performance just as we do about its management quality, strategic direction, or human capital management.'

Questions

- Has your organisation joined the UN Global Compact?
- Which SDGs are most relevant to your organisation?
- Are key regulations, frameworks and standards applied in your organisation?
- How can they help drive a more positive ethical impact?

Notes

1. Carney, M. (2021) *Value(s)*. William Collins, p. 191.
2. See: https://www.taylorfrancis.com/chapters/edit/10.4324/9781351279086-27/cannibals-forks-john-elkington-1997.
3. See: https://www.imd.org/ibyimd/audio-articles/regenerative-business-three-rs-are-new-triple-bottom-line/.

4 See: https://unglobalcompact.org/compactjournal/25-years-un-global-compact-legacy-impact-and-call-bold-action#:~:text=On%2026%20July%202000%2C%20then,environmental%20stewardship%20and%20anti%2Dcorruption.
5 See: https://forwardfaster.unglobalcompact.org/home.
6 See: https://unglobalcompact.org/about.
7 See: https://documents1.worldbank.org/curated/en/280911488968799581/pdf/113237-WP-WhoCaresWins-2004.pdf.
8 See: https://sdgs.un.org/goals#icons.
9 See: https://www.legislation.gov.uk/ukpga/2006/46/section/172.
10 See: https://www.gov.uk/guidance/equality-act-2010-guidance.
11 See: https://www.frc.org.uk/library/standards-codes-policy/corporate-governance/uk-corporate-governance-code/#who-does-the-uk-corporate-governance-code-apply-to-9b7c5b9b.
12 See: https://commission.europa.eu/business-economy-euro/doing-business-eu/sustainability-due-diligence-responsible-business/corporate-sustainability-due-diligence_en.
13 See: https://www.unepfi.org/industries/banking/china-embarks-on-a-journey-of-esg-disclosure/.
14 See: https://www.ft.com/content/02ed56af-7595-4cb3-a138-f1b703ffde84?shareType=nongift.
15 See: https://www.sec.gov/newsroom/press-releases/2024-31 and https://www.google.com/url?sa=t&source=web&rct=j&opi=89978449&url=https://www.sidley.com/en/insights/newsupdates/2025/04/sec-ends-defense-of-climate-related-disclosure-rules%23:~:text%3DOn%2520March%252027%252C%25202025%252C%2520the,investors%2520(the%2520climate%2520rules).&ved=2ahUKEwjBzaD3tq2NAxXjU0EAHZuMHeAQFnoECBkQAw&usg=AOvVaw3vMExf9wo7uiexd1l26g4r.
16 See: https://www.globalreporting.org.
17 See: https://www.ifrs.org/sustainability/knowledge-hub/.
18 See: https://integratedreporting.ifrs.org/resource/international-ir-framework/.
19 See: https://www.unepfi.org/impact/interoperability/european-sustainability-reporting-standards-esrs/.
20 See: https://eur-lex.europa.eu/eli/reg/2019/2088/oj/eng.
21 See: http://antigreenwashcharter.org/what-you-need-to-know-about-the-eus-green-claims-directive-and-how-the-anti-greenwash-charter-can-help/.
22 See: https://sciencebasedtargets.org/how-it-works.
23 See: https://www.planetmark.com.
24 See: https://sciencebasedtargetsnetwork.org/resources/faqs/.
25 See: https://www.unpri.org/about-us/what-are-the-principles-for-responsible-investment.
26 See: https://www.sse.com.
27 See: https://www.sse.com/about-us/our-culture/.

28 See: sse-inclusion-and-diversity-report-2025.pdf.
29 See: https://careers.sse.com/inclusion.
30 See: https://careers.sse.com/our-employee-led-communities.
31 See: https://www.sse.com/about-us/leadership-and-governance/.
32 See: SSE plc Annual Report 2025, p. 98.
33 See: sse-sustainability-report-2025.pdf.
34 See: https://www.sse.com/media/4bzijbrj/sse-net-zero-transition-plan-2025.pdf.
35 See: https://www.sse.com/media/jgvbbw45/doing-the-right-thing-june-2024.pdf.
36 See: https://www.sse.com/media/4i1bzat0/sustainable-procurement-code_no-links-final.pdf.
37 See: https://www.sse.com/news-and-views/2025/03/sse-joins-irma/.
38 See: https://onlinelibrary.wiley.com/doi/full/10.1111/fima.12413.

chapter 19

Non-government standards

'Businesses that adopt transparent and ethical practices tend to build stronger relationships with customers and stakeholders, leading to long-term success.'

Jason Holt CBE

In this chapter you will learn:

- How voluntary ethical standards can improve ethical performance
- How two case studies have applied them
- How professional standards support employees who belong to professional bodies

Introduction

ESG frameworks and standards have come from government collaboration in the United Nations and have mainly influenced large, listed companies.

At the same time, businesses of all sizes have looked for other ways of improving their ethical performance through non-government initiatives.

What is B Corp certification?

The most prominent initiative, B Corporation (also known as B Corp) certification, was started by B Lab in 2006.[1] There are now over 9,000 B Corps in 102 countries.

B Lab believes that a different kind of economy is not only possible, but necessary, and that business could lead the way towards a new, stakeholder-driven model. It has become known for certifying B Corps, which are companies that meet B Lab's standards of social and environmental performance, accountability and transparency.

B Lab aims to address society's most critical challenges by changing our economic system, creating standards, policies, tools and programmes that shift the behaviour, culture and structural underpinnings of capitalism. It is designed to advance a new model that moves from concentrating wealth and power to ensuring equity, from extraction to generation, and from prioritising individualism to embracing interdependence.

B Corp certification evaluates and verifies performance, accountability and transparency on factors from employee benefits and charitable giving to supply-chain practices and input materials. In order to achieve certification, a company must:

- demonstrate high social and environmental performance and pass a 'risk review'
- make a legal commitment by changing its corporate governance structure to be accountable to all stakeholders, not just shareholders
- exhibit transparency by allowing information about its performance measured against B Lab's standards to be publicly available on its company profile on B Lab's website
- re-certify every three years.

Note that B Corp certification sets a higher ethical bar than 'Benefit Corporation' status, which is a class of company available in most US states and some other countries including British Columbia, Italy, France, Spain and parts of Latin America. In both cases, the corporate constitution must show accountability to all stakeholders, not just shareholders.

In 2025, the B Corp standards were raised and now cover seven criteria:[2]

- **Purpose and stakeholder governance:** companies act in accordance with a defined purpose and embed stakeholder governance in decision making. By doing so, they contribute to an inclusive, equitable and regenerative economic system for all people and the planet.
- **Fair work:** companies provide good quality jobs and have positive workplace cultures.
- **Justice, equity, diversity and inclusion:** companies have inclusive and diverse workplaces and contribute to just and equitable communities.
- **Human rights:** companies treat people with dignity and respect their human rights.
- **Climate action:** companies take action to combat the climate crisis and its impacts.
- **Environmental stewardship and circularity:** companies demonstrate environmental stewardship and contribute to the circular economy in their operations and value chain. They both minimise negative impacts, to help stay within ecological thresholds and pursue positive impacts.
- **Government affairs and collective action:** companies play a leadership role in fostering shared understanding and implementing solutions towards an equitable, inclusive and regenerative economy. This role includes a fair and responsible contribution to their operating countries' economies and infrastructure.

Case study – Patagonia[3]

Patagonia was the first California company to sign up for B Corp certification in 2012 and was one of the early pioneers of operating and advocating high standards of social and environmental responsibility. It was founded by Yvon Chouinard as an outdoor clothing business in 1973, having evolved from the founder's climbing equipment business. It now has a turnover estimated at over $1 billion and is owned by a charitable trust.

The key features of the business are as follows:

- **Long-term decision making:** it prioritises long-term environmental and economic sustainability, with a healthy respect for profits and competitive advantage. 'We strive to balance the funding of environmental activities with the desire to continue in business for the next hundred years.'
- **Innovation:** 'When I look at my business today, I realise one of the biggest challenges I have is combating complacency. I always say we're running Patagonia as if it's going to be here a hundred years from now, but that doesn't mean we have a hundred years to get there.'
- **Product and service focus:** it does not follow fashion cycles and trends, but focuses on product sustainability, quality, testing and innovation. It uses recycled materials and offers customers a free repair service with no lime limits.
- **Promoting its values over selling:** 'We have three general guidelines for all promotional efforts: 1) Our charter is to inspire and educate rather than to promote. 2) We would rather earn credibility than buy it. 3) We advertise only as a last resort and usually in sport-specific magazines.' Its use of multiple sales channels, dealerships, retail stores and e-commerce have helped it ride out recessions successfully.
- **Hiring and training employees for their values more than their qualifications:** 'We don't want drones who will simply follow directions. We want the kind of employees who will question the wisdom of something they regard as a bad decision.'
- **Environmental action:** it donates 1% of its sales to environmental action groups.[4]

What other standards are there?

While not an exhaustive list, the following is a broad picture of key non-government initiatives.

ISO Standards[5]

ISO, the International Organization for Standardization, is a non-profit founded in 1946 and based in Switzerland. It brings global experts together to agree on best practice for anything from making a product to managing a process.

It has published over 25,000 standards and operates in 174 countries. To be certified as meeting an ISO standard, an organisation has to prove its compliance, normally every three years.

Environmental and social responsibilities are features across its standards, but two have a particular focus and a third is in development.

- **ISO 14001 (environmental management)**

    Provides a framework for organisations to manage their environmental impact, reduce waste and ensure compliance with environmental regulations. Note that the European Commission established EU Ecolabel[6] in 1992 to support one aspect of the ISO 14001 standard, certifying non-food products for sale in the EU which effectively meet the international standard ISO 14024 of environmental performance. EU Ecolabel has so far certified over 100,000 products.

- **ISO 26000 (social responsibility)**

    Offers guidance on social responsibility practices, helping organisations address the impacts of their decisions and activities on society and the environment.

- **PAS 808:2022 and ISO 37011 (purpose-driven organisations)**

    PAS 808 focuses on helping organisations prioritise social and environmental purpose alongside profit. It is the precursor to a full standard (ISO 37011) likely to be launched in 2027. It will add to the '37000' range of standards which include Governance of Organisations (37000), Anti-Bribery Management (37001) and Whistleblower Management (37002).

> ### Case study – Anglian Water Group[7]
>
> Anglian Water is the lead sponsor of the work on PAS 808:2022 as part of its commitment to the public interest.
>
> It is one of the largest water and water recycling companies in England, supplying 7 million people in 14 counties. It has a turnover of £1.6 billion, employs about 6,000 people directly and 30,000 indirectly, operating 38,996 km of water mains and 76,355 km of sewers.

It was one of the original regional water companies privatised by the British Government in 1989. Its current shareholders are the Osprey Consortium, a private alliance of long-term investors including the Canada Pension Plan Investment Board, which bought the business for £2.25 billion in 2006.

The natural environment

The counties it serves are the driest and lowest lying in the UK, with over 1,200 km of coastline. This makes it particularly vulnerable to the effects of climate change, exposed to the risks of both more droughts and more flooding. Anglian Water therefore has commercial and ethical reasons to prioritise reduction of environmental risks and has a long history of doing so.

As an example, the business was instrumental in the Osprey Project. Their involvement began in 1996 and, five years later, saw the first wild ospreys to hatch in central England for over 150 years.[8]

In 2015, the business was awarded the Queen's Award for Enterprise: Sustainable Development and, in 2017, it was named Responsible Business of the Year.[9] In 2017, it became the first business in the UK utility sector to launch a Green Bond.

Public Interest Commitment

It was instrumental in the development of the water industry's Public Interest Commitment, published in April 2019. Each signatory committed to enshrining public interest in the company's purpose and meeting five priorities to tackle leakage, carbon emissions, plastics, affordability and social mobility.

Anglian Water was the first water company to follow through and change its constitution by legal changes to its Articles of Association and a commitment to quantified goals for each of the five priorities by 2030. The enhanced Articles of Association were approved by the shareholders. They require the business to operate for the benefit of shareholders while also delivering long-term value for the company's customers, the region and the communities it serves, and seeking positive outcomes for the environment and society.

Overall, it is summed up in the Statement of Purpose: 'Our Purpose is to bring environmental and social prosperity to the region we serve through our commitment to Love Every Drop.'

It reports publicly through its Annual Integrated Report which reflects the complexity of a large, regulated business. However, it goes well beyond its narrow regulatory obligations. This is illustrated by two frameworks.

Social Contract

The first is its 'Social Contract' which is based on The UN's 17 Sustainable Development Goals. Anglian Water has mapped their work to the UN goals and drawn out the 10 components that have the most material impact on their work. The result is 10 commitments on which they invite stakeholders to hold them to account. They are:

Customers and communities:

- Fair charges, fair returns
- Delighted customers
- Safe, clean water
- Positive impact on our communities.

Going further for our people and partners:

- Resilient business
- Our people: healthier, happier, safer.

Doing the right thing for our environment and planet:

- Investing for tomorrow
- A smaller footprint
- Flourishing environment
- Supply meets demand.

Six Capitals

The second is its 'Six Capitals' framework, ensuring it keeps its responsibility to customers, communities and the environment when making business decisions, together with a set of metrics for each of the capitals to help the business understand, track and report impact. The Six Capitals taken from its report are:

> *'Natural – The health of the natural systems and resources that we rely on and impact in our region and beyond; the availability and quality of water in our rivers and aquifers, the protection of our soil and biodiversity and our impact on carbon emissions.*

'Social – The value of our relationships with stakeholders, including customers, communities and other organisations, the impacts we have on people and society (both positive and negative) and the trust they place in us as a result.

'Financial – The financial health and resilience of the organisation and our access to and use of sustainable finance.

Manufactured – The ability of our infrastructure to provide resilient services to meet the current and future expectations of our customers.

'People – The knowledge, skills and wellbeing of our people; and the health, happiness and safety of our working environment; our organisational culture and our ways of working.

'Intellectual – The knowledge, systems, processes, data and information we hold, create and share within our business and with our alliance partners.'

Incentives

To align executives to these priorities, Anglian Water reviewed its performance metrics to identify those that directly contributed to the purpose. Senior managers' financial bonuses now rely entirely on the purpose measures, with regulatory metrics recognised non-financially.

External frameworks

When looking for responsible business principles, Anglian Water considered several methods including the Global Compact and B Corp certification. They wanted something that would help drive positive change as well as specific biodiversity initiatives. For their context, they needed to design something new and chose to work with the British Standards Institute (BSI).

As a result, BSI, Anglian Water as lead sponsor, a group of like-minded companies, academics, charities and sustainability organisations co-created a 'Publicly Accessible Specification' (PAS) on embedding purpose in organisations. The result is PAS 808:2022 'Purpose-driven organisations – Worldviews, principles and behaviours for delivering sustainability'.[10] This is a step towards creating an International Standard (ISO 37011) which is now under development.[11]

The goal is to set out the characteristics of a leading organisation that is pursuing a sustainable purpose at the core of their business. When fully developed, it will play a key role in driving positive change and holding to account organisations that have a sustainable purpose.

> ## The Better Business Act[12]
>
> As part of its advocacy of positive change, Anglian Water also supports the Better Business Act coalition (BBA), a business-led campaign calling for a change to Section 172 of the UK's Companies Act 2006. It would require directors of every medium and large company in the UK to align their activity with the interests of wider society and the environment, in the way that Anglian Water has chosen to do.

Fairtrade[13]

Fairtrade is a movement to get better prices, safe working conditions, local sustainability and fair terms for farmers and workers. It certifies products, including tea, coffee, flowers, bananas and gold, and works with producers, retailers and governments to build a more ethical and sustainable system.

After decades of local initiatives, Fairtrade certified its first products in 1994 and established the umbrella international body Fairtrade International, a German-registered charity, in 1997. It is now an international movement working in partnership with 2 million farmers and workers, in more than 1,900 producer organisations. It certifies 6,000 products worth about $10 billion across 68 countries.

Living Wage[14]

The Living Wage Foundation is a charity created in 2011 following a 10-year campaign by Citizens UK[15] to encourage employers to pay a wage based on a reasonable cost of living. It is a leading example of 'civil regulation' where campaigners and businesses agree voluntary standards that support and encourage businesses to go beyond legal obligations, in this case paying more than the legal minimum. It now has 16,000 accredited employers, of which 94% report net business benefits alongside paying an extra £3.8 billion to their lowest paid workers since 2011.[16] Civil regulations for Living Hours and Living Pensions have now been developed and the Living Wage is one of the components of the Good Business Charter.

Good Business Charter[17]

The Good Business Charter (GBC) is a UK-registered charity, designed to highlight responsible businesses to members of the public. Founded in 2020 by retailer, Julian Richer, it aims to give a straightforward answer to the growing question from customers, 'Am I buying from a responsible business?'

Response to the Research shows that customers value responsible organisations. GBC research, in collaboration with TSB Bank, revealed:

> *'We found that 97% of people think it is important that a business acts responsibly. Most consumers want more consistent information from businesses and more than half polled would value a simple independent certification. This is exactly what the Good Business Charter seeks to be. It is independent, it is a certification, and it is simple to understand. 10 components, businesses need to commit to all 10 in order to achieve GBC accreditation.'*

The 10 components are:

1. Real living wage.
2. Fairer hours and contracts.
3. Employee well-being.
4. Employee representation.
5. Diversity and inclusion.
6. Environmental responsibility.
7. Pay fair tax.
8. Commitment to customers.
9. Ethical sourcing.
10. Prompt payment to customers.

1,300 organisations have been accredited since 2000.

Good Shopping Guide[18]

The Good Shopping Guide (GSG) is a UK business focused on the consumer market, started by the Ethical Company Organisation in 2001.

It audits the ethical credentials of businesses that put themselves forward under the headings of environment, people, animals and other. It publishes the ratings of the top 200 ethical businesses every year.

Case study – Aviva plc[19]

Aviva is an active member of the UN Global Compact, accredited under the Good Business Charter and highly rated in the Good Shopping Guide.

It is a major insurance company based in the UK. It is listed on the London Stock Exchange and is one of the largest 100 companies in the FTSE100. It has 20.5 million customers mainly in the UK, Ireland and Canada, with a turnover of £22.4 billion and about 26,000 employees.

It has evolved through a number of mergers and acquisitions dating back to the start of the first industrial revolution in 1696.[20]

Aviva's purpose is 'with you today for a better tomorrow' with a strategy under four headings:

- **Growth** – accelerating growth in capital-light Wealth and Insurance, disciplined in Retirement.
- **Customer** – growing our customer base, serving more needs and transforming experience.
- **Efficiency** – driving operating leverage with technology and artificial intelligence at the core.
- **Sustainability** – committed to climate and social action, and being a sustainable business.

This is underpinned by four values:

- **Care** – we care deeply about the positive difference we can make in our customers' lives.
- **Commitment** – we understand the impact we have on the world and take the responsibility that comes with it seriously.
- **Community** – we recognise the strength that comes from working as one team, built on trust and respect.
- **Confidence** – we believe the best is yet to come for our customers, our people and society.

> Speaking with David Schofield, Aviva's sustainability director, the commitment to climate and social action comes from three centuries of seeing the business as part of, not separate from, the communities it serves. It is also enlightened self-interest, helping Aviva understand the unmet needs of current and future customers, and build a 'go to' trusted brand – overall, it's a good long-term investment.
>
> Aviva committed to being a Living Wage employer in 2014, later adding Living Hours and Living Pension commitments.[21] These were particularly significant for its employees in the UK's cost of living challenges from 2021 when basic living costs grew faster than wages, disproportionately affecting the lowest paid.
>
> In 2021, Aviva was the first insurance company to secure Good Business Charter accreditation[22] and the first major global insurer to commit to net-zero carbon emissions by 2040.
>
> When considering frameworks and kitemarks, David Schofield looks to drive practical impact that both helps Aviva improve performance and demonstrate its ethics in action. For example, the Living Wage commitment increased wages for the lowest paid, and having ethical accreditation in the Good Shopping Guide,[23] where Aviva is in the top 200 ethical businesses, has a positive impact on customer trust.
>
> The majority of consumers continue to expect businesses to act responsibly in light of the challenges we all face.[24] David explains, 'Glib messages about climate and social action run the risk of oversimplification. We are serious about systemic risks and opportunities and need to explain them with care, so stakeholders understand what we are doing and why it's important for our customers and for the long-term success of our business.'
>
> Aviva's broader actions to support system change in this area include membership of the Institute of Business Ethics and support for smaller businesses to meet the Living Wage commitment, through Aviva's supply chain and a business community pilot in the North-East of England. David also chairs the UN Global Compact Network in the UK.

Cradle to Cradle[25]

Cradle to Cradle is a US-registered non-profit organisation started in 2010 to support the shift to a circular economy. It provides product certification to over 500 businesses and 70,000 products globally, grading them at one of four levels – platinum, gold, silver and bronze.

Stakeholder feedback

Customer and employee feedback from Google, Facebook, Tripadvisor, Trustpilot, Indeed, Glassdoor and other individual-facing rating services are also becoming de facto standards from customers' and employees' viewpoint.

What is the role of professional standards?

Professional standards play a key role supporting and challenging ethical behaviour and culture. Individuals who are both employees and members of a professional body, for example lawyers, accountants and governance professionals, have a dual obligation to their employer and the standards of their profession.

The role of governance, ethics and compliance professionals has changed significantly in the last 20 years. Increased public and regulatory scrutiny, as well as prioritisation of ethical standards, means the role typically has more breadth, responsibility and focus on organisational culture. The 2025 report on 'The Importance of Values for Governance'[26] by the Worshipful Company of Chartered Secretaries and Administrators (WCCSA) and Leeds Beckett University explains: 'Understanding the culture and values of organisations and how they can truly be lived across the entire organisation is an increasingly important pre-requisite of effective governance.'

Key professional organisations include the Chartered Governance Institute, based in the UK with a global network of 40,000 members,[27] the Ethics and Compliance Officer Association, based in the USA with over 1,000 members globally[28] and the Ethics and Compliance Initiative in the USA.[29]

Other professions are also having to adapt. Speaking to Malcolm Bacchus, president of the Institute of Chartered Accountants in England and Wales (ICAEW), he said, 'Ethics are not always served by more rules, they must be proportionate.' The ICAEW Code of Ethics[30] reflects this with five principles – integrity, objectivity, professional competence and due care, confidentiality and professional behaviour – alongside specific rules on gifts and separation of audit and advisory services. Malcolm also talked about 'ethical pain thresholds': 'The chief financial officer (CFO) is often regarded as gatekeeper of the company's conscience because of their code of professional ethics. They should have a lower ethical pain threshold than other executive colleagues. Non-executive directors, and the chair in particular, have similar obligations. They are a key route for whistleblowers, must avoid 'groupthink' and confirmation bias and be prepared to challenge, calling on root-cause analysis when necessary.'

Professional bodies also provide confidential ways of exploring ethical dilemmas, such as the Institute of Accountants of Scotland (ICAS) 'Ethics Buddy' service.[31] Speaking to James Barbour, director of Policy Leadership at ICAS, he highlighted 'moral courage' as a key enabler, explained in the ICAS Cose of Ethics as 'the need to act in accordance with the fundamental principles, especially in situations where there is risk of suffering adverse personal consequences'.

Conclusion

The market in non-government kitemarking and support for ethical performance is growing in response to business and consumer demand.

Well-established systems, such as ISO Standards and professional bodies, are adapting and new civil regulations, such as Living Wage, are growing out of grassroots initiatives.

The challenge for businesses of all sizes is to choose the most relevant standards to help them improve ethical performance and stand out in the market.

Questions

- Which ethical standards would provide most benefit to your organisation?
- Do your competitors use standards to demonstrate their ethical credentials?
- Do employees who belong to professional bodies make active use of their ethical codes?

Notes

1 See: https://www.bcorporation.net/en-us/.
2 See: https://www.bcorporation.net/en-us/news/blog/b-lab-new-standards-impact-topic-purpose-stakeholder-governance/.
3 See: https://www.patagonia.com/home/; Chouinard, Y. (2016) *Let My People Go Surfing*.
4 See: https://eu.patagonia.com/gb/en/actionworks/about/.
5 See: https://www.iso.org/home.html.

19 NON-GOVERNMENT STANDARDS

6. See: https://environment.ec.europa.eu/topics/circular-economy/eu-ecolabel_en.
7. See: https://www.anglianwater.co.uk/corporate/ and author's interview with Andy Brown, group chief sustainability officer, Anglian Water Group.
8. See: https://www.lrwt.org.uk/rutlandospreys.
9. See: https://www.ft.com/content/68b26566-5bf7-11e7-b553-e2df1b0c3220.
10. See: https://www.bsigroup.com/en-GB/insights-and-media/insights/brochures/pas-808-purpose-driven-organizations-for-delivering-sustainability/.
11. See: https://www.iso.org/standard/86112.html.
12. See: https://betterbusinessact.org.
13. See: https://www.fairtrade.org.uk.
14. See: https://www.livingwage.org.uk.
15. See: https://www.citizensuk.org.
16. See: https://www.livingwage.org.uk/real-living-wage-civil-regulation-assessment.
17. See: https://goodbusinesscharter.com/what-is-the-good-business-charter/.
18. See: https://thegoodshoppingguide.com/how-we-rate/.
19. See: https://www.aviva.com/investors/annual-report/ and author's interview with David Schofield, sustainability director, Aviva plc.
20. See: https://clicktime.symantec.com/15w2KP5Qa37epVFrABvPE?h=dxC1mnUBFvtTJLMb16qa6aKNcM8RuLttiQbUOoYltxI=&u=https://web.archive.org/web/20120917194123/http://www.aviva.com/about-us/heritage/events-timeline/non-flash/.
21. See: https://www.livingwage.org.uk.
22. See: https://goodbusinesscharter.com/our-10-components/.
23. See: https://thegoodshoppingguide.com/brand-directory/aviva-insurance/.
24. See: https://clicktime.symantec.com/15w2QDGh2eoFES5mhkKXr?h=EPzJEPtDHSrrM9MZHk0sgf7DIMRr-JEclOXoiCyBnw8=&u=https://www.ipsos.com/en/people-and-climate-change.
25. See: https://c2ccertified.org/certified-products.
26. See: https://www.leedsbeckett.ac.uk/research/sustainable-business-research-institute/importance-of-values-for-governance/.
27. See: https://cgi.org.uk/about-us/.
28. See: http://ecoass.org.
29. See: https://www.ethics.org.
30. See: https://www.icaew.com/technical/trust-and-ethics/ethics/code-of-ethics.
31. See: https://www.icas.com/regulation-technical-resources/regulation/ethics/ethics-buddy-service.

chapter 20

Making a positive impact

'The future can't be predicted,
but it can be envisioned and brought
lovingly into being.'

Donella Meadows

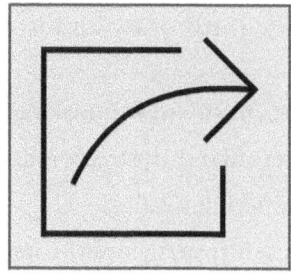

This final chapter invites you to take action.

It brings together:

- Key networks you can join to learn and collaborate outside your organisation
- Further reading
- All the toolkits in one place to make a positive impact

Key networks

Learning and development for leaders is a practical endeavour. Work by Morgan McCall, Michael Lombardo and Robert Eichinger[1] uncovered the 70:20:10 model of learning in executive development where:

- 70% of learning comes from practical experience, projects and trial and error
- 20% comes from networks, team interactions and professional relationships
- 10% comes from training, coursework and reading.

The leaders I spoke to are members of networks, learning with other leaders and influencing system change beyond their organisation.

There are myriad organisations that provide rich opportunities to learn and influence, including standard-setting and certifying organisations, described in Chapter 19, and professional bodies.

The following are other key non-profit organisations and networks where you can share and influence best practice:

- Blueprint for Better Business (https://www.blueprintforbusiness.org)
- Business in the Community (BITC) (https://www.bitc.org.uk)
- Business Roundtable (https://www.businessroundtable.org)
- Chambers of Commerce (https://www.britishchambers.org.uk; https://www.uschamber.com)
- Future Fit Business (https://futurefitbusiness.org/about-us/)
- Institute of Business Ethics (IBE) (https://www.ibe.org.uk)
- Net Impact (https://www.netimpact.org)
- Society for Business Ethics (https://sbeonline.org)
- Tomorrow's Company (https://www.tomorrowscompany.com)
- UN Global Compact (https://unglobalcompact.org/about)
- 1% For The Planet (https://www.onepercentfortheplanet.org/about/story; https://www.forbes.com/sites/afdhelaziz/2023/05/09/how-businesses-and-individuals-are-leading-the-way-with-1-for-the-planet-in-environmental-giving/).

Further reading

Business ethics

Black, L. (2023) *How to Lead with Purpose*.

Carney, M. (2021) *Value(s)*. William Collins.

Chouinard, Y. (2016) *Let My People Go Surfing*.

Edmans, A. (2020) *Grow The Pie*.

Elkington, J. (1997) *Cannibals with Forks*.

Elkington, J. (2024) *Tickling Sharks, How We Sold Business On Sustainability*.

Garrett, J. (2023) *Equality vs Equity*.

Greasley, D. and Alderson, R. (2025) *Integrity Etc*.

Jennings, M. (2018) *Valuable*.

Luckerath-Rovers, M. (2023) *Moral Dilemmas in the Boardroom*.

Mackey, J. and Sisodia, R. (2014) *Conscious Capitalism*.

Nelson, J.S. and Stout, L.A. (2022) *Business Ethics*.

O'Brien, J. and Cave, A. (2017) *The Power of Purpose*.

Palazzo, G. and Hoffrage, U. (2025) *The Dark Pattern, The Hidden Dynamics of Corporate Scandals*.

Richer, R. (2018) *The Ethical Capitalist*.

Richer, J. (2017) *The Richer Way*.

Rozenthuler, S. (2024) *Now We're Talking*.

Rozenthuler, S. (2020) *Powered by Purpose*.

Seldon, A. (2009) *Trust*.

Sisodia, R., Wolfe, D. and Sheth, J. (2014) Firms of Endearment, 2nd edition.

Spencer-Cooke, A. and van Dijk, F. (2015) *Creating a Culture of Integrity*.

Steare, R. (2019) *Ethicability*.

Taylor, A. (2024) *Higher Ground*.

Wallis, N. (2021) *The Post Office Scandal*.

Economics

Hickel, J. (2020) *Less is More*.

Kay, J. (2024) *The Corporation in the 21st Century*.

Marx, K. and Engels, F. (1888) *The Communist Manifesto*.

Keynes, J.M. (1936) *The General Theory of Employment Interest and Money*. Atlantic Publishers (2016).

O'Rourke, P.J. (2007) *On The Wealth of Nations*. Raworth, K. (2022) *Doughnut Economics*.

Sandel, M. (2012) *What Money Can't Buy*.

Smith, A. (1776) *The Wealth of Nations*.

Stiglitz, J. (2024) *The Road to Freedom*.

Philosophy

Buxton, R. and Whiting, L. (2020) *The Philosopher Queens* (eds).

Hall, E. (2018) *Aristotle's Way*.

Rawls, J. (1971) *A Theory of Justice*.

Smith, A. (1759) *The Theory of Moral Sentiments*.

Psychology

Brown, B. (2018) *Dare to Lead*.

Haidt, J. (2012) *The Righteous Mind*.

Kahneman, D. (2012) *Thinking, Fast and Slow*.

Lindeblad, B.N. (2022) *I May Be Wrong*.

All the toolkits

All the toolkits are presented together in this section.

Toolkit A: Ethical decision making
How do you apply the key ethical principles to decisions?

Toolkit B: Ethical health
What is the ethical health of your organisation?

Toolkit C: The natural environment
What is your organisation's responsibility for the natural environment?

Toolkit D: Social equity
What is your organisation's responsibility for social equity?

Toolkit E: Emerging technology
What is your organisation's responsibility for applying emerging technology?

Toolkit F: The Ethical Compass (ETHIC)
How do you apply the Ethical Compass?

Toolkit G: Ethical culture (employer viewpoint)
How can you improve your organisation's culture?

Toolkit H: Improving ethical practice (ILEAP: employee viewpoint)
How do you influence ethical practice as an employee?

Note

1 See: https://www.ccl.org/articles/leading-effectively-articles/70-20-10-rule/.

Toolkit A: Ethical decision-making

How do you apply the key ethical principles to decisions?

Every leader and organisation face ethical dilemmas in their decisions and builds a reputation on their response.

This toolkit is in two sections – process and principles. It supports and challenges decision-makers, helping meet their responsibility to make well-balanced decisions ethically and commercially. You should adapt it to complement your organisation's policies and processes.

How to use the toolkit

Section 1 is for the person leading the decision-making process to ensure it is effective.

Score it individually or as a small group and ensure you have evidence for each score.

A total score of 60 or more provides a high level of confidence.

A score of 40–60 shows that there are significant areas which need improving.

A score below 40 indicates that a systemic change may be needed to get to a reliable decision.

In any case, the scores against each individual question will highlight individual areas to improve.

Section 2 is for individuals involved in the decision to complete to ensure ethical rigour.

Dilemmas will rarely score a maximum of 12 marked 'yes', a score of 9 or more is sound.

The discussion about areas of disagreement or improvement are more important than the score.

Section 1 – Process

Heading	Key Process Questions Ratings: 4 very high, 3 high, 2 medium, 1 low	Level of confidence Rate 1–4
Diagnose the problem	1. How well defined is the problem and its measure of success? 2. How will it contribute to our long-term purpose? 3. Which stakeholders are affected? 4. What are the commercial and ethical dilemmas? 5. What is needed to reach a balanced decision?	
Apply due process	6. Who is accountable for the decision? 7. Who should be involved to reduce bias? 8. Which process and regulations should be applied? 9. What are the inputs and assessments of risk? 10. Which organisational values apply?	
Evaluate benefits, costs and options	11. How well have ethical principles been applied? (Section 2) 12. How can risks be reduced or eliminated? 13. Which options maximise long-term impact? 14. How effectively have options been weighed up? 15. What is the right decision?	
Follow-through, explain and learn	16. Who is affected and needs to know the decision? 17. How do we explain how and why we made the decision? 18. How do we ensure we deliver the intended impact? 19. What adjustments should we make during implementation? 20. What can we learn for future decisions?	
Total Score		**Max 80**

Section 2 – Principles

Everyone involved in the decision can test their conscience as follows in order, to decide whether ethical principles have been applied effectively, i.e. to answer Question 11 above. This can also be used as a standalone toolkit for personal dilemmas.

Key Questions of Principle See Chapter 1 for definitions of the four key principles	Yes/No
Integrity – honesty, self-control, accountability	
1. Would you want someone else to copy your decision?	
2. Would you make the same decision if it was openly published?	
3. Have you followed due process including consultation and taking advice?	
Duty – commitment to the common good	
4. If everyone did the same as you, would it serve the common good?	
5. Are you observing recognised laws, regulations and norms?	
6. Are you focused on the common good despite organisational/personal loyalties?	
Fairness – compassion, care, justice	
7. Have you thought through the benefits and costs with validated information?	
8. Will you achieve the greatest benefit for the greatest number of people?	
9. Have you adjusted to compensate for others' disadvantage or vulnerability?	
Freedom – autonomy, enlightened self-interest, imagination	
10. Have you been courageous enough?	
11. Have you taken account of risks to you and those close to you?	
12. Have you applied imagination to maximise benefit and avoid compromise?	
Total 'Yes'	Max 12

A dilemma is, by definition, likely to have some questions answered 'no'.

Consider changing your decision in response to any 'no' answers, particularly if your score is below 10.

Note: the effectiveness of the toolkit depends on how rigorously you apply it and follow through.

Toolkit B: Ethical health

What is the ethical health of your organisation?

Background

This toolkit will help you assess ethical health at a high level. You should adapt it to complement your organisation's policies and processes.

Organisations demonstrate ethical behaviour in three broad categories. Some businesses demonstrate all three depending on the context.

1. Consistency – complying with commitments and regulations.

   The organisation meets its obligations to legal and good practice, for example protecting the safety and rights of employees and meeting its quality and service commitments to customers and other stakeholders. If it falls short of its commitments, it accepts responsibility and takes compensating action. It builds a reputation for doing what it says it is going to do.

2. Conscience – going beyond obligations to do what is right.

   The organisation goes beyond legal and contractual obligations by observing principles which define an 'organisational conscience'. It treats stakeholders with care and compassion even if that incurs additional short-term costs or uncomfortable truths. For example, it may provide assistance to employees or suppliers experiencing hardship. It builds long term relationships, guided more by shared purpose than contractual terms.

3. Cause – pursuing system change for a cause beyond the organisation.

   The organisation applies pressure externally for an ethical cause, while living by its principles inside the business. It may include activism to raise awareness, lobbying for more rigorous regulation and collaborating on voluntary standards. It builds a reputation for moral courage.

How to use the toolkit

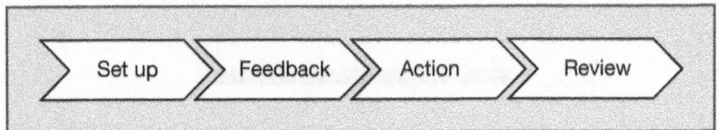

- **Set up with colleagues**
    - Discuss the toolkit with a cross-section of colleagues, ideally at a time when you are planning next year's priorities or the long-term strategy.
    - Work out how this toolkit can benefit the business, for example reinforcement of values, stakeholder trust and risk reduction.
- **Gather feedback**
    - Ask a group of colleagues to complete the toolkit including examples to back up their answers. If you think colleagues will answer more honestly by completing it anonymously then set up an online poll to collect anonymous answers.
- **Take action**
    - Review the feedback as a group and identify strengths and areas to improve.
    - Identify actions to make improvements, use the other toolkits in this book if necessary.
    - Assign responsibilities and follow through.
- **Review the impact**
    - Revisit this toolkit when you have planned or made changes to test the effect on your scores.
    - Take action to improve further.

Note: the effectiveness of the toolkit depends on how rigorously you apply it and follow through.

Ethical Health Questions Ratings: 4 consistently/always, 3 often, 2 sometimes, 1 rarely/never	Rate 1–4	Evidence
Consistency		
1. Does the organisation deliver on its commitments?		
2. Does this create competitive advantage?		
Conscience		
3. Are the values (or principles or ethics) clearly understood?		
4. Do values take priority over rules when necessary?		
5. Are customers more loyal because of the values?		
6. Are employees attracted and retained by the values?		
7. Are suppliers more loyal because of the values?		
8. Do the values create competitive advantage overall?		
Cause		
9. Does the organisation stand for an ethical cause or causes?		
10. Is the organisation respected for moral courage?		
Total Score	**Max 40**	
Notes: ● Answer these from either the viewpoint of the whole organisation or of a division or team. ● This refers to 'values', it works equally well referring to 'principles' or 'ethics'.		

Answer the questions individually, validate the evidence as a group, discuss and agree a score for each of the 10 questions, then add them up (maximum 40).

Total Score	How to improve ethical health
30–40	The organisation has sound ethical health. Consider whether there are any areas to improve, in particular if the competitive advantage is not consistently high.
20–30	The organisation can improve its ethical health. Use the other toolkits in this book or other methods to identify specific areas to work on further.
Below 20	The organisation is carrying ethical risks or missing out on ethical potential or both. Use the other toolkits in this book or other methods to identify areas where work can start to develop ethical health.

Toolkit C: The natural environment

What is your organisation's responsibility for the natural environment?

This toolkit enables you to create or test your organisation's plans. You should adapt it to complement your organisation's policies and processes.

How to use the toolkit

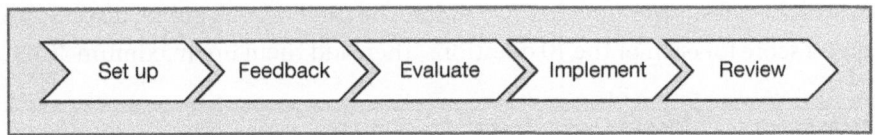

- **Set up with colleagues**
  - Discuss the toolkit with a cross-section of colleagues, ideally at a time when you are planning next year's priorities or the long-term strategy.
  - Work out how this toolkit can benefit the business, for example reinforcement of values, stakeholder trust and risk reduction.
- **Gather feedback**
  - Ask a group of colleagues to complete the toolkit including examples and evidence to back up their answers. If you think colleagues will answer more honestly by completing it anonymously then set up an online poll to collect anonymous answers.

- If the feedback identifies key risks 'which are hard to discuss', consider creating an independent review. It may need to report to a governance director or senior independent non-executive director to ensure objectivity.
- **Evaluate actions**
  - Review the feedback as a group and identify strengths and areas to improve, looking at case studies in this book for inspiration if necessary.
  - Identify actions to make improvements.
  - Evaluate each action against potential benefits, costs and risks, then rank the actions in order of net benefit. Decide which actions to take forward and which to drop or defer.

  Note: Use your organisation's normal project evaluation process; if you do not have one, use the *Benefits Scoring Matrix* below.
- **Implement**
  - Identify risks and enablers and who needs to be consulted and directly involved to achieve the benefits, reduce risks and unlock the resources to deliver the changes.
  - Secure commitment to make changes based on the actions which achieve greatest benefit.
  - If costs and investment are required, secure the budget required.
  - Assign responsibilities and follow through.
- **Review the impact**
  - Revisit the impact of your actions.
  - Take action to improve further.

Benefits Scoring Matrix (if needed)

Heading	Ethical	Financial	Total
Benefits (eg Low = 1)	1–4	1–4	2–8
Costs & Risks (eg Low = 4)	1–4	1–4	2–8
Total	2–8	2–8	4–16

- Use judgement to decide criteria for 'Very High', 'High', 'Medium' and 'Low'.
  - Use your stated purpose (or mission), values and behaviours as criteria for the ethical column. If you do not have these, use 'stakeholder trust' as a proxy.

- Score 'Benefits' as Very High 4, High 3, Medium 2, Low 1
- Score 'Costs & Risks' as Low 4, Medium 3, High 2, Very High 1
- Add up total scores in the right-hand column, out of a maximum of 16
- Rank the highest scoring action at the top and the lowest scoring at the bottom.

Note: the effectiveness of the toolkit depends on how rigorously you apply it and follow through.

The Natural Environment Ratings: 4 very high, 3 high, 2 medium, 1 low	Priority Rate 1–4	Current Effectiveness Rate 1–4	Action to Improve Effectiveness
Process			
Strategy and Planning • Set environmental strategy and principles • Evaluate benefits, ethics, costs, risks and impact • Prioritise against overall purpose and values • Set targets including emissions • Join external collaborative networks • Regularly review against best practice			
Governance and Compliance [Note 1] • Agree governance and oversight process • Understand and comply with regulations • Determine external review or audit process • Report against benefits, costs, risks and impact			
Management & Reporting • Assign responsibilities, targets and resources • Set operational processes and controls • Manage performance and risks • Track and report benefits, costs, risks and impact • Learn and improve against best practice			

The Natural Environment Ratings: 4 very high, 3 high, 2 medium, 1 low	Priority Rate 1–4	Current Effectiveness Rate 1–4	Action to Improve Effectiveness
Engagement and Training • Consult and communicate with stakeholders • Inform and train employees and suppliers • Set performance incentives and sanctions • Publish and promote plans and performance			
Actions			
Energy and Resources • Reduce emissions overall • Improve efficiency and insulation of property • Increase renewable energy sources • Increase use of biofuels • Reduce travel • Increase locally sourced suppliers			
Waste, Pollution and Circular Economy • Reduce waste and pollution overall • Apply 9R [Note 2] principles • Reduce production waste • Reduce packaging • Reduce use of non-recycled material • Reduce use of consumables eg paper, ink • Increase water conservation • Segregate and recycle waste			
Biodiversity • Source animal and plant supplies sustainably • Increase sustainability of business-owned land, plants and animals			

The Natural Environment Ratings: 4 very high, 3 high, 2 medium, 1 low	Priority Rate 1–4	Current Effectiveness Rate 1–4	Action to Improve Effectiveness
Supply Chain and Distribution Channels • Set standards for suppliers and partners • Adapt procurement and partnering criteria • Set performance incentives and sanctions • Manage performance and risks			
Note 1: See Chapters 18 and 19 for information on ESG-related regulations and voluntary standards. *Note 2:* The 9Rs of the circular economy comprise 10 strategies numbered 0–9; they are: Refuse, Rethink, Reduce, Reuse, Repair, Refurbish, Remanufacture, Repurpose, Recyle and Recover[1]			

Note

1 https://www.weforum.org/stories/2022/05/the-circular-economy-how-it-can-be-a-path-to-real-change/

Toolkit D: Social equity

What is your organisation's responsibility for social equity?

This toolkit enables you to create or test your organisation's plans. You should adapt it to complement your organisation's policies and processes.

How to use the toolkit

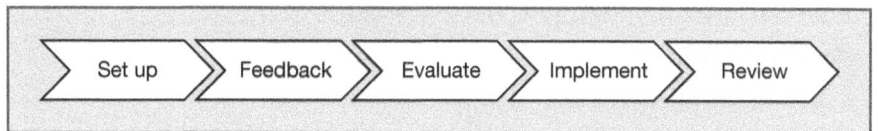

- **Set up with colleagues**
    - Discuss the toolkit with a cross-section of colleagues, ideally at a time when you are planning next year's priorities or the long-term strategy.
    - Work out how this toolkit can benefit the business, for example reinforcement of values, stakeholder trust and risk reduction.
- **Gather feedback**
    - Ask a group of colleagues to complete the toolkit including examples and evidence to back up their answers. If you think colleagues will answer more honestly by completing it anonymously then set up an online poll to collect anonymous answers.
    - If the feedback identifies key risks 'which are hard to discuss', consider creating an independent review. It may need to report to a governance director or senior independent non-executive director to ensure objectivity.

- **Evaluate actions**
  - Review the feedback as a group and identify strengths and areas to improve, looking at case studies in this book for inspiration if necessary.
  - Identify actions to make improvements.
  - Evaluate each action against potential benefits, costs and risks, then rank the actions in order of net benefit. Decide which actions to take forward and which to drop or defer.

  Note: Use your organisation's normal project evaluation process; if you do not have one, use the *Benefits Scoring Matrix* below.

- **Implement**
  - Identify risks and enablers and who needs to be consulted and directly involved to achieve the benefits, reduce risks and unlock the resources to deliver the changes.
  - Secure commitment to make changes based on the actions which achieve greatest benefit.
  - If costs and investment are required, secure the budget required.
  - Assign responsibilities and follow through.

- **Review the impact**
  - Revisit the impact of your actions.
  - Take action to improve further.

Benefits Scoring Matrix (if needed)

Heading	Ethical	Financial	Total
Benefits (eg Low = 1)	1–4	1–4	2–8
Costs & Risks (eg Low = 4)	1–4	1–4	2–8
Total	2–8	2–8	4–16

- Use judgement to decide criteria for 'Very High', 'High', 'Medium' and 'Low'.
- Use your stated purpose (or mission), values and behaviours as criteria for the ethical column. If you do not have these, use 'stakeholder trust' as a proxy.
- Score 'Benefits' as Very High 4, High 3, Medium 2, Low 1.
- Score 'Costs & Risks' as Low 4, Medium 3, High 2, Very High 1.
- Add up total scores in the right-hand column, out of a maximum of 16.

- Rank the highest scoring action at the top and the lowest scoring at the bottom.

Note: the effectiveness of the toolkit depends on how rigorously you apply it and follow through.

Social Equity Ratings: 4 very high, 3 high, 2 medium, 1 low	Priority Rate 1–4	Current Effectiveness Rate 1–4	Actions to Improve Effectiveness
Process			
Strategy and Planning - Set social equity strategy and principles - Evaluate benefits, ethics, costs, risks and impact - Prioritise against overall purpose and values - Set targets - Regularly review against best practice			
Governance and Compliance - Agree governance and oversight process - Understand and comply with regulations - Determine external review or audit process - Report against benefits, costs, risks and impact			
Management and Reporting - Assign responsibilities, targets and resources - Set operational processes and controls - Manage performance and risks - Track and report benefits, costs, risks and impact - Learn and improve against best practice			
Engagement and Training - Consult with employees and communities - Develop regular dialogue and feedback - Inform and train managers and employees - Publish plans, targets and performance			

▶

Social Equity Ratings: 4 very high, 3 high, 2 medium, 1 low	Priority Rate 1–4	Current Effectiveness Rate 1–4	Actions to Improve Effectiveness
Actions – diversity, equity and inclusion of…			
Employees … hiring of new employees … pay and incentives … promotions … support and development of skills and health … access for disabled			
Communities … engagement with relevant [Note 1] communities			
Customers … adaptation of products and services			
Supply Chain and Distribution Channels … procurement and partnering criteria … performance incentives and standards … performance and risks			
Note 1: 'relevant' means local or related to the sector in which the business operates.			

Toolkit E: Emerging technology

What is your organisation's responsibility for applying emerging technology?

This toolkit enables you to create or test your organisation's plans. You should adapt it to complement your organisation's policies and processes.

How to use the toolkit

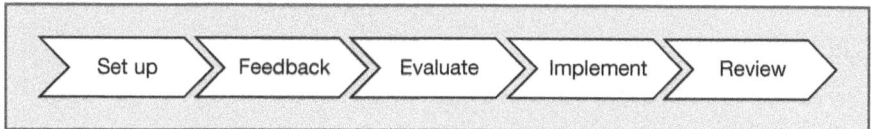

- **Set up with colleagues**
  - Discuss the toolkit with a cross-section of colleagues, ideally at a time when you are planning next year's priorities or the long-term strategy.
  - Work out how this toolkit can benefit the business, for example reinforcement of values, stakeholder trust and risk reduction.
- **Gather feedback**
  - Ask a group of colleagues to complete the toolkit including examples and evidence to back up their answers. If you think colleagues will answer more honestly by completing it anonymously then set up an online poll to collect anonymous answers.
  - If the feedback identifies key risks 'which are hard to discuss', consider creating an independent review. It may need to report to a governance director or senior independent non-executive director to ensure objectivity.

- **Evaluate actions**
  - Review the feedback as a group and identify strengths and areas to improve, looking at case studies in this book for inspiration if necessary.
  - Identify actions to make improvements.
  - Evaluate each action against potential benefits, costs and risks, then rank the actions in order of net benefit. Decide which actions to take forward and which to drop or defer.
  - Note: Use your organisation's normal project evaluation process; if you do not have one, use the *Benefits Scoring Matrix* below.
- **Implement**
  - Identify risks and enablers and who needs to be consulted and directly involved to achieve the benefits, reduce risks and unlock the resources to deliver the changes.
  - Secure commitment to make changes based on the actions which achieve greatest benefit.
  - If costs and investment are required, secure the budget required.
  - Assign responsibilities and follow through.
- **Review the impact**
  - Revisit the impact of your actions.
  - Take action to improve further.

Benefits Scoring Matrix (if needed)

Heading	Ethical	Financial	Total
Benefits (eg Low = 1)	1–4	1–4	2–8
Costs & Risks (eg Low = 4)	1–4	1–4	2–8
Total	2–8	2–8	4–16

- Use judgement to decide criteria for 'Very High', 'High', 'Medium' and 'Low'.
  - Use your stated purpose (or mission), values and behaviours as criteria for the ethical column. If you do not have these, use 'stakeholder trust' as a proxy.
- Score 'Benefits' as Very High 4, High 3, Medium 2, Low 1
- Score 'Costs & Risks' as Low 4, Medium 3, High 2, Very High 1

- Add up total scores in the right-hand column, out of a maximum of 16
- Rank the highest scoring action at the top and the lowest scoring at the bottom.

Note: the effectiveness of the toolkit depends on how rigorously you apply it and follow through.

Emerging Technology Ratings: 4 very high, 3 high, 2 medium, 1 low	Priority Rate 1–4	Current Effectiveness Rate 1–4	Actions to Improve Effectiveness
Process			
Strategy and Planning • Set technology strategy and principles • Evaluate benefits, ethics, costs, risks and impact • Prioritise against overall purpose and values • Set targets • Regularly review against best practice			
Governance and Compliance • Agree governance and oversight process • Understand regulatory obligations • Determine external review or audit process • Report against benefits, costs, risks and impact			
Management and Reporting • Assign responsibilities, targets and resources • Set operational processes and controls • Manage performance and risks • Track and report benefits, costs, risks and impact • Learn and improve against best practice			
Engagement and Training • Consult and communicate with stakeholders • Inform and train employees, suppliers and partners			

▶

Emerging Technology Ratings: 4 very high, 3 high, 2 medium, 1 low	Priority Rate 1–4	Current Effectiveness Rate 1–4	Actions to Improve Effectiveness
Actions			
Purpose and Impact • Define purpose, ethics and benefits of each application • Communicate benefits and ethics to stakeholders • Test impact on employees and customers and adjust			
Accuracy and Fairness • Ensure outputs are accurate and consistent • Risk-assess limitations [Note 1] • Test outputs for bias and adjust • Ensure 'human in the loop' where necessary			
Accountability and Transparency • Visibly label use of technology to users • Openly report limitations of accuracy • Ensure human accountability for decisions • Provide clear channels for feedback and concerns			
Privacy and Safety • Set ethical standards • Comply with privacy, safety and mis-use standards • Test, report and improve compliance			
Note 1: 'Model Cards' are an example of a framework for providing transparent information about AI and machine learning models[1]			

Note

1 https://www.techtarget.com/whatis/definition/model-card-in-machine-learning

Toolkit F: The Ethical Compass (Ethic)

How do you apply the Ethical Compass?

Background

The 'Ethical Compass' is derived from the experience and insights of 50 leaders. It does not attempt to define right and wrong but supports and challenges an individual or team to develop an ethical direction. You should adapt it to complement your organisation's policies and processes.

The labels for the five challenges spell out the acronym ETHIC:

1 Empathy – how do you build trustful relationships with stakeholders?
2 Traction – how do you take an organisation with you and deliver?
3 Higher purpose – how do you create an ethical direction?
4 Ingenuity – how do you find ethical answers to business questions?
5 Courage – how do you find the courage to follow your conscience?

The five challenges help you build ethical practice into day-to-day actions. Each challenge relies on your leadership competence which can be learned and developed. It recognises that business ethics at its best is a team activity, fuelled by challenge, diversity of thought and ingenuity.

The following preparation is recommended to use this toolkit effectively:

- Complete Toolkit B (Ethical Health)
- Read Chapters 7–12.

The toolkit is in two sections.

- Section 1, Ethical Visibility, is for individuals to understand the visibility of your ethics as a leader.

- Section 2, The Ethical Compass, is a group exercise to help you work with your team on five challenges to make a greater impact as an organisation.

In both sections you are invited to test your scores with colleagues, look for evidence of impact and identify areas to developed further.

Section 1 – Ethical Visibility (as a leader)

Most of the leaders I have spoken to see themselves striving to be 'ethical'. However, the examples they give showed that it is often a tightrope between pressures of business performance and principles or, more subtly, competing principles.

Many businesses have ethical codes, often with regulatory obligations. This toolkit does not replace those codes but focuses on leadership behaviour and visibility of ethics in day-to-day work.

How to use the toolkit

The group who will work together on section 2 should also complete this 10-point questionnaire individually, to establish the visibility of your ethics (or values or principles) as a leader. To get a rigorous result, look for evidence or validation from colleagues for each of your scores.

Section 1 Ethical Visibility (as a leader) Ratings: 4 consistently/always, 3 often, 2 sometimes, 1 rarely/never	Rating 1–4	Evidence
1. Do you consider the ethical impact you make as a leader?		
2. Do colleagues see you as a values-driven leader?		
3. Do you prioritise values above short-term profit when necessary?		
4. Do you share stories of other people putting values into action?		
5. Do you formally recognise colleagues who demonstrate values?		
6. Do you discuss and debate values with key stakeholders?		
7. Do you call out colleagues who do not meet your values?		
8. Do you include values in hiring decisions and appraisals?		
9. Do you learn about better ways of applying values?		
10. Do you apply values in the same way whether in or out of work?		
Total Score	**Max 40**	
Note: for these purposes 'ethics', 'values' or 'principles' can be used interchangeably.		

Total Score	How to make your values (or ethics or principles) more visible
30–40	Your values have high visibility. Consider whether there are any areas to improve and how you can support colleagues in their ethical development.
20–30	You can improve the visibility of your values from a sound starting point. Use Section 2 of this toolkit to identify specific areas to work on and consider pairing up with a colleague to encourage each other.
Below 20	You can improve the visibility of your values from a low starting point. Use Section 2 this toolkit to identify specific areas to work on and consider working with a mentor or coach to develop this aspect of your leadership.

Section 2 – How to apply The Ethical Compass (as an organisation)

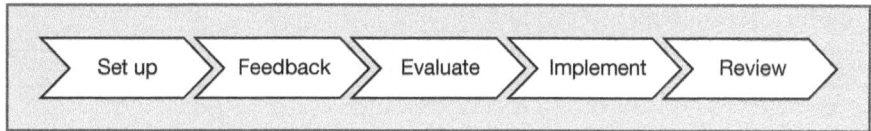

- **Set up with colleagues**
  - Discuss the toolkit with your team, ideally at a time when you are planning next year's priorities or the long-term strategy.
  - Work out how this toolkit can benefit the business for example reinforcement of values, stakeholder trust and risk reduction.
- **Gather feedback**
  - Ask your team to complete the toolkit including examples and evidence to back up their answers. If you think colleagues will answer more honestly by completing it anonymously then set up an online poll to collect anonymous answers.
- **Evaluate actions**
  - Review the feedback as a team and identify strengths and areas to improve, looking at case studies in this book for inspiration if necessary.
  - Identify actions to make improvements.
  - Evaluate each action against potential benefits, costs and risks, then rank the actions in order of net benefit. Decide which actions to take forward and which to drop or defer.
  - Note: Use your organisation's normal project evaluation process; if you do not have one, use the *Benefits Scoring Matrix* below.

- **Implement**
  - Identify risks and enablers and who needs to be consulted and directly involved to achieve the benefits, reduce risks and unlock the resources to deliver the changes.
  - Secure commitment to make changes based on the actions which achieve greatest benefit.
  - If costs and investment are required, secure the budget required.
  - Assign responsibilities and follow through.
- **Review the impact**
  - Revisit the impact of your actions.
  - Take action to improve further.

Benefits Scoring Matrix (if needed)

Heading	Ethical	Financial	Total
Benefits (eg Low = 1)	1–4	1–4	2–8
Costs & Risks (eg Low = 4)	1–4	1–4	2–8
Total	2–8	2–8	4–16

- Use judgement to decide criteria for 'Very High', 'High', 'Medium' and 'Low'.
  - Use your stated purpose (or mission), values and behaviours as criteria for the ethical column. If you do not have these, use 'stakeholder trust' as a proxy.
- Score 'Benefits' as Very High 4, High 3, Medium 2, Low 1
- Score 'Costs & Risks' as Low 4, Medium 3, High 2, Very High 1
- Add up total scores in the right-hand column, out of a maximum of 16
- Rank the highest scoring action at the top and the lowest scoring at the bottom.

Note: the effectiveness of the toolkit depends on how rigorously you apply it and follow through.

Section 2 The Ethical Compass (ETHIC)				
Challenge and Features (refer to Chapters 7–12)	Questions Ratings 4 very high, 3 high, 2 medium, 1 low (refer to Toolkit B)		Rating 1–4	Potential Actions

Section 2 The Ethical Compass (ETHIC)			
Empathy Compassion Balance	How much trust and loyalty do our customers, employees, suppliers, shareholders and communities demonstrate?		
Traction Autonomy Rules	How consistent is our ethical and financial health across the organisation?		
Higher Purpose Authenticity Teamwork	How well is our purpose embedded in our products and services and what is our impact beyond the organisation?		
Ingenuity Incentives Imagination	How well do we find ingenious solutions to business problems which are both ethically and commercially sound?		
Courage Power Temptation	How well do we stand out as an ethically courageous and collaborative organisation?		
Total Score		**Max 20**	

Total Score	How to improve
15–20	Your leadership as a team is delivering effective ethical and business performance. Consider any areas which are inconsistent and need improving.
10–15	You can improve from a sound starting point. Identify and rank potential actions to make improvements.
Below 10	You can improve from a low starting point. Identify and rank potential actions to make improvements and consider systemic changes.

Toolkit G: Ethical culture (employer viewpoint)

How can you improve your organisation's culture?

This toolkit helps you apply the lessons from responsible cultures and business failures. The toolkit highlights the features of ethical cultures, which focus on building an 'organisational conscience' leading to long-term relationships. You should adapt it to complement your organisation's policies and processes.

How to use the toolkit

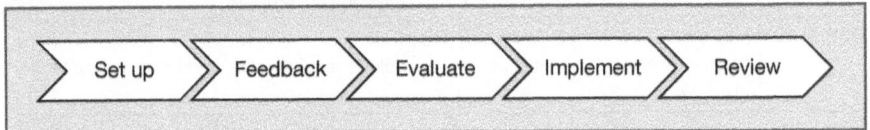

- **Set up with colleagues**
  - Discuss the toolkit with a cross-section of colleagues, ideally at a time when you are planning next year's priorities or the long-term strategy.
  - Work out how this toolkit can benefit the business, for example reinforcement of values, stakeholder trust and risk reduction.
- **Gather feedback**
  - Ask colleagues to propose potential improvements in the right-hand column, look at the examples given below and case studies in Chapter 14 for inspiration if necessary.

- **Evaluate actions**
  - Evaluate each proposed improvement against potential benefits, costs and risks, then rank the actions in order of net benefit. Decide which actions to take forward and which to drop or defer.
  - Note: Use your organisation's normal project evaluation process; if you do not have one, use the *Benefits Scoring Matrix* below.
- **Implement**
  - Identify risks and enablers and who needs to be consulted and directly involved to achieve the benefits, reduce risks and unlock the resources to deliver the changes.
  - Secure commitment to make changes based on the actions which achieve greatest benefit.
  - If costs and investment are required, secure the budget required.
  - Assign responsibilities and follow through.
- **Review the impact**
  - Revisit the impact of your actions.
  - Take action to improve further.

Benefits Scoring Matrix (if needed)

Heading	Ethical	Financial	Total
Benefits (eg Low = 1)	1–4	1–4	2–8
Costs & Risks (eg Low = 4)	1–4	1–4	2–8
Total	2–8	2–8	4–16

- Use judgement to decide criteria for 'Very High', 'High', 'Medium' and 'Low'.
  - Use your stated purpose (or mission), values and behaviours as criteria for the ethical column. If you do not have these, use 'stakeholder trust' as a proxy.
- Score 'Benefits' as Very High 4, High 3, Medium 2, Low 1
- Score 'Costs & Risks' as Low 4, Medium 3, High 2, Very High 1
- Add up total scores in the right-hand column, out of a maximum of 16
- Rank the highest scoring action at the top and the lowest scoring at the bottom.

Note: the effectiveness of the toolkit depends on how rigorously you apply it and follow through.

Ethical culture (employer viewpoint)

Feature	Leading with consistency	Leading with conscience	Improvements
1 Products and services	Reliable	...and considerate	
2 Suppliers and partners	Reliable	...and considerate	
3 Speaking up	Safe ways of reporting concerns	...and visible action on breaches of values	
4 Interaction with leaders	Regular communications	...and consult on key decisions	
5 Recruitment of employees	Test for competence	...and for potential and mindset	
6 Employee support and development	Focus on knowledge, skills and behaviour	...and wellbeing and career development	
7 Pay, terms and conditions	Clear and transparent	...and flexible	
8 Employee recognition and incentives	Based on personal performance	Based on team performance	
9 Ethical codes and procedures	Clear rules	...and autonomy to 'do the right thing'	
10 Support charitable causes	Limited	Paid time off	

Examples from cultures with an 'organisational conscience':

Feature	
1 Products and services	Free repairs on products returned, with no time limit
2 Suppliers and Partners	Increasing prices paid to suppliers to enable payment of living wages to their employees
3 Speaking up	Paying rewards for valid concerns raised
4 Interaction with leaders	C-suite leaders hold a meaningful dialogue with all employees every month and meaningful union representation
5 Recruitment of employees	Example question: What do you do to support your local community or care for people in need?
6 Employee support and development	Employees have a regular review of their long-term ambitions, prospects and well-being
7 Pay, terms and conditions	Duration of sick pay is determined case by case with no upper limit

8 Employee recognition and incentives	No sales commission, profits shared among all employees
9 Ethical code and procedures	Do what is right and seek forgiveness not permission
10 Support charitable causes	All employees have two paid days off work every year to support a charitable cause

Toolkit H: Improving ethical practice (ILEAP) – employee viewpoint

How do you influence ethical practice as an employee?

This toolkit is a guide to help you make proposals to influence and improve ethical practice. It is **NOT** suitable for whistleblowing about potential corruption (see Chapter 16).

It does not attempt to define right and wrong but supports and challenges you to make a positive impact when you are not in a position of authority. It has five stages under the acronym ILEAP:

1 Idea – turn your idea into a proposal.
2 Learning – test and improve the proposal.
3 Evaluation – add rigour and ingenuity.
4 Allies – find supporting allies.
5 Persuasion – apply leverage.

How to use the toolkit

- Read Chapter 16 before applying the toolkit.
- Go through each step in turn.
- Repeat Steps 1, 2, 3 and 4 if your proposal is complex or fails to attract support.

- Before committing to Step 5, weigh up the risks and benefits of going ahead.
- Whether you are successful or not, reflect on what you have learnt at the end of the process.

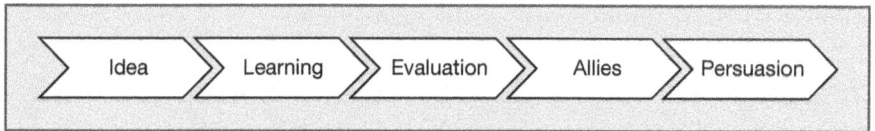

ILEAP	Improving Ethical Practice Note: **NOT** suitable for whistleblowing about potential corruption.	Employees are incentivised to sell insurance to new customers. Customers are starting to complain because they feel coerced. You want to find a way to improve customer trust.
Step	See Chapter 16	
1 Idea turn your idea into a proposal	Define the change you want to see and its impact.	Your initial idea is to reduce incentive scheme targets so that customer complaints reduce and trust in the organisation increases.
2 Learning test and improve the proposal	Test the proposal with others. Understand your motivation. Work on stakeholders' viewpoint. Improve the proposal.	You learn that the insurance product is profitable, some customers value the product, the emerging problem of customer complaints is not widely known. You change the proposal by keeping the incentive scheme but reducing the price to customers but less profitable for the business.
3 Evaluation add rigour and ingenuity	Understand the organisation's goals and where this fits. Work out benefits, costs, risks, barriers and enablers. Use imagination and ingenuity to improve further.	You find that the cost of insurance from your suppliers is too high, so it is possible to renegotiate terms to reduce the price to your customers and maintain the margin for your organisation.
4 Allies find supporting allies	Find allies to test and support your proposal. Let your proposal become part of a bigger change if the opportunity arises.	You find that another team is working on product structuring and pricing and agree to work together. By sharing your proposal, it is more likely to be agreed as part of a wider initiative to increase customer trust.
5 Persuasion apply leverage	Understand decision-makers' viewpoint to make your case. Follow organisational processes if appropriate. Call on support from allies.	The full proposal is put to the board, highlighting the organisation's value of 'being trustworthy'. Customer prices are reduced, supplier costs are reduced offset by higher volumes.
What did you learn?		

Part 4 Regulations, standards and impact: Quick read summary

Chapters 17–20 are summarised here in bullet points.

Chapter 17 Directors' duties and anti-corruption laws

- In most jurisdictions, directors broadly have a duty to act in the best interests of the company that employs them, although the details of their duties are not the same in all jurisdictions.
- Obligations to stakeholders, not just shareholders, are increasingly reflected either in law or in commonly accepted practice.
- Despite decades of increasing legal and ethical effort, corruption is more than 3% of the global economy. Aspects of anti-corruption enforcement in the USA has now been paused.
- Some regions and markets are still prone to corruption. There are ways of acting ethically and competitively in any case.

Chapter 18 The UN Global Compact, ESG and SDGs

- The United Nations (UN) has created a business network, the UN Global Compact, which has developed environmental, social and governance (ESG) standards since 2004.
- The standards work alongside strategic development goals (SDGs) for countries and businesses to achieve long-term social and environmental objectives.
- Individual member states have started to introduce laws and regulations to support these standards.
- Concerns about over-regulation, particularly in the USA since 2023, have challenged the momentum behind UN initiatives.
- Whether called ESG or not, the 50 leaders interviewed mostly appreciated external standards because they help to level the playing field, help translate goals into action and communicate ethical messages.

Chapter 19 Non-government standards and Chapter 20 Making a positive impact

- There is a growing market in voluntary ethical standards and civil regulations for large and small business.
- Many businesses now recognise that mandatory standards lag market expectations. To create ethical, high-trust organisations in a volatile market, they are choosing to collaborate on voluntary standards to raise and be seen to raise the ethical bar.
- Professional standards, for example for lawyers, accountants and governance professionals, are increasingly providing ethical support and challenge.
- Networks to support collaboration are also growing.

Conclusion

I hope you have found insights and tools to bring business ethics into the foreground of your work and, as Lauren said in the foreword, the courage to do what's right in all our interests.

Index

1% For The Planet 232
9/11 89–90
70:20:10 model of learning in executive development 232
100 Best Companies to Work For in America 26

ABF The Soldiers Charity 103
Accenture 55
accountability 5, 6, 27
   lack of 166
AlphaFold 71
altruism 6, 9, 132–4, 185
Amazon 70
American Express 56
Ampa 83, 97, 176
   case study 152–3
Anglian Water Group (case study) 219–23
Anscombe, Elizabeth 9
anti-corruption laws 78, 195–6, 266
APSCo Global 105, 106
Arctic Shores (case study) 70
Ariely, Dan 133
Aristotle 9, 10, 11
Arthur Andersen LLP 161
artificial intelligence 36, 67, 68, 71
Asch, Solomon 137
Association of Employment and Learning Providers 111–12
authenticity 102, 116
autocratic command-and-control leaders 166

AutogenAI 69, 112
autonomy 5, 7, 96–8
Aviva plc (case study) 225–6

B Corp certification 36, 151 152–3, 194, 216–17
B Lab 216
Bacchus, Malcolm 227
balance 90
   case studies 91–2, 93
   stakeholder needs 32
Bank of England 18, 27
Bank of Scotland 27
Barbour, James 228
Barclays Bank 20
Baring Brothers & Co (Barings) 160
   case study 161–2
Baring Foundation 162
Basel III commitments 196
Beeby, Peter 93
   case study 110
Bell, Sir David 89
Ben & Jerry's 35, 154
Benefits Scoring Matrix 49, 63, 74, 124, 169, 243, 248, 252, 258
benefits, long-term vs. short-term 136
Bentham, Jeremy 10
Better Business Act 153, 193, 223
Biltcliffe, Simon (case study) 110–11
bioengineering 36
B-Lab Global 36
Black Diamond 28

BlackRock 22
Blueprint for Better Business 232
Bourneville Estate, Birmingham 20
Bourneville Village Trust 20
BP plc (case study) 163
Branson, Richard 150
Branston, Lauren 3, 143
Bregman, Rutger: *Moral Ambition* 179
bribery 117, 197
　case study 117, 118
British Academy
　'Principles for Purposeful Business' 22
British Airways 105
Brown, Brené 115
Brown, Michael 138
Buffett, Warren 6
Bullock, Mike (case study) 102–4
Bunyan, Tabby 47
Business in the Community (BITC) 232
Business Roundtable 22, 194, 232

Cadbury 20
Canada Pension Plan Investment Board 220
care 5, 7, 10
Carney, Mark 54, 201
Cascade Engineering 59–60
Categorical Imperative 9, 10
CAUKIN Studio (case study) 46
cause xv, 35, 78
Celtel International 197
CFO Coalition for Strategic Development
　Goals (SDGs) 202
Chambers of Commerce 232
charities 29, 103
Charles III, King 102
Chartered Governance Institute 227
Chartered Institute of Personnel and
　Development (CIPD) 56
Cheese, Peter 56
Childline 106
China 19, 206
Chouinard, Yvon xiv, 28, 29, 217
circle of care 104
Citizens UK 223
City Lit 89
Citysearch 176

civic spirit 132
Civil Rights Act (1964) 55
Clarks footwear 20
class differences 136–7
Climate Change Conference (2015)
　(COP21) 44
Cohn, Alain 133
Combat Stress 103
common good 5
company limited by shares 18
compassion 5, 7, 88
　case study 89, 90
competitive advantage xiv, 8
Conference of the Parties (COP) 44
confirmation bias 132, 228
Confucius 9
Conn, Charles 82, 132, 176
conscience xv, 6, 34, 78
consistency xv, 27, 34, 78
Consumer Protection Act 196
Cook, Robin 4
corporate responsibility 4, 22, 77
corporate social responsibility (CSR) 4
Corps of Commissionaires 102
Corps Security 102–4
corruption 195
corruption perception index 197
courage xv, 9, 115–20, 194
cover-ups, risk of 160
Covery, Stephen 175
COVID-19 pandemic (2020) 32, 54, 90, 91–2
Cradle to Cradle 26
crony capitalism 23
cryptocurrency 68
cultural numbness xv, 138
culture, definition 130
culture of urgency and necessity 166
Curry, Oliver 131

Da Costa, Alastair (case study) 99
Davis, Dr Brian 27
Davis, Michael 82
Dawkins, Richard: *Selfish Gene, The* 133
death-in-service benefit 103
Deepwater Horizon oil rig 163
Deltic Group 91

deontology 9
DeSteno, David 132
  'Who Can You Trust?' 135
'dictator' game 132–3
Dieselgate scandal 164, 165
directors' duties 189, 191–8
  in EU countries 194
  general duties 190–1
  to stakeholders 194–5
  in UK 191–3
  UK vs USA 193
discrimination 117
dishonesty 133
Disney, Walt (case study) 151
distributive justice 10
diversity, equity and inclusion (DEI) 55–6
Dodd-Frank Wall Street Reform 196
Doerr, John 105
Dolata, Uwe 159
Donoghue v Stevenson (1932) 35
Dowling, Ben 30
'dropped wallet' experiment 133
Dunne, Ronan 84, 109, 176
  case study 97
duty 5, 6, 9, 77
duty of care 191
duty of confidentiality 191
duty of good faith 191
duty of loyalty 191

East India Company 18, 19, 77
Edison, Thomas 95
Edmans, Alex 26, 211
Eichinger, Robert 232
Elkington, John 22
  Cannibals with Forks 202
emerging technology (Toolkit E) 3–6, 36, 68, 78, 251–4
emotional intelligence 57, 67
emotional return 111
empathy xv, 69, 87–8, 93
ends justify the means 166
enlightened self-interest 11
Enron 196
  case study 160–1

environmental, social and governance (ESG) 22, 23, 29, 202–5, 211
  frameworks and standards 206–7
  regulations 206
equality 56–7
equity 56–7
Esprit 28
ETHIC (acronym) 84, 85, 121, 126
ethical bar 69
ethical business, definition 4, 26
Ethical Company Organisation 224
ethical compass xv, 81–5, 100
  Toolkit F 121–6, 255–9
ethical cost versus benefit 10
ethical culture (employer viewpoint) (Toolkit G) 168–71, 260–3
ethical decision-making (Toolkit A) 13–15, 236–8
ethical failures, learning from 157–66
ethical health (Toolkit B) 39–41, 239–41
ethical leadership xv, 82–3
ethical pain thresholds 227
ethical practice, improving
  Step 1: Idea 175
  Step 2: Learning 175
  Step 3: Evaluation 175–6
  Step 4: Allies 177
  Step 5: Persuasion 177–8
ethics
  definition 4, 26
  reason for xiv
  trust and competitive advantage 26, 78
Ethics & Compliance Initiative (ECI) 179, 180, 227
Ethics and Compliance Officer Association 227
European Central Bank 196
European Sustainability Reporting Standards (ESRS) 207
European Union
  Artificial Intelligence Act (2024) 69, 70
  Corporate Social Reporting Directive (CSRD) 207
  Corporate Sustainability Due Diligence Directive 206
Ecolabel 219

272   INDEX

European Union (*continued*)
   Sustainable Financial Sustainable
      Disclosure Regulation (SFDR) 207
   Whistleblowing Directive 2019/1937 181
exploitation 68
Exxon Valdez oil spill 207
EY Beacon Institute 26

Fabreco® 47
Facebook 227
fairness 5, 7, 10, 55, 77
Fairtrade 55, 223
Fairtrade International 223
Fallon, John 89
fiduciary duties 191
financial crash (2008) 27, 32, 54, 68
financial return 111
Financial Stability Board (FSB) 196
Fink, Larry 22, 23
Fischer, Peter 137
fluidity 99
Forward Faster initiative (2023) 202
Fox, Caroline (case study) 104
Fox, Jacqui 104
'Frankenstein' risk, 68
freedom 5, 7, 10–11, 77
Freeman, Edward 21, 77
French Revolution Committee of Public
     Safety (1793) 17
Friedman, Milton 21, 77
Friends Provident 20
Furness Withy transport 20
Future Fit Business 232
future truth 111, 112

Generation Z (Gen Z) 32–3, 78
generational differences 32–3
generative AI systems 68
generosity 6, 132
Gibb's reflective cycle 132
Gillard, Sarah 43
Gilligan, Carol 10, 131
Gini Index of income 54
Glassdoor 227
Global Business Ethics Survey (GBES®)
     179–80

global connectivity 36
Global Reporting Initiative (GRI) 207
Golden Rule 9, 10
Good Business Charter (GBC) 223, 224, 225
Good Shopping Guide (GSG) 224–5, 226
Good to Great 26
Google 227
Google DeepMind 71
greenhouse gases 44
groupthink 228
GRP Solutions (case study) 149–50
Guiding Principles on Business and
     Human Rights (2011) 54

Hadden, Judy (case study) 57
Haidt, Jonathan 131, 132, 141
Halifax 27
Hamilton, W.D. 133
Hamilton's Rule 133
hard landscaping of processes and
     rules 100
Harpur, Brian 87, 149–50
Hassabis, Sir Demis 71
Heaven Company 134
Heaven, Veronica (case study) 134
Hegel, Georg 11
higher purpose xv
Hill, Katie 36, 53
Holt, Jason 215
honesty 5, 6
human rights 54–5
Hume, David 5
Huntley & Palmers 20
Huxley, Mark (case study) 105

Ibrahim, Mo 197
IFRS International Sustainability
     Standards Board (ISSB) 207
ILEAP acronym 183
   Toolkit 183–4, 264–7
Imagination 5, 7
impact statements 29, 78
impatience 136
impatience bias 136
incentives 96, 109, 110–11, 166
industrial revolution, first 19

ingenuity xv, 109–12
Institute of Accountants of Scotland (ICAS) 'Ethics Buddy' service 228
Institute of Business Ethics (IBE) 142, 226, 232
Institute of Chartered Accountants in England and Wales (ICAEW) 227
institutional power 178
integrity 5, 6, 9, 77
intellectual property 19, 20, 69
intellectual return 111
International Bill of Rights of 1966 54
International Integrated Reporting Council (IIRC) framework 207
intuition 132
ISO Standards 218–19, 228
    14001 (environmental management) 219
    26000 (social responsibility) 219
    37000 (Governance of Organisations) 219
    37001 (ISO, Anti-Bribery Management) 219
    37002 (Whistleblower Management) 219
    37011 (purpose-driven organisations) 219, 222

Johnson & Johnson 163
    case study 164
joint stock company 18
justice 5, 7
justified neglect 138

Kahneman, Daniel 132
Kant, Immanuel 9, 130
Kell, George 165
Keller, Fred (case study) 59–60
Kennedy, Jessica 135
Kennedy, John F. 6
Keynes, John Maynard 136
Kickstarter 46
Kidder, Rushworth 8
kindness 138
Kohlberg, Lawrence 130–1, 137
Kolb's reflective cycle 132

Lakat, Maxime 33
Lamont, Douglas 153–4
leadership 83–4

Leeson, Nick 162
Lewis, John 34
licence to operate 22, 190
limited liability companies 20, 77, 190
livery companies 19
Living Hours 223
Living Pensions 223
Living Wage 103, 104, 223, 226, 228
Living Wage Foundation 223
Lloyds Banking Group 20, 27
Lombardo, Michael 232
long-term focus 27
Löscher, Peter 159
Lynch, Luann 165

Malcomson, Mark (case study) 89, 90
Manzoni, Sir John 208
Maréchal, Michel 133
Markkula Center for Applied Ethics 11, 68
Marks, Peter 91–2
marshmallow experiment 136
Marx, Groucho 189
Marx, Karl and Friedrich Engels: *The Communist Manifesto* 19
Marxist principles 110
Mastercard 56
McCall, Morgan 232
McKee, Kevin 138, 157
Meadows, Donella 231
Microsoft 111
Midgley, Mary 7
    Beast and Man 133
Milgram, Stanley 135
Mill, John Stuart 11
misogyny 117
missionary versus mercenary model, 105
Moore, Celia 83
moral courage 35, 40
Moral Foundations Theory 131
moral hierarchy 35
moral judgements 132, 185
moral psychology 129–38
moral reasoning 130–1
    conventional reasoning 130
    postconventional reasoning 131
    preconventional reasoning 130

morality as co-operation 131
morals
    definition 4
    empiricist view 130-1
    intuitionist (or nativist) view 130, 131-2
Moscow, Sheppard 96
motivation 180
Mueller, Matthias 165
Murgia, Madhumita 71

National Centre for Social Research 82
national differences 136-7
Nationwide Building Society (case study) 27, 29
natural environment, corporate responsibility for 43-7
    Toolkit C 48-52, 242-6
NEOS 91
Net Impact 232
Newry, Robert 70
Nightingale, Florence 102
non-government kitemarking 228
non-governmental organisations (NGOs) 83, 205
North Face 28
Northern Rock 27
not for profit 102
NSPCC 106

O2 84
Octopus Group xv, 88, 98, 176
    case study 143-4
Oliver, Roy 151
omnipotence 138
organisational conscience xv, 34, 39, 185
organisational culture 137-8
    bystander effect 137
    change in 151
    majority must be right 137
    stereotyping 137
Osprey Consortium 220
over-regulation 78

Palantir 56
Paris Agreement 44
Patagonia xiv, 82, 88, 132, 176, 194
    B Corp certification in 217-18
    case studies 28, 29, 217-18

patience 136
Pearson Group 89-90, 96
Peasley, Josh 46
Planet Mark 207
power 116-17, 134-6
    case study 116, 117
practical wisdom ('*phronesis*') 10
Principles for Responsible Investment (PRI) 202, 207
professional support 181
prospect theory 132
Prospectus 93, 110
prudence 9
psychometric assessment 70
Public Benefit Corporations (PBCs) 194
Public Interest Disclosure Act (1998) (PIDA) 181
Publicly Accessible Specification' (PAS)
    PAS 808:2022 219, 222
purpose and values 29, 32
purpose of business 17-23

Quaker capitalism 20

RAF Benevolent Fund 103
rationality 132
Rawls, John
    Theory of Justice, The 10
    Veil of Ignorance 35
Ray, Amit 67
RE_CONSIDERED (case study) 46, 47
reciprocity 35
recruitment problem, solving (case study) 58-9
recycling 47
Re-generation 33
regional differences 136-7
REKOM 92
REKOM UK 92
relevance 27
remote stakeholders 36
representative power 178
responsibility of organisation 162-4
responsible business, definition 4
restraint 9
Richer Sounds 177
    case study 145-8

Richer, Julian 145, 224
right-right dilemmas 8
risks 180–1
  courage and 116
Rix, Justin (case study) 98
Rogerson, Simon xv, 88, 143–4
  case study 98
roots
  of today's markets 19–20
  of trade 18–19
Ross, James 163
Rowland, Ben (case study) 111–12
Royal Marines Charity 103
Royal Navy 103
Royal Society: 'Basics of Climate Change, Basics' 44
Rozenthuler, Sarah 101
rules 5, 6, 98–9

S&P Global 56
Salesforce 56
Sandel, Michael 132
Sarbanes-Oxley Act (2002) (USA) 161, 196
Saxton, Sharon 150, 151
Scardino, Dame Marjorie 89, 90
Schofield, David 226
Science Based Targets Initiative (SBTi) 202, 207
Securities and Exchange Commission (SEC) 196, 206
self-awareness 132, 138
self-control 5, 6
self-interest 5, 7
shareholder primacy 17, 21–2, 77
Sheth, Jag 26
Siekaczek, Reinhard 159
Siemens 197
  bribery scandals 158
  case study 159–60
Sinek, Simon 25
Single Supervisory Mechanism (SSM) 196
Sisodia, Raj 26
Smith, Adam 7, 9, 19, 23, 68
  Theory of Moral Sentiments, The 9, 19
  Wealth of Nations, The 9, 19, 77
Snarey, John 137

social enterprises 29
social equality 54
social equity 36, 62, 78
  corporate responsibility for 53–60
  Toolkit D 62–5, 247–50
social welfare fund 103
Society for Business Ethics 232
soft landscaping of autonomy and storytelling 100
solid values 104
solidarity 132
speaking up (employee viewpoint) 117, 142–3, 173–81
SSE plc 207
  case study 208–10
  'Just Transition Strategy', 209
stakeholder
  definition 35
  feedback 227
  key 88
  needs, balancing 32
  value 17, 21–2, 77
Stanford Prison Experiment 135
Stanford Research Institute 21, 77
Statement on the Purpose of a Corporation 194–5
Steare, Roger 173
  Ethicability 11
Stern, Stefan 107
storytelling 97
Straw, Jack 4
Swain, Ann (case study) 106

Tajfel, Henri 137
Taylor, Alison 166, 180
  Higher Ground 55
Taylor, Hayden 30–1
teamwork 105–6
technology, emerging
  investment in 103
  responsibility for 67–71
temptation 117–19
Tett, Gillian 23
Theory U, 132
Theranos 111
third sector organisations 29

Thornton, Grant 98
Tomorrow's Company 232
Tompkins, Doug 28
Tony's Chocolonely 35, 153
traction xv, 15, 95–100
training 96
Transocean 163
Transparency xiv
Transparency International 197
Trevino, Linda 138
Tripadvisor 227
Truman, Harry 177
trust 8
  of business leaders 83
  in governments and businesses 54
  see also balance; compassion
Trustpilot 227
TSB Bank 224
Tversky, Amos 132
Twin Group 104

UK Bribery Act (2010) 195–6
UK Companies Act (2006)153, 191, 193, 206, 223
UK Corporate Governance Code 193, 206, 209
UK Equality Act (2010) 55, 206
UK Hospitality 91
UK Post Office 'Horizon Scandal' 68, 162–3
ultimatum game 132–3
United Nations (UN) 22, 44
  Declaration of Human Rights (1948) 54
  Global Compact 54, 165, 202–3, 204, 207, 225, 226, 232
  Intergovernmental Panel on Climate Change (IPCC) 44
  Six Capitals 221–2
  Sustainable Development Goals (SDGs) 205–6, 208, 221
  'Who Cares Wins' report 204, 206
Unilever 154
universal test of reciprocity 10
universality, principle of 7
Unloc (case study) 30–1
upcycling 47

US Foreign and Corrupt Practices Act (FCPA) (1977; amended 1988, 1998) 196
utilitarianism 10

values, definition 4
Veil of Ignorance 10
Verizon Wireless 84
Vernell, Sean 116
  case study 178
Virgin Airlines 105, 150
Virgin Atlantic (case study) 150–1
Virgin Money. 27
virtuous circle 149
Vital Farms 194
Vitsoe (case study) 45
Volkswagen (VW) 164
  case study 165

Walker-Smith, Sarah 81, 83, 152, 153
  case study 97.
Wall Street Journal's corporate ranking 55
Walter, Captain Sir Edward 102
Warnock, Mary 129
Webmart 110–11
Wedell-Wedellsborg, Merete xv, 138
Wells Fargo (case study) 158–9
Western capitalism 19
whistleblowing 8, 117, 158, 159, 161, 180
white lie 119
Williams, Sean 69
  case study 112
willpower 136
Wolfe, David 26
Women's Empowerment Principles (2010) 202
World Benchmarking Alliance 55
World Economic Forum's (WEF) 44
  Digital Trust Framework 69
World Values Survey (WVS) 137
WorldCom 161
Worshipful Company of Chartered Secretaries and Administrators (WCCSA)
  'Importance of Values for Governance, The' 227

Zimbardo, Philip 135